THE
JOKE
MAN
BOW TO STERN

THE JOKE MAN

BOW TO STERN

JACKIE MARTLING

Foreword by Artie Lange

A POST HILL PRESS BOOK

The Joke Man:
Bow to Stern
© 2017 by Jackie Martling
All Rights Reserved

ISBN: 978-1-68261-389-4
ISBN (eBook): 978-1-68261-390-0

Cover Photo by Peter M. Budraitis, PMBPhoto.com
Interior Design and Composition by Greg Johnson/Textbook Perfect

Post Hill Press
New York · Nashville
posthillpress.com

Published in the United States of America

This book is dedicated to my parents,
John and Dot

SPECIAL THANKS TO

Artie Lange, Peter Steinberg, Anthony Ziccardi, Michael Wilson, Will Vitka, Jon Ford, Billie Brownell, Ruth Tarlow, Nancy Sirianni, Carl Caprigolio and Oglio Records, Ian Karr, Howard Stern, Fred Norris, Rory Rosegarten, Toby Ludwig, Frank Weimann, Mel Berger, Barry Jerkowitz, Frank Baer, Karen Bunone, Jane Akre, Mark Simone and WOR 710AM, Jim Kerr and Shellie Sonstein and Joe Cristiano and Q104.3FM, Roger and JP and Brett and WBAB 102.3FM, Phil Iazzetta and iHeart Radio, John Fugelsang and SiriusXM, Rita Beglin, Peter Martling, Jake LaGrange, Mike Hunt, and, of course, Katie, Jessica, and Brendan Dunn, and Kevin Kelly.

And a *very special thanks* to Barbara Klein.

CONTENTS

FOREWORD

by Artie Lange

Jackie asked me to write the Foreword to his autobiography. If somebody told me twenty years ago I was going to be doing this, I'd have said, "Do I have to?"

I'm kidding . . . I'd have thought it was amazing.

The truth is, I immediately told him, "Yes, of course, it'd be my honor."

After all, we have the bond that both our deaths have been fraudulently broadcast over the radio.

So, Jackie shows up here at my apartment for me to record the foreword and the first thing he does is bitch at me for him having to wait a few minutes for me to do him this favor.

That says it all. I have to admire his balls. Round and small.

He's always on time and on schedule. I'm not. Shoot me.

So, he's here sitting on the floor. To him, even at however old he is, everything's still a beach party.

The other thing we have in common is somehow, individually, we both lasted many years on a show that had two nocturnal comedians getting up at the crack of dawn. And that still puzzles us both. Nobody who's never walked in those shoes can ever in any way join in our discussions the horror that is the hours of *The Howard Stern Show*.

Oh, and both of us are no longer welcome on the show.

Here I am, trying to dictate this foreword, and my old friend Mario Bosco is here and won't shut the fuck up, even after my producer Danny [Falato] turned off his microphone. I'm such an easy mark. I'm feeding Mario as he's annoying me and I'm doing a huge solid for a whining Jackie. This is making getting up for Stern sound like a party.

The room just leapt off topic and after a quick hello to Sam Simon in hell, we're discussing getting it on with Tina Fey. Is that pussy-dropping?

My author Anthony Bozza just showed up. Anthony writes my books, which I have because of a job Jackie created, but continuing to ignore the foreword, we've irresistibly jumped to Stuttering John's political career and him canceling his appearance on my podcast two days ago. This session has blossomed into more brouhaha than the creation of a book foreword, so we decide we'll roll, this will be my next *Artie Quitter* podcast (#343) and we'll kill two birds with one sitting.

To keep you current, Mario just stormed out—after he finished eating, of course—because I won't let him chime in and slow us up while we're attempting to be funny.

We're having a few chuckles at Stuttering John's expense and he really should have no problem with it. After Jackie left the *Stern Show* and I had arrived months later, at the mere mention of Jackie's name, John would run into the studio and joyously join in the Jackie bashing, piling on and crapping all over Jackie on the air, stammering with glee that Jackie was b-b-broke and h-h-homeless. But I would never join in his and their frolic.

Conan is a listener, and my first appearance on his show, he mentioned he'd noticed how I'd sidestepped it. I told him I've never jumped on trashing people I like and respect, and me and my friends always really dug Jackie. I don't think Howard was thrilled, but I never played along with that stuff.

Before we got to know each other in the last few years, I had only met Jackie the time I did the *Stern Show* with Norm [MacDonald].

Norm said to Jackie, "Artie wants to tell you a joke," and he said, "I have to go to the bathroom."

No, he fake laughed and it was great. I was very excited about that.

From a fan's perspective, I'd always enjoyed all of Jackie's contributions to the show and had no reason to crap on him. All I had to say about him was positive and they sure didn't want to hear that.

We just decided the first stand-up show Jackie and I do together will be at one of John's political rallies. As tough as it is to stop talking about angry author Senator Melendez, who thinks he needs a running mate, Sam Simon wearing blue eyeliner in hell, my next book, and Bensonhurst

Mario pacing downstairs in a huff, it's back to the job at hand . . . Wait, now we're onto Jackie's editor being a white guy and African-American pilots . . .

I can't wait to read this book. The little he's shared with me so far has me hooked . . . Michigan State University in the late sixties, over a decade of playing in rock and roll bands, early eighties comedy stories, his eighteen-year *Stern* run, all flavored with healthy doses of booze and pot—and I know me and my friends would love to read about his childhood. Should be good, no?

To me, one of the most golden parts of the *Stern Show* was the dynamic of Jackie writing for the Jackie Puppet and Billy West doing the Jackie Puppet voice, goofing on Jackie and Conan O'Brien (Conan's late-night show had just completed a not-so-hot first year and the Stern gang was throwing him a goodbye party). The Jackie Puppet was goofing on Jackie while Jackie wrote the lines. It was one of the greatest E! TV shows and may be one of the funniest things I ever saw.

I'm thrilled to hear that Jackie and Billy are still great pals. Not for nothing, Billy West is another guy who was formerly on-air, a huge part of the Greatest Show on Earth, but is no longer welcome on the Stern show. Do you see a pattern forming?

Now we're back off track. Jackie's got the Jackie Puppet being responsible for Triumph the Insult Comic Dog and it leads to frightening and wonderful Otto and George stories. This foreword may suck, but it's going to be a great podcast.

Way back, if you asked any of my buddies who we'd like to hang out with, it always would have been Jackie. In my stand-up and talk show appearances and even the sketches I wrote on Howard Stern, the biggest influence was probably Jackie Martling. Because of what he brought to Stern, the political incorrectness, the subtle stuff he used to do in the background . . . That's what all my premises were. He was truly dangerous.

On Howard's Channel 9 show, when Richard Simmons was a guest, Jackie had them lower a fully cooked turkey from the ceiling until it was a few inches from the 600-pound guy who was Richard's work-in-progress, after which Howard held a fishing pole with a bag of potato chips on the line and waved that in front of him, too. That's comedy, friend.

There's a thing now, if you talk about religion in Hollywood, they think it's a dangerous thing. It's not. Everybody in Hollywood's anti-religion, nobody believes in God, and if you do an anti-God bit, you're among friends.

It's like people thinking if Dave Chappelle talks about race it's dangerous. It's not. It's the safest thing you can do. If *I* talk about race it's dangerous.

It's like Caitlyn Jenner . . . Bruce Jenner becomes a hot chick and gets a brave award, a courage award. That's not brave. If *I* become a chick, *that's* courage.

Jackie just said, "You want to get a Purple Heart, strap on a vagina," and Dan screamed with glee.

The idiot's punching up what I'm supposed to be writing for his dopey book.

This has to be in the foreword.

Hey, I'm writing it . . . of course it'll be in it.

When Howard got to New York, almost instantly, my father had become a huge fan.

He said, "Art, you have to listen to this guy on the radio. He's outrageous, so damn funny. And I love this guy on his show, this comedian Jackie Martling."

So one of the first times I'm listening, my favorite moment maybe ever, Howard had a listener on the line ready to go, both of them ready to embarrass the hell out of Jackie.

He takes the call and the guy says, "Howard, ask Jackie about the time in college when he was mooning from a moving car and took a dump out the window."

Howard said, "*No.* Not *really*, Jackie . . . that's disgusting."

Before even a beat passed, so casually—he might even have been eating something when he said it—like a throwaway line, Jackie said, "Yeah, a harvest moon."

I was completely blown away. They're thinking Jackie's going to curl up into a fetal position with a story like that going out to millions of people, but not only is he totally unfazed, he had a fucking *name* for it.

"A harvest moon."

I said, "Look, I don't know what Jackie makes a year—it's gotta be more than me—if I can be that guy, I won in life."

I thought, "If this guy's ever dumb enough to leave . . . ."

That was the epitome of what I wanted to do. That attitude.

I saw Jackie do stand-up at Rascals in 1989 and the walls moved, he was killing so hard. The place kept erupting. And then he was going to this great radio gig.

I said out loud, "What a life. He's doing stand-up and he's on *The Howard Stern Show*."

And that happened to me! What a country.

Then I saw Jackie almost a year ago today do stand-up at Gotham and again the walls moved. And they were the same jokes.

Which is a great compliment, because I laughed just as hard. Jackie proves it's the art of his presence up there. It's him. Seventy-five percent of stand-up is your presence on stage.

Richard Pryor tells stories any black person would have if they grew up in a whorehouse.

Wait a minute . . .

The point is, when Richard Pryor had a microphone in his hand, it was part of his body. Like chubby Jackie Gleason's Minnesota Fats holding a pool cue, it was part of his arm.

And when you watch Jackie he's supposed to be there. He's supposed to be on stage doing stand-up.

I found out later my influence wasn't Howard. It was Howard a lot, but it was the sensibility Jackie brought to the show, the guy who says, "It was a harvest moon," that thing. That's been my style, with much thanks to him.

When we did "Best of Gotham Live" together in December 2015—along with Gilbert Gottfried, Mario Cantone, and Orlando Jones, the greatest lineup I've ever been a part of, what Mark Cuban told me was his best-ever AXS TV show—and as they were saying his name, everybody's applauding, and Jackie's slowly walking up to the microphone, I said to myself, "This is probably what it was like to watch Babe Ruth walk from the on-deck circle to home plate." Then he'd take a few practice swings and then hit it out of the park.

We seem to remember people by their greatest quotes . . .

Alexander Graham Bell: "Watson, come here, I need you . . ."
Abraham Lincoln: "Four score and seven years ago . . ."
Jackie Martling: "Two flies land on a piece of shit . . ."

That's Jackie's practice swing:
"Two flies land on a piece of shit."

INTRODUCTION

I've had a wild and silly and fun and offbeat and relatively successful life. I hope you enjoy the hunks of it I relate in this book.

Of course, there's a better than excellent chance the reason you're holding this book is to read the parts about my years on *The Howard Stern Show*. Which is, of course, fine by me.

I decided that though I sincerely believe you'd thoroughly enjoy many more of the wacky tales that have been my life than I've included here, the bulk of this book should be about my experiences with the show that put me on the map, made me lots of money, and got me to you. I know I owe it to the fans. Hopefully, with this read, you'll get to know me like you never have and will grab for the sequel.

Countless millions have listened to and watched Howard Stern and *The Howard Stern Show* over his lengthy span on radio and television. And many have listened so often, so religiously they feel they know the show inside out, that they're totally aligned with and in the know of all that went on.

But I had the vantage point of the best seat in the house, perhaps the best seat in show business, what has come to be known as "the Jackie Chair."

I saw it all, contributed to it all, lived and loved it all. It was a dream job. I was the kid sitting in the back of the class passing notes and disrupting the goings-on whenever it seemed like a good idea . . . only with the full encouragement of the teacher.

Other than Howard, no one has told stories of *The Howard Stern Show* from the inside, from the belly of the beast, from the perspective of, say, the pitcher's mound or the director's chair or the judge's chambers.

I'm going to share with you much of the experience the way I experienced it. Not the dirt and gossip (not to be redundant), though I'm sure it'll necessarily forage into those areas a bit, but the rarefied excitement and fun that filled that room every minute of every show.

I'm not exaggerating when I type "every minute of every show." It's no accident, no quirk Howard rose so spectacularly. No matter where he is, there's cutting-edge magic when his microphone goes on, and being an important part of it for so long, just a few feet away, filled me with a bottomless vault of outrageous and funny and hard-to-believe memories. And here it is, from my perspective, a first helping of that treasure trove. I'm thrilled to be sharing it with you.

Close to five hours a day, five days a week, for fifteen years I was in the thick of it as we churned along, as tight and amazing as an ensemble could be, becoming a radio behemoth as Howard Stern became a radio star of unprecedented magnitude. It continued in all its glory after I left, and does to this day.

When I was aboard, the handpicked cast like no other anywhere relentlessly picked at each other's bones when we weren't hosting on-air guests that the word "eclectic" didn't do justice, all to the delight of a staggering and constantly growing legion of loyal listeners and viewers—and readers—coast to coast.

Endless infighting and ball breaking and practical jokes, movie and television and musical stars, tabloid wonders, crazy fans, legendary remote broadcasts, a lifelike female doll, puppets, scads of little people, drunks, sluts—even the commercials were fun. Anything and everything and everyone that entered Howard's studio or sphere instantly became part of the mix, a magnificent stew like had never been served, ever.

So welcome to many tales of an unparalleled existence and a healthy dose of what life was like as head writer for The King Of All Media.

Please grab a drink, fill the bowl, and get comfortable.

I love you for reading my book.

1859

A ROOSEVELT?

My father was John Coger Martling. His mother, Dorothy Hall (Martling), and her five younger brothers and two younger sisters grew up near the corner of Cove Road and Moore's Hill Road in what was then known as "Dutch Hollow" in Oyster Bay Cove, Long Island, a stone's throw from President Theodore Roosevelt's summer retreat (and eventual Summer White House), Sagamore Hill. Starting in 1897, their father, Franklin Hall, worked at Sagamore Hill, and his family had the run of the place, his children often frolicking with Teddy's children.

The youngest of the Hall children, Leonard Wood Hall, was born at Sagamore Hill on October 2, 1900. At her father's suggestion, Teddy's then eight-year-old daughter Ethel named him for her father's favorite general and fellow Rough Rider, Leonard Wood. Ethel Roosevelt was soon to be designated little Leonard's godmother. Len Hall was to graduate from Georgetown Law School at nineteen, become county sheriff, a congressman, national chairman of the Republican Party, and Dwight D. Eisenhower's campaign manager for the '52 and '56 presidential elections, with Ike winning each in a landslide.

Great-Uncle Len and Ethel Roosevelt Derby, who were very close lifelong friends, were loved and respected locally as well as nationally and

1

were to lead the successful 1948 push to have Sagamore Hill declared a National Historic Site.

My grandmother was also very close to Ethel, and to Theodore's second wife, Edith. Side by side, their families had weathered a lot of heartache, and I have some very loving letters my grandmother received from each of the Roosevelt women.

When we were little kids, my brothers and sister and I, as well as our many first cousins of varying ages, were somewhat aware of our family's history, but it never went any further than that. Clem Platt was married to my father's sister Edith and during summers in the 1950s, we'd all often go to Uncle Clem's in Bayville, a few houses from Long Island Sound and only a few miles from our home in East Norwich. Weekends, we kids and the moms would swim all day, the men remaining in the house to drink and watch the Yankees. Sundays, they'd frequently watch *Meet the Press*, when Great-Uncle Len was on the panel. We were all pretty young and had no idea how prominent he was.

As we got older, it started to sink in that Uncle Len was a pretty big deal, as was great-grandfather Franklin's job at Sagamore Hill. I have no idea why it didn't have more of an impact on me when I found them in the attic of my childhood home in East Norwich, but when I realized the Roosevelt letters to my grandmother were priceless, I had them framed and started to ask questions. At the time, I had no idea of the very probable reason for their close relationships.

In the late 1980s, after my father's sister Eleanor told us that, at holidays, the Roosevelt family would have presents for all of Dorothy Hall Martling's children, I said, "Pop, you sat on Teddy Roosevelt's lap in the incredible living room of Sagamore Hill when you were five and he gave you a Christmas present? He wasn't just a president, Pop, for Christ's sakes, he's on *Mount Rushmore!* And we find out *now?* You're seventy-five. You didn't think it was worth mentioning?"

A very soft-spoken and humble man, he said, "Not really, no."

Then, in 1998, when the Bill Clinton and Monica Lewinsky scandal hit, there was an editorial in a local weekly newspaper, the *Locust Valley Leader.*

The piece was about how sex and politics have always gone hand in hand. It cited the indiscretions of Franklin Roosevelt and John F.

Kennedy, and at one point it read, "It is hard to believe, but from time to time we have heard the rumor that Leonard Hall, a long-time resident of Locust Valley, was the illegitimate son of Theodore Roosevelt."

My first cousin Dotty (Platt) Frederick had been very close to Great-Uncle Len. He had taken her under his wing in Washington, DC, financially and spiritually helped her get through college, and had always been there for her, as well as the entire family. And when she read the editorial she was outraged. She sat down and wrote a scathing letter to Edith Wycoff, the publisher of the paper. How *dare* they besmirch that wonderful man!

She thought it wise that before she sent it, she'd run it by Eleanor, Dorothy Hall Martling's last living child.

Dotty read the editorial to Aunt Eleanor, a nondrinking, hospital-volunteering salt-of-the-earth type, and said, "There's nothing to this TR rumor, is there, Aunt Ellie?"

Dotty's heart sank when Aunt Ellie took a deep breath and said, "Well . . ."

Aunt Eleanor said, "Actually, that wasn't the rumor. The rumor in the family for generations was always that Grandfather [Franklin] Hall was the illegitimate son of Teddy's *father.*"

That was the first any of our generation had heard "the rumor."

Should that be the case, my great-grandfather Franklin Hall was Theodore Roosevelt's illegitimate half-brother. Wow.

I dug in a bit and soon found out enough to convince me that with the information we know as hard facts, the mystery, the rumor, absolutely screams for a final answer. Is it true or is it conjecture?

Here are the facts, see what you think:

Theodore Roosevelt's frail mother had a very difficult time giving birth to little Teddy in New York City on October 27, 1858. It's well documented that in the month before Teddy's birth, her husband Theo had been hunting in Maine. (Theodore Roosevelt's father's name was Theodore Roosevelt . . . it can get confusing.)

Theo and his four brothers were known throughout New York City to be great partygoers and ladies' men.

According to Franklin Hall's death certificate and other official documents, my great-grandfather was born in New Gloucester, Maine, on May 16, 1859, to William Henry Hall and Harriet Carle, and was thus conceived in August or September 1858.

However, in Leonard Hall's unpublished autobiography, he states that his father was born in England and came to Maine as a child. Uncle Len absolutely knew that wasn't true . . . so did he throw in that red herring to nip in the bud anyone wondering about his father's personal history?

In 1882, Franklin Hall married Mary Garvin from Centre Island, New York, and soon thereafter, Theodore Roosevelt got Franklin a job working with Judge William J. Youngs. The Youngs had been situated in Oyster Bay Cove since the 1600s and had been family friends of the Roosevelts for many years.

In 1897, after Judge Youngs moved his law practice to Garden City to be closer to the office of his new job as Queens County district attorney, Theodore Roosevelt hired Franklin Hall to work for him at his Sagamore Hill estate.

In a March 1956 *Time* magazine cover story on Uncle Len, as well as other places, Franklin Hall was cited as Roosevelt's "coachman." However, in 1898, Theodore Roosevelt wanted to run for governor of New York State. But he had filed as a resident of Washington, DC, to avoid the high Oyster Bay and New York taxes. His competition protested: How could he run for governor if he wasn't a resident? Roosevelt had Franklin Hall pull the proof of the Oyster Bay 1898 property tax payments he had made to help verify his residency. That was hardly an assignment for a coachman. Also, in 1902, Franklin was financial chairman of the President Roosevelt Welcome Home Celebration.

And then, after William McKinley's assassination in 1901, Theodore Roosevelt became, at forty-two, the youngest president in the history of the United States. In late 1901 he asked Franklin Hall to come to work with him in Washington, offering him the job of White House messenger.

Franklin's wife said there was no way she was uprooting eight children (Dorothy, Helen, Franklin Jr., Edith, William, Frederick, Theodore Roosevelt, and Leonard Wood) and moving to Washington. But he went anyway, returning to Oyster Bay with Theodore summers, holidays, and whenever else he could. When Teddy's term was up in 1909, Franklin stayed on with Presidents Taft and Wilson, until just before he died in 1916. At the time, he was still employed as a clerk in the White House.

Theodore Roosevelt was present at both Franklin Hall's funeral and his burial—the only Roosevelt employee funeral he ever attended.

It's easy to see why such a rumor emerged from this series of events. It certainly seems like Teddy took very good care of a random guy who was born in Maine and for no apparent reason wound up in Oyster Bay on Long Island. It appears he treated him . . . like a brother.

There are many more intriguing details, but that's the nuts and bolts of the story.

And the question could easily be answered with a very simple DNA test. Thanks to my dear friend Syd Mandelbaum, a genetics expert and the founder of the wonderful charity Rock and Wrap It Up, I even have DNA sampling kits. But, so far, I haven't been able to get a Roosevelt descendant to give me the simple swipe of a Q-tip from their inner cheek.

Contrary to what many believe, you can't do a DNA sampling on a piece of hair from a barbershop floor or via similar strategies. It's a very specific test. And the test can't be done surreptitiously. It has to be done with the full cooperation of the DNA source.

Twice we've been very close to getting a Roosevelt's cooperation when the participant had a change of heart. So my quest continues.

Once we get a participant from their family, it'll be easy and definitive. A swipe of a Roosevelt's DNA, a swipe of my DNA, and off to the lab they go. And very soon we'll get the call, a match or not a match.

My cousin John Hammond, Town of Oyster Bay historian and acclaimed researcher of all things local and all things Roosevelt, is very close to absolutely sure the rumor is fact. The timeline is too perfect and the simplest of questions are bafflingly unanswered. Such as, what drew young Franklin Hall to the tiny and out-of-the-way Long Island hamlet of Oyster Bay from the wilds of Maine in 1880? And where did he meet and/or how did he know Theodore Roosevelt, a member of one of the richest families in Manhattan? What was his *entrée*?

It makes me bonkers that the folks we could have asked about this (relatives, locals, whoever) are no longer with us. It could have been so, so easy. There might be simple explanations for each of the coincidences.

What's really interesting is how very much times have changed. I'm sure that if this rumor's indeed fact, everyone in both families—as well as many people in the area—*knew*. But, years ago, people just didn't talk, didn't spew around the gossip that fuels the world nowadays. Or, at the very least, they played it very close to the vest.

If you know a Roosevelt, please ask them to read this, to give a brother a swab. I know they're not falling over each other to help solve this. And should the rumor unfold to be true, I'm sure they won't be anxious for the world to know that Theodore Roosevelt's father—by all accounts his hero, the greatest man he ever knew—sired an illegitimate son.

Oyster Bay was built on Theodore Roosevelt. Majestic Sagamore Hill, Roosevelt Park, Theodore Roosevelt School, the statue of Teddy as you drive into our delightful little village, Theodore Roosevelt's gravesite. . . it goes on and on.

And I'm a fairly well-known local, in quite a different genre. If this should pan out, it's going to be pretty, pretty interesting local news. Am I the illegitimate great-great-grandson of Theodore Roosevelt's father Theo?

I'm hoping the sequel to this book will feature the answer.

1950

FOUR PARENTS

My father, John Coger Martling, was the second brother of three. There were also three sisters, one of whom died when he was very young. On February 20, 1913, he was literally born in the kitchen of the East Norwich, Long Island, house his father Percy had built in 1900, and lived there his entire life but for two years of college and his participation as an army engineer in the Philippines during World War II.

A few years after the war was over, his cousin Joan Hall introduced him to one of her neighbors in Mineola, Dorothy Poole. They dated a while, pretty quickly they introduced John's brother Leonard to Dot's sister Janet, and they became an item, too.

My parents married on July Fourth, 1947. The fireworks that were going off that day and night were certainly an omen.

Len and Janet got married in late 1947, the boys' mother moved out to go live with one of their sisters, and the happy foursome set up house in the family home, John and Dot downstairs and Len and Janet upstairs. It was the Kramdens and the Nortons.

John Coger Martling, Jr. (that's me) was born a little more than seven months after my parents' nuptials, on Valentine's Day, 1948, the first child to enter the world of these two Martling boys and their wives, all living under the same roof.

7

So for the first two years of my existence, I had four doting parents. I'm sure every time I pooped, every crawl, every step, every utterance, that whatever I did was headline news at the corner of Whitney Avenue and Oyster Bay Road (one of the first homes in our tiny hamlet, our house didn't even have a number until the sixties).

Two years later, my brother Bobby was born, my aunt gave birth to my cousin Lenny, my father got a second job and was drinking a bit more, and in a heartbeat I went from four parents to none, the center of attention having shifted drastically.

So here I am, sixty-seven years later, still screaming, "Where the fuck did everybody *go?*"

It's just fascinating to attempt to piece together what made us who, what, and how we are. My entire life my mother never stopped telling me how spoiled I was/am.

"You're a willful, spoiled brat."

I swear I can still hear her. I hated it, *hated* it, and have always *really* really despised that word. I recoil at the mere utterance of the word "spoiled."

But maybe I am.

My mother told me that when I was almost two years old I started saying, "Mommy, I want somebody to play with. I want a brother."

Needless to say, I had no idea she was very pregnant, and a few weeks later she brought home my brother Bobby. Who knows? Maybe that set me on the path of always expecting to get whatever I wanted.

Hmm . . . I always wanted to write a book . . .

1966

MY MICHIGAN STATE ROOMMATE

I arrived at Snyder Hall, my Michigan State University dormitory, in September 1966. I couldn't have been more excited, not having any idea what to expect on any front. At some point, Nick Puscas walked in. He was to be my roommate. Nick was blond, well built, and handsome as hell. I very quickly learned he was from Livonia, a middle-class suburb of Detroit. He had a quick smile and a great sense of humor.

The first laugh we shared was when I hurt myself. Our room was where the building had an eave, so there was an angled hunk of wall and I smacked my head on it.

I went, *"Owch!"* and in the Midwest accent I was to become so damn familiar with, Nick said, "What'd you cob your melon, Jaaack?"

Always a fan of colorful speech, we were best buds from that second onward.

Nick had been smart in high school, yet rode motorcycles with some of the ruffians where he was from—a wonderful mix of both worlds.

One day, he walked in and said, somewhat proudly, "I just saw a high school pal and he asked me if I was up here working construction."

His girlfriend called him "Pudge," and mine called me that, too, though neither of us was pudgy. And they were both named Patti. We ran

9

parallel on so many fronts that we almost immediately started referring to ourselves as "the Blond Bombers of 302" (our dorm room).

We were both pretty intimidated by the whole college thing, so it was a little while before we started chasing after beer and babes. A few days, a month, I truly have no idea how long before we loosened up. I do know we both wanted to make a good go of college.

The very first weekend, on Sunday, Nick's parents and his nephew Sookie came up to visit. His folks were easily two of the nicest people I had ever met. They're Croatian, and when his father walked in, he kissed Nick on the lips. It took me a minute to process that.

Then his father asked him how his weight was, and Nick said something like, "I'm one hundred seventy-two, Pop, doing good."

Again, I was taken aback. His father asked him about his *weight?* I stood there wondering if my father even knew I had left for college.

They took us to dinner at the Jack Tar Hotel, across the street from the state capitol, which was about ten miles down the road from the dorm. We ate and drank and laughed, and it was really terrific, as I was far from home and they were already like family.

On the drive back to the dorm, after all that eating and drinking and laughing (especially at my own stories), I suddenly felt the churnings of gas in my belly. And it got worse and worse pretty quickly.

Nick's father was driving, his mother was riding shotgun, little Sookie was sitting between them, and Nick and I were in the backseat, me on the left and him on the right . . . Needless to say, close quarters. No longer able to hold it back, I silently sneaked out a whopper of a fart.

A few seconds later, little Sookie goes, *Sniff! Sniff!* ". . . Grandpa?"

Without flinching, Nick's father shakes his head and says, "Wasn't me, Sookie."

"Grandma?"

"Nope, not me, Sook."

"Pudge?"

Nick said, "Wasn't me, Sook. Must have been Jaaaack."

Aside from Nick laughing his ass off, I have no idea what happened next. Usually, nothing bothers me, but I was mortified. To this day, I wonder what went through their minds right then. My God, they treated me to a beautiful steak dinner and drinks and this was my payback?

A few weeks later, Nick and me and our newly anointed third Blond Bomber, Chris Hoffman, went down to Ann Arbor, to the University of Michigan, where Chris's older brother Joe was sharing a house. It was Michigan State University's biggest football game of the year, pitting MSU against staunch rival U of M, and I was quick to find out it's a huge deal.

We, of course, had no tickets, so we watched it on television, taking our first drink as they kicked off.

By that night, we were really hammered. We went to a party and on the way out, the front walkway of the apartment building was swarming with college kids.

In the middle of these very electric surroundings I was probably going, "Yay, Michigan State," or something like that, there in the heart of enemy territory, just asking for it, and somebody came out of the crowd and coldcocked me.

I immediately started yelling and complaining that somebody had hit me.

There were cops all over, and they said to Nick and Hoffman, "Hey, try to calm down your friend."

They couldn't. They all shrugged and the cops cuffed me, loaded me into their car, and took me off to jail. When I woke up, I tried to piece together why I was in there. It's hard to describe how I felt, freezing and hungover and in what, for all purposes, was a foreign jail.

I got one phone call. What do I do?

I have no idea how . . . I must have asked the police to locate "a Puscas in Livonia," but remarkably, I got the number and called Nick's house, which was forty-five minutes away. His father got on the phone. I explained I was in jail and needed to be bailed out, and along with whatever else, his father said, "I'll be there as soon as I can."

An hour or so later, Mr. Puscas was there. He bailed me out and drove me back to East Lansing, seventy miles north. Again, who knows what we talked about on that trip, but though we were terrific pals already, man, did that seal the deal.

Nice way to pay back a guy for a steak dinner, eh? A vicious fart in his car and a marathon Sunday drive when a hardworking man wants to be with his family.

That Christmas, Nick came to visit me on Long Island. My family immediately loved him and I set out to show him the fun that was to be had in my neck of the woods.

I took him to the Empire State Building and the Staten Island Ferry—my first time for both. We were equally knocked out.

One night, we went to a party and got beyond bombed. I had a huge 1961 Chrysler Imperial, got lost up in the fancy hills of Mill Neck Estates, and tried to do a three-point turn on a one-lane road that was bordered by a steep slope on one side. Next I knew, the car was mostly hanging off the cliff. We attempted to jack it up, but there was, of course, no way to set up the jack on a hill. So we abandoned ship and hitchhiked the four miles home to East Norwich.

The next morning, I was awakened by my father asking me, "*Wake up!* What the hell did you do?"

I opened my eyes and there was my old man and, in full uniform, Officer Jarvis, a local cop who was a good friend of the family (it's a very small town).

My father wasn't an excitable guy, but he was so furious it scared me.

He fumed, "You left the car blocking the road in Mill Neck. Where are the keys?"

My head was splitting and I had no idea what had happened or where the keys were. Not really going way out on a limb, as I got very drunk very often and in the past the keys always had found their way to the same place, I said, "They're in the kitchen cabinet where I always put them."

I remember walking down the stairs with Pop and the cop behind me, panicking that the keys might not be there . . . but they were.

Officer Jarvis said he wasn't going to arrest me or press any charges and they took off to rescue the car. In the other twin bed, Nick had slept through the entire episode.

There's so much more, but I'll put out the chutes here for now.

Nick and I had two years together in Snyder Hall: 1966–1968. By the end of year two, he had pretty much had his fill of me and my loud mouth and my drinking. After sophomore year, though we remained pals, for two guys who had been so damn close, we rarely communicated and saw very little of each other.

I'm so glad to say we've never lost our love for one another and have recently (as of spring 2016) gotten back in touch. Wow, does it feel great to revisit this stuff. I wonder if Nick remembers these adventures the way I do . . . That's why I wanted to get some of this down. I guess his book will be the rebuttal.

1968

CLAIMS BAD KNEE

What a tale this is. Summer 1968 my longtime pal Michael Iacovelli and I had been playing in the same bar band, the Secrets (our secret was that our drummer, though he was six foot five, was only sixteen, and shouldn't have been playing in the boozy dives we worked at), but we had broken up because we had relentlessly tortured my best friend, our guitar player Chris Bates, about his girlfriend and he had angrily quit.

So Mike and our nut job pal Red McCreedy and I were cruising down the Long Island Expressway in Mike's white 1964 Chevy Impala en route to a party in the city being thrown by Red's wealthy girlfriend, Cynthia's friend Joyce.

(To this day, Red is the only person I know who actually saw the Beatles at Shea Stadium, due to Cynthia's rich father's connections.)

(Update 2017: I'm up to knowing three people who saw them.)

Suddenly, there in the middle of the right lane was a full-size beer keg.

I yelled, "Iacovelli, pull over."

I figured it'd make a great table for my room in my parents' cellar, where I was living while I was home from Michigan State University for the summer. Plus, it would be the Good Samaritan Thing to Do, because the thing was certainly going to cause an accident sooner rather than later.

It wasn't until a ways up, of course, but Ikey was finally able to pull off onto the shoulder and we ran back. I went out onto the highway to the keg and it was ice cold and full!

I figured there was no way a keg would ever fall out of a beer truck, so it must have been in a caterer's van, tipped over, rolled, and smashed out through the rear doors, or something to that effect. I immediately pictured a stoned delivery boy, still zipping along, totally oblivious.

The keg couldn't have been out there long, because it was still ice cold and it was a broiling August day.

No small task, we rolled it to the car and put it in the trunk.

We were (still are, I guess) assholes, so it never dawned on us that beer is homogenized, like milk, and that leaving it in the trunk of the car all night wasn't a great idea if you planned on eventually drinking it. Not that we could have done anything about it, short of heading home, which would have been out of the question.

Our little party that night was one for the books. We had a bottle of gin and no mixers and no money. So we drank gin and water. Did you ever try to drink gin and water? It's damn near impossible to get down, unless you're college kids determined to get drunk. Luckily, we filled that bill, so we also filled our glasses with gin and water.

Joyce had a nice apartment—she was wealthy, too—and I very clearly remember (this is important to the story) that she had a cloth seat cover on her toilet seat. And she had stereo speakers standing up on the floor to either side of her turntable, and each had some kind of decorative material on top of them.

One of the living room sofas pulled out to become Joyce's bed. We must have been way too loaded to even consider driving home, so we stayed over. Plus, I think I was trying to get with Joyce. Actually, it's a safe assumption. As I remember, she was a lot older—only in her mid-twenties, but I was just twenty, and at that age a few years was a big gap.

When I began to come to in the morning, lying on the room's other couch, which was ninety degrees to where she lay, my head was pounding as badly as I can ever remember (gin and water? My God . . .).

And into my mind came this very foggy memory of a dream I had that I had been sitting on one of the speakers—it was cloth, so maybe I had made the connection that it was the cloth of the toilet seat . . . I'm trying to extrapolate and fill in the blanks of a very drunk guy who had to take a leak in an unfamiliar dark apartment in the middle of the night . . . I had been sitting on a speaker, and had awakened when Joyce screamed, *"What the hell are you doing?"*

My hazy memory started to recall that in my dream when she screamed I had snapped to a bit and realized that I was sitting on the speaker with my pants down to my ankles, relaxed and pissing like a racehorse on the living room rug.

And as this all was slowly coming into focus in my gin-soaked mind, as I opened my eyes and glanced over toward where the closest speaker was . . . in front of the speaker was a huge wet spot, about three feet in diameter. It hadn't been a dream. I had pissed her rug.

When I got up and around, she was needless to say way beyond mad (even I couldn't type "pissed"). Plus, though she wasn't especially attractive or sexy, she thought she was superior to us due to her age and her financial status, thought she *was* attractive and sexy, and accused me of sitting on the speaker and jerking off as I watched her sleep. What a fucking idiot. But what a great story. We roared all the way home.

We get back to Oyster Bay and put the keg in the downstairs cooler where the kegs were stored at Ida's Folly, the bar-restaurant by the old Oyster Bay train station owned by Michael's parents, Eddie and Ida Iacovelli. Ida said we could keep our keg down there until we were ready to drink it.

One night, Mike and I walked into the bar and the customers were talking about the rotten beer they'd been served. Our good friend Charlie Brezinski, a long-time conductor on the Long Island Railroad and the chief cook and bottle washer at Ida's between shifts, had been drunk when he went down to tap a new keg and accidentally tapped ours. And it was nasty. The official bar term is "skunked." It had gone bad, very bad, sitting in the hot car trunk for a full day.

It was pretty funny when we put it all together. And we told Ida it was only fair that we get a keg to replace it. How the fuck that was fair I'll never understand, but she said okay.

Believe it or not, this story is the chronicling of my military career.

A week or so later, my dear friends the DeGuzman family were having a big Sunday afternoon party at their home on Main Street in

Oyster Bay, with the family's many kids and friends, their relatives the Biggarts' many kids and friends, and of course all the local hippies, who wound up at every party any of us had back in those great, great days that were the late sixties. It was the perfect party for our windfall, the rescued keg of beer, so we decided to donate it. We dragged one up from Ida's cellar and brought it to the party.

We of course got smashed as hell, and it had rained a bit, so the outdoor party was a sloppy mess.

While my brother Bobby and Peter DeGuzman and I were wrestling in the mud, one of them smashed against my left leg from the side, it bent the way it wasn't supposed to, and something ripped. Man, did that hurt. *Wow.* But I was drunk, and eventually the pain subsided. A week or so later, I turned on my left leg a bit too quickly or something, and I got hit with the same pain. My knee killed me for about an hour and then again it subsided.

What I didn't know was when I got hit from the side, the cartilage in my left knee had partially torn, and the second time I had torn it a bit more.

I went back to college, and in January I was walking up the stairs of my rented house, caught the heel of my left boot on a stair, and it was like someone shot me in the knee. The cartilage had finally totally ripped and the pain was triple what it had been the other two times. My God. I started guzzling beer much faster than usual, somehow hobbled over to my pal Jan Beers' apartment across the street, and got naked with her.

I vividly remember saying to her as she was riding on top of me, "As much as I'm enjoying this, it isn't helping. My knee is really killing me."

The next day I actually limped all the way to class, with no crutches. But I couldn't even sit. Unable to stand it any longer, and realizing I might be being an idiot, I dragged myself to Olin Health Center on campus. They X-rayed me, gave me crutches, and told me I needed a knee operation.

It was there, though it was ever so slight, I had my first and last brush with serious drug addiction. Nowadays the operation I had would be done laparoscopically and leave a pinprick in my knee. But it was 1968, and they had chopped into my knee but good. When I woke after the carnage, in indescribable agony, I rang for the nurse and she quickly came in and gave me a shot. The trippy Jefferson Airplane song "White Rabbit" had just started on my eight-track player, and before it ended I was smiling and enjoying it as I never had. A few hours later I awoke in pain again, rang for the nurse, and got another shot. *Ahhh.* The next time I rang for her, I swear I watched a goddess in white walk through the door carrying a red velvet pillow with my needle riding on top, which she used to once again put me on Mars.

The next time I was hurting, I rang, and this time the goddess was carrying a red velvet pillow . . . but there was a white pill on top of it.

I said, "What's that?"

She said, "No more shots. It's too dangerous. Morphine can be very, very addicting."

Man, they knew their stuff. *Whew.*

I dropped out of school, and my equally thirsty pal Bill Paterson dropped out, too, so I wouldn't have to drink alone. The tales of those few months—waking up shaking like leaves in his Volkswagen Bug in the middle of a cornfield off Route 17 in the throes of winter, on our way to chase girls we knew at upstate New York colleges—well, I have to save something for the sequel. Maybe by then I'll be able to recall some of it.

After the operation, my knee was weird. I'd be walking down the halls of the Engineering Building (yes) and suddenly be on the ground. My knee would just give out. I thought to myself, "This really wouldn't be good if I was in combat."

Our country was a very scary place for someone my age in 1969. The war in Vietnam—and the domestic protests against it—was raging. I knew there was no way I could ever put on a uniform or carry a gun. For God knows what reason when I got to school for summer orientation I had signed up for ROTC (Reserve Officers' Training Corps), and after a few fish-out-of-water weeks, and with no small amount of holding my ground with military lifers trying to intimidate me, I had dropped out of that frightening mess.

One day lined up for inspection the sergeant had said, "Martling, you're the most slovenly soldier I've ever seen," and gave me five demerits. The worst guys get perhaps three over the course of the two-year program. Obviously, the entire concept was alien to me. Boy Scouts had been all the regimentation I needed.

By the beginning of my (first) senior year, fall 1969, I had a ponytail down to the middle of my back and often walked barefoot in the Engineering Building with my dog Goopie at my side. I drank too much, smoked pot, did acid here and there, and took speed mainly for band jobs, but I did well in school and had a great tech average (your GPA, or grade point average, for the technical courses like atomic physics and mechanics).

In 1969 there was still a military draft, and that year they initiated a lottery system based on birthdays. The first draft lottery was December 1. My roommates and I decided we'd plant ourselves in front of the TV in our house and watch them pull the dates out of the hopper together. I did the beer run, but for obvious reasons, there was a long line at the package store.

When I got back, it was a few minutes after the lottery had started, they all said, "Martling, you better start drinking. They already pulled February 14 . . . you're number four."

Fuck. I was a social science student assistant (we turned on the TV for the lectures, took attendance, and led the class discussions at the end of each lecture), and the next day when I walked into the classroom someone said, "Mr. Martling, were you affected by last night's lottery?"

I was incredibly hungover and, needless to type, very freaked out.

I leaped up on my desk and, stomping with my boots, I screamed, "I'm number four!"

I had my college deferment. But by 1970, I had dropped out a term here and there (I had actually dropped out spring term 1969 à la "tune in, turn on, and drop out"), so the army wanted me. But I had enrolled in school again after, of all the crazy things, I met a terrific sorority girl that spring, fell in love in Cape Cod over the summer, and went back to finish and get my degree that fall. After I graduated, the military was right back on my case.

Actually, ever since I had become number four in the draft, they had tried many times to get me to go for a physical so I could be classified and it could be determined whether I had a deferment. (If you didn't, you were classified as 1-A, meaning available for military service.) When they sent me a notice to appear for a physical in Michigan, I told them I was in New York, and vice versa. I had the records of my operation, my doctor visits, and lots of documentation of what had happened with my knee, and the government had been repeatedly sending it back and forth from New York to Michigan.

March 1971, I got a notice, the long and short of it being you better show up for this physical or we'll come get you.

So I figured I better go this time, so I boarded one of the two busses that were to take our group of future soldiers from Lansing to Detroit. All the way down, guys were showing off their big, thick folders with psychiatrist's notes, doctor's notes, all kinds of excuses and whatever they thought could help their case. I had nothing. My file was hopefully waiting for me at the recruitment center in Detroit, where it had been sent from New York.

We got there, I went and got my folder, and it contained one thin piece of paper. Aside from my name, there were no notations on it whatsoever, except in the comments box at the very bottom, where all it read was "claims bad knee." Nothing about my knee operation, falling down whenever my knee gave out, nothing. I shit my pants.

The physical was a hoot. Hundreds of naked guys, mostly us college ball breakers, with just towels wrapped around us. If you remember folk singer Arlo Guthrie's physical down at Whitehall Street in the movie *Alice's Restaurant*, it was exactly like that. We were herded like cattle, and though we were all scared to death—we all had friends who had died in Vietnam at this point—we laughed our asses off for hours.

I quickly stopped laughing when I realized I was in the final line and they were about to classify us. I was a perfect physical specimen, if I do say so myself. A former gymnast, no matter how much I drank and debauched, the rock and roll had kept me trim and powerful. I'd make the perfect killer. I was freaking.

And then one of the recruiters said something to the effect of, "If any of you has any last-minute questions before you're classified, please go through this door."

I'm glad I was paying attention. I got out of line and walked into that room. What follows is as vivid a memory as anything in my little head.

There was a small Asian doctor, and I said, "Doc, my knee is screwed up. They don't have any of my documentation. I had an operation, and sometimes I fall down when my knee doesn't catch right."

He told me to sit on his table. He saw the big scar on my knee and he felt around it. Then he felt around my other knee. My heart sank like a stone.

I said, "Come on, doc, it's *this* one, the one with the scar."

He said, "Yes, I know," turned around, grabbed his pen, bent over a form, checked a box, scribbled his name, and handed it to me. With no communication or sign of emotion whatsoever.

I looked at the form, and he had checked "#47—unstable left knee." I swear I can still see it. I wasn't really sure what the form would do for me, but my first inclination was to hug the little fella, which didn't thrill him.

I said, "Thanks, doc," and he of course again showed no sign of emotion whatsoever.

I left the room and got back in my place on line. When I got to the front, I handed the form to the recruiter sitting there, he looked at it, and stamped me 4-F. Which meant unsuited for military service.

My friend Jimmy Mehrtens used to say that if you were classified 4-F, "They'd take women and children first, and in case of war, they'd hold you as a hostage."

It hit me slowly at first, but when I had digested it, it banged me over the head profoundly. They had not just given me two years of my life, they had probably given me my *life*. I was smart, so odds are I would've been made a first lieutenant, who were biting the dust the fastest over there, some of them killed by their own troops.

On the way back in the bus, I was very quiet, much like the kid who hides his report card full of As from his fuck-up pals. Almost all of the guys with thick dossiers and surefire outs had all been classified 1-A. In other words, start packing. Only two or three of us had pulled a 4-F.

When I got back to Lansing, my sweetheart Darlene was there waiting for me. I got off the bus with a long face, looking like my world had ended. She came running up and when she saw my expression, she immediately got incredibly upset.

She hugged me tight and said, "Sweet pea, what happened?"

I said, "I'm 4-F. They'll take women and children before me, and in case of war they'll hold me as a hostage."

She said, "You *bastard*," and started pummeling me.

We laughed and cried and did our best to assess what had happened. It was surreal.

I'll never know what I would have done had I been accepted for military service. I wonder if I'd have run to Canada. I know I could never, ever have been a soldier. To this day I shudder every time I think about it . . . and then take a deep breath and once again thank my lucky stars . . .

As for the guy who was driving for the caterer that day, I'll always wonder where that keg came from. I've always hoped that one day the jerk-off(s) who so poorly packed up that van will read or hear this story. Whoever it was would have to remember showing up for a catered affair and the keg of beer not being there when he (or she) went to unload it.

Whoever and wherever you are, thanks.

1970

THE ONE-LEGGED WOMAN

This is a tale I told the *Stern Show* boys early on, but only got to relate on the air after they'd gotten to know me well enough to realize there was a more than good chance it was true.

It was a typical spring weekend in 1970 as I was winding up my (first) senior year at Michigan State University. My band was playing Friday and Saturday at fraternity parties, and my good friend, James Wolanin, whom I'd known from Snyder Hall, the dormitory where I lived on campus for my first two years, was coming up from Detroit on Saturday night. As per our usual game plan, he'd be bringing along a small gang who we'd get into the party to drink free and then meet back at our house for the late and most likely into-the-early-morning festivities.

This night, however, for whatever reason, the Detroit crew didn't make it to the frat party, and I wondered what had happened to them. It wasn't like them to not show.

When we were through playing, we packed up, loaded the equipment in our sorry blue truck, and headed for the house. We were already pretty toasted.

A few minutes after we got home, James finally pulled up with his entourage and tons of booze. Beer, wine, and whatever else. He and his friends were working folk in Detroit City, actually had jobs and paychecks, so they had loot to blow on weekends. Needless to say, supplying the goods for the festivities at our nuthouse in the college town was a terrific way for them to waste their hard-earned money. It was the perfect wedding: we supplied the frat party and then the house for the after-party, and they brought the hooch.

They had gotten hung up in Detroit for a while, and almost didn't come. Well, in the end, they did, and it had ridiculous long-range impact on my life. Almost immeasurable.

As they came through the front door lugging the goodies, I quickly assessed the potential pairing-off situation, as the few girls we already had at our house I'm sure I already knew, carnally or otherwise, so that would basically have been a rerun or a dead end.

About five guys and maybe three girls walked in. As I remember, one of the girls was with one of the guys, and another wasn't too hot. The third was definitely very cute.

I pulled James to the side and said, "What's *her* story?"

He said, "That's Debbie. She's rich. She was in a really bad car accident a few years ago and got a huge settlement. She's available. She's a great-looking chick, but she's got an artificial leg."

Well, I looked around. She was by far the best-looking woman in the place. I checked her out, and her legs looked fine to me. They certainly seemed to match, under her tight blue jeans.

I can still remember thinking, "Damn, she has a great face and a great body . . . *hmm . . .*"

So, I set my sights. Knowing I'd need fortification for this romance, I started wailing it down, and the next thing I knew, it was morning and I woke up next to a very pretty girl. At this point, my eyes barely open, the night before was still pretty much a foggy dream.

I pulled myself out of bed and dragged my still half-drunk self in to take a leak. When I'm a mess in the morning, I often sit down to pee. It just seems easier than hovering and leaning and aiming. So, I sat down, and as I brought my head up, there, leaning against the corner of the bathroom—I swear I can still see it—was Debbie's prosthesis. A fucking fake leg. Flesh-colored, with a foot on it, and a metal knee joint, and straps coming out of the thighs, I guess to attach it to however much of her real thigh remained. Needless to say, it was an eye-opener.

The night before quickly shot through my brain. It was blurry, but there I was, half-bombed, checking her out, realizing that she was the night's best choice and deciding to make a play for her even though she had an artificial leg . . .

My God, I'd succeeded.

Of course, everybody asks, "So what was it like?"

And I have no idea. I have to assume we had sex, as we were both naked when I woke up, and in those days I'd have banged a night table, and liquor had never seemed to deter my prowess.

And no, I hadn't peeked at her stump. Before I got to the bathroom, I had no idea how interesting it would have been under those covers.

I was freaked out. For at least thousand reasons, the foremost probably being that I didn't especially want to help her strap that thing on. I left the bathroom through the other door, went through the other bedroom and down the stairs, shook my roommate Red awake, and said, "I'm taking your car." I called my dog Goopie, and the two of us ran outside, jumped in the convertible, and bolted away from the scene of whatever you'd call what had taken place.

I had no idea where to go. I think I figured the first thing to accomplish was to get the hell out of the house, and then I'd deal with what to do next.

For a few months I'd been dating Darlene Stone, a cute little Kappa Delta with a drinking problem that rivaled mine. We had lots of fun together but we weren't too involved. We did like each other enough that we never went for the drunken sex but had put it off for the right time, should that ever arise. Or possibly we were always so bombed we forgot, though that didn't really fit my MO.

We were both class of '70, and she had just graduated, whereas I hadn't, due to various fuck-ups along the four-year route. I knew she was leaving town any day. Should I maybe go over and say goodbye? It seemed like as good an idea as any, so I headed for Sorority Row.

I knocked on the door of Kappa Delta, a pretty girl answered it and let me in, and I asked for Darlene. She came into the foyer and lit up when she saw me. She was incredibly tickled that I had come over to see her one last time. A bunch of the girls were in the next room, sitting around the piano singing "Leaving on a Jet Plane," and it was a really sentimental time that I had somewhat randomly stumbled into.

Obviously caught up in the moment, Darlene said, "My grandmother gave me her car for a graduation gift, and Suzie and I are leaving for Cape Cod tomorrow. Do you want to come?"

Pretty quickly, I realized I did. It was one of the more spontaneous decisions I've ever made. And for once, I'm pretty sure I never vacillated even a little.

It's hard to believe that at any place in a person's life they could be that free to just take off, but I was, and I said, "My friend Bobby DeVine got here last week from New York. We just planted a garden and were planning on staying here for the summer, but he's usually game for anything. Can he come, too?"

She said, "Why not? Then Suzie'd have somebody to talk to."

I asked Bobby, and he simply smiled and said, pretty much exactly as I imagined he would, "Sure. I'll go with the flow."

I told my roommate Wimpy (still my good pal and former drummer in the college incarnation of the Off Hour Rockers, Jim Santino) to take good care of Goopie and the pot garden and that I'd see him in the fall. The next day, Darlene pulled up, Bobby and I jumped in, and off we went.

And it blossomed into my first real relationship. We fell in love in storybook Falmouth Heights on Cape Cod, moved back to East Lansing so I could finish school, and stayed together for a little over two years.

I'm not sure that I ever told her exactly how I wound up at her door that Sunday morning.

The craziest part of this story—yeah, I know, so far it's been pretty nutty—is that three years later, after Darlene and I had broken up and I was still living in our house in the Lansing ghetto with a drunk and a drug addict, two different guys, I dragged myself downstairs one morning to pee, stumbled into the bathroom, pulled down my pants, eased myself onto the toilet, and . . . there in the corner . . . *dèjà vu*.

It turned out the night before, my very drunken roommate Billy had picked up a girl at a bar, danced with her all night, then brought her home and into his bed, all the while having no idea she had a fake leg.

So, once again, here I was, sitting on the bowl, staring at a flesh-colored fake leg, with the foot, the knee joint, and the straps, the whole nine yards. I swear it was exactly the same. Maybe even the same one, who knows?

Twice. Not once. *Twice*. Yikes.

1972

THE INFAMOUS
URINE TOSSING INCIDENT

I hope you enjoy this story. I told it on *The Howard Stern Show* many times, and everyone's always asking me if it's true, what really happened . . . So here it is, in all its wacky detail, once and for all.

I graduated from Michigan State University as a mechanical engineer in spring 1971 but had stayed in the college town to seek musical fame by getting demolished and playing in my college rock and roll band at bars and frat parties. Yes, to avoid mainstream work and growing up.

In late spring 1972, I left the band (the Pillowcayse . . . with a *y*, we don't know why) in East Lansing, Michigan, and came back to Oyster Bay on the premise I was going to spend the summer earning enough money to buy a secondhand electric piano, the sound of which, I had convinced the guys, would greatly enhance our band. The fact I was totally inept at playing piano must have escaped them. Maybe they were as sick of our noise as I was . . . but, at any rate, home to Long Island I came.

Happily ensconced in the cellar of my childhood home, I worked as a cement hauler during the day and a waiter in a really happening bar at night, played on a local softball team (Oyster Bay Beverage, believe it or

28

not), pretty much avoided the girl I had been seeing, and mostly stayed smashed for about two months.

At the end of the summer, the fog cleared and I had no money. I convinced a girl I worked with at the bar to lend me the money for the piano, found a used one in Queens, where you can find, used, anything you need twenty-four hours a day, she drove me in and we bought it. A Fender Rhodes 88. Ahhh. Now, all I had to do was get it back to Michigan.

I had no car, so I asked Carl Dincesen, the six-foot-five drummer from my high school band the Sonics and then the Secrets and still a good friend, to drive me and my new old piano back to the Midwest in his '64 Mustang convertible.

At some point I guess my mother decided she wanted to go with us and we said okay. Looking back on the situation with some perspective I'm sure it was more like she told me she was coming, and I can only guess that she either kicked in some for the piano or volunteered gas money so I couldn't say no.

At any rate, I can't see me just saying, "Hey, Dot, hop in, we're going cruising." I mean, she could be fun, but I was a twenty-four-year-old screaming asshole and Carl wasn't much better. You know, now that I write this, I have to correct myself. We definitely might've said hop in. The more the merrier. Always.

We got a few cases of beer, put a lot of it on ice, secured a fifth of rye whiskey for ma, put the piano in the trunk as best we could, and then packed us and the booze into the car somewhere around ten in the morning. We wanted to get to East Lansing before the bars closed.

My mother was sitting on the right in the backseat, I was shotgun, and huge Carl was at the wheel. The Mustang had a tiny trunk and I remember at least half of the big, rectangular Fender Rhodes sticking out like a shelf.

Carl had to have his seat all the way back in the tiny car, and that left no room behind it. So on my mother's left, in the middle of the backseat, was the cooler, and she played bartender.

Being an experienced traveling beer drinker from driving back and forth to Michigan all those years, I had an open-top pitcher with me so we wouldn't have to pull over every time I had to pee. That would've stretched the fourteen-hour trip considerably.

As ridiculous as this may read, these are the facts and that was my actual thought pattern at the time. Jesus.

So we were barreling down either Interstate 80 or whatever thoroughfares were being used in the sections of I-80 that weren't finished yet, drinking, laughing, and having a merry old time. Dot had a bottomless glass of rye on ice, and we had only to reach out for her to hand us another ice-cold chillie, which is what we called a beer at any temperature when I was in college. In a Mustang convertible, even with the top up, wailing along at eighty miles per hour, we had to talk pretty loud to be heard, so the energy level was high and higher.

At some point, I'd imagine somewhere between beer five and beer six, winding through the mountains of eastern Pennsylvania, I had to take a leak. You put off that first one as long as you can, because it breaks the seal and you then start needing to go more and more often.

I grabbed the pitcher, turned around, and got up on my knees on the seat facing my mother, unzipped and pulled out my willie, the conversation and party never skipping a beat. I remember talking to her and laughing as I commenced to peeing into the pitcher, with Carl in total disbelief. He'd been six foot five since eighth grade, so he was cursed with having had to act like an adult his entire life—whereas I had yet to even try it.

When I was done, still yakking away, I turned around and sat down, simply opened the window, stuck the pitcher out as far as I could reach—so none would get on the car—and turned it upside down, 180 degrees. Honestly, again, that was the thought process and the move.

Of course, as I did this, I was still talking and looking at Carl, when we heard a bloodcurdling yelp from the backseat.

I turned around as Carl looked into his rearview mirror. The wind rushing past the car had blown the bulk of the pee back in the window, a healthy amount of it splashing right in Dot's face. By the time we saw her, it was dripping off her nose and down her cheeks and forehead. She was laughing uncontrollably, and so was I, and at the sight of her soggy face in his mirror, Carl erupted so violently into hysterics he almost lost control of the car. We were swerving down the road like a snake with a piano tail. Thank God no one was driving next to us. Or watching.

For the life of me, I don't remember what happened immediately after that, or even after we caught our breath. And neither does Carl. I'm sure we raced to the nearest exit, cleaned her up, wiped off the backseat as best we could, got in, set up another round, and were on our way. What else could we do?

A classic story. My mother didn't get pissed off, even when she got pissed on.

I guess I should've asked her if she remembered the incident, but hey, she never remembered any of the old tales anyway, and it drove me nuts. Wouldn't you remember that if it happened to you?

Well, it's too late now. The so very intelligent and incredibly funny Dot left us in 1998.

1978

A GREAT
RODNEY DANGERFIELD STORY

At the very beginning of my comedy career, I spent two weeks on the road with Rodney Dangerfield. He was my favorite comedian of all time when we met, and he still is. There's never been anyone like him, before or since. I cherish the time we spent together. In late 1978, he bought some jokes from me, we got somewhat close for a while, and at Easter in 1980, he took me with him—all expenses paid—on a week's vacation in Fort Lauderdale. Then he took me to his weeklong engagement at the Aladdin Hotel in Las Vegas, where he was co-headlining with songwriter Paul Williams. To this day, I'm recalling things that happened in that short span that have been long buried in the haze of a once-in-a-lifetime trip.

Rodney and I had been brought together thanks to a fellow fledgling comedian's fib.

In the late seventies, Rodney Dangerfield was a household name, but he hadn't done TV commercials or movies yet. He had been regularly featured on the Dean Martin television shows for a while, but that had been years back, and at this point you only caught him every couple of months on *The Tonight Show with Johnny Carson*.

For me, as well as many of us, Rodney's appearances on *The Tonight Show* were terrific events. His seven minutes of stand-up, and then seven more minutes of stand-up while he was sitting down with Johnny, were always nonstop brutally funny. Yes, there actually was a time when you were glad to see a stand-up comic on television.

One night, in late 1978, my new friend Richie Minervini, another freshly minted comedian, walked into my grandmother's house, where my girlfriend and I were squatting for free since Grandma had passed away. He told me he had gone on at Dangerfield's, Rodney's comedy club on the Upper East Side in Manhattan, the night before. He told me that he had not only killed (done really well with the audience), but that Rodney had watched him and had spoken to him about using him on a TV show. I was so jealous I could have exploded.

Of course, Jackie the Hustler immediately sat down at his typewriter, stuck in two sheets of paper and a carbon—always a carbon for the loose leaf—and methodically went through every joke he knew, switching and molding the ones that he thought would work for Rodney and the "I don't get no respect" Dangerfield persona.

Let us break briefly for a very important insert:

A few weeks earlier, I had been awakened at about five o'clock in the morning by the phone. In retrospect, that seems like nothing, considering the asshole hours I kept for the fifteen years I was on *The Howard Stern Show* every day, but at the time, it stuck out in my mind as a very weird time to be awake unless I was screaming drunk somewhere.

I tell people that before *The Howard Stern Show* went to morning drive in February of 1986, I had gotten up at 4:30 a.m. precisely twice in my life. Once to go fishing, and once to catch farmer's mass in Saratoga with a friend's family before we drove home, to miss the traffic. It sucked then, and it sucked for the fifteen years I was a regular on the show. Nowadays, I wake up and smile at my silent clock. I set the alarm as rarely as I can get away with.

The phone call was from Jackie Ratcliffe, a close friend who was calling from, of all places, Peru. He was down there either doing or buying cocaine, or both, and had met some wild guy from the Deep South in the US who had told him something he thought was really funny and he just had to tell it to me.

As fucked up as he was, he knew enough to keep me on the phone until I was conscious enough to be sure to remember what he told me, as it was a safe assumption I had gone to bed with a snoutful myself. And then he hit me with it.

He said, "Chief [which is what my guys called me back then, with absolutely no respect intended], this girl was so ugly that she was known as a 'Tennessee Two-Bagger.' That's a girl who's so ugly, you not only have to put a bag over *her* head, but you have to put a bag over your *own* head, in case her bag rips."

Of course, I fell out of bed, woke up my girlfriend and told it to her, wrote it down, and went back to sleep.

and we're back . . .

So as I typed away, I was going through my jokes and tailoring and typing out the ones I thought would work for Rodney, now that I had a direct channel to him. When I got to the "Tennessee Two-Bagger," it struck me as, "Yeah, this is great for him," but it didn't leap off the page. You see, as I typed, I was trying to convince myself that everything I was writing was perfect for him. Hell, in my fraudulently optimistic mind, I was spitting out his new act. And when I was done, there they were: six delightful pages, the pages that would be my entry to Real Show Business.

When Richie walked in, I handed the pages to him in an Off Hour Rockers envelope—while I couldn't even afford to eat, I had company stationery—and said, "Do me a favor and hand this to your new pal Rodney Dangerfield."

Richie looked at me sheepishly and said, "Oh, man, I didn't meet Rodney the other night. He wasn't there. I didn't even get on stage."

"So I guess your spot on his TV show is on the back burner."

"I'm sorry, man."

"You weren't even there, were you?"

"Yeah, yeah, I was there. I swear. They told me to come back, that I'd get on next time. Look . . ."

He reached in his pocket and pulled out a matchbook. It read "Dangerfield's, 1118 First Avenue, New York, New York." It had the phone number and the caricature of Rodney sweating and pulling at his tie. It was authentic. He had at least been there.

This makes Richie sound like an incredible bullshit artist, which he is, but that's strictly a coincidence. In Richie's defense, all starting comics, maybe all comics period, lie about their shows and how their careers are going.

There's a classic joke about two Catskill comics who live together. As a joke-teller by trade, you'll find I call jokes "classic" because it has a nicer ring to it than "old."

> *Two Catskill comics live together.*
>
> *One guy goes out to work, and when he gets back that night, his room-mate says, "So how'd it go?"*
>
> *He says, "You wouldn't believe it. The best show I ever had. It was unbelievable."*
>
> *"I was there. You weren't so hot."*
>
> *"The band fucked me up."*

So, I immediately forgave Richie. But I still had this envelope with six pages of jokes for Rodney.

Then I thought to myself, "Wait. The address of Rodney's club is on the matchbook. I'll just send it to the club. I've got a carbon copy of my work, so even if it gets tossed, I've got nothing to lose except the price of a stamp."

I sat back down and typed a quick note to Rodney, "Here's a few jokes I hope you can use," and gave him Nanny Appy's, I mean, my dear departed grandmother's, phone number. I stuck it in the envelope with the jokes, wrote the address and "attention: Rodney Dangerfield" on it, and stuck it in the mail on my way to my job at Workshoppe Recording Studios.

Two days later, my girlfriend and I were sitting in Grandma's kitchen when the phone rang. We'd only been there a month or so, and very few people had the number, so it was an event when we got a call.

I answered. "Hello?"

"Hello, Jackie? This is Rodney."

"Rodney who?"

"See that? You're funny. I knew you were fucking funny . . ."

Meanwhile, I'm cupping the phone and telling my girlfriend, "It's Rodney Dangerfield!" And she of course wasn't buying it for a second.

She said, "Tell Richie I say 'hi.'"

I said, *"It's fucking Rodney Dangerfield!"*

I was about as excited as I've ever been. This wasn't just a celebrity, this was my *hero,* my *idol,* one of the funniest guys *ever.*

He went on, "I got the jokes. Some really funny stuff here. I'm gonna send you a check for four or five of these. Want to come meet me? I'm at Westbury Music Fair Friday night."

"I'll be there."

"That two-bagger, that's a funny fucking joke. See you Friday. Just tell them you're with me."

At the Westbury show, the two-bagger joke brought down the house. In his dressing room after the show, Rodney almost shit when he saw I had a ponytail down my back and was in ragged blue jeans, but he couldn't have been nicer. I guess it didn't hurt that my girlfriend was young and attractive. Rodney was, of course, all over the place.

"Look at your fucking hair. And the jeans. Jesus Christ. She's beautiful. Want a piece of fruit? Have a piece of fruit. Some funny stuff. A ponytail? She's gorgeous. Send more jokes, send 'em to my house. I'll put my home address in the letter with the check. You want something to drink? She's a knockout. Have a piece of fruit. Look at you. I like that fucking two-bagger. Yeah. Send more . . ."

A few days later, I got a letter listing the four jokes he was buying and a check for two hundred dollars. Signed by Rodney Dangerfield. And we were pals. Not bosom buddies by any stretch, but in some form of the word, pals.

Over the next year or so, he bought a few scattered jokes, here and there . . .

"I know I'm getting old. My last birthday cake looked like a *prairie fire.*"

Every time I sent Rodney a batch of jokes, I'd throw in a quick note, which always included, "Hey, Boss, why not take me on the road some time. We could write jokes and have a few laughs . . ."

By February 1980, my band had been dissolved for a little over a year. We had been a three-piece band, and after one of our gigs at Neptune Pub in East Meadow, Long Island, where we raked in a hundred dollars—total—we were in the dressing room. Well, uh, the room where they stored the cases of beer. The other two guys told me they were leaving the band to start their own band. Now, I told most of the jokes and wrote ninety percent of the songs, but if you're in a three-piece band and two of the guys "leave to start their own band," that's kicking me out of the band. The rest is semantics. So even though I had already started my move to comedy, and it was most likely the single best thing that ever happened to me, it hurt like hell.

So it was much to my delight that my ex-partner, the other guitar player in the band, my oldest friend, a guy I went to kindergarten with, Chris Bates, was sitting in my office in my mother's attic. He was right next to, at this point, the four "Use Your Finger! (516) 922-WINE" phone lines, talking to me, when I answered the phone. It was Rodney calling.

Rodney said, "Hey, you keep asking. You ever been to Vegas?"

I said, "Not since passing through as a kid in 1966."

"Want to go to Vegas?"

"Well, fuck *yes* I want to go to Las Vegas!"

"Yeah, come to Vegas, the week after Easter. I gotta go to Fort Lauderdale first. What about Fort Lauderdale? I'm not working there, just going for a week with my daughter and her friend during their school vacation. Want to go to Lauderdale, too? Yeah, come to Lauderdale. Then we'll go on to Vegas. I'm working the Aladdin. You come for both weeks, yeah, it's all on me. First class, the whole bit, it'll be good. I like that two-bagger joke."

Knock me over with a feather. I hadn't been to Fort Lauderdale since my Michigan State spring breaks in 1967 and 1968, when we ruled the turf. And now I would be returning in grand style. Well, as a hanger-on, but it certainly didn't suck.

And I'd be going back with Rodney Dangerfield. First class.

And then on to Las Vegas, not only with a major headliner, but my *comedy hero.* Wow. All that nagging got to him. No, he appreciates the jokes. Maybe a bit of each. But *fuck!* I was going.

Needless to say, Batesy's jaw dropped. I don't like myself for it, but it made me feel better about the band thing. We remain the dearest of friends. It's been sixty-three years and we just might go all the way.

Me being invited to travel with Rodney Dangerfield was somehow good news for all of us locals, a really positive event. The other Long Island comics actually held a benefit at the East Side Comedy Club to raise some spending money for me. I know it makes no sense, but they did it. They were as excited for me as I was. Man . . . even as I type that it's hard to believe.

The plan was I'd fly down with the girls, Rodney's sixteen-year-old daughter Melanie and her pal Debbie, rent a car at the airport, drive us to the hotel—the spectacular Bahia Mar at the south end of the Lauderdale strip, that had a walking bridge over Route A1A to get to Fort Lauderdale Beach—and then pick up Rodney at the airport the next day.

I remember the morning I went to pick up the girls at Rodney's apartment on York and Seventy-Fifth Street so, so vividly.

I had been there before, of course. Many other comedians had been there, too, and then forever told the tale of Rodney answering the door in the same ratty blue bathrobe, the robe hanging open and his balls nearly dragging on the floor . . .

One time, I had the good fortune of talking with him at his dining room table as he ate his non-varying concoction of chopped chicken and salad from a huge bowl, shoveling it in like the world might end. After I met Thelma, his long-time Jamaican housekeeper, he told me how he and his great pal Joe Ancis—a legend in comedy circles—would stand behind a door in his apartment that was just barely cracked open and watch Thelma watch her game shows, screaming like mad at the television when she didn't like somebody's decision. Rodney swore it was he and Joe's favorite thing in the world to do.

Joe Ancis never took the stage in his life, but anyone and everyone who knew him claimed he was the funniest guy ever. And his gang in the '50s was Rodney (Jack Roy at the time), Lenny Bruce, Buddy Hackett . . .

Joe was always at Rodney's club, Dangerfield's, on First Avenue in New York City, and Rodney performed there pretty often in those days. (As of 2017, Dangerfield's is still there, with comedy shows nightly. Rodney's original partner, Tony Bevacqua, still runs it.)

Joe had a job when Rodney did his act at Dangerfield's. At some point when Rodney was nearing the end of his show, Joe would yell from the back of the room, "So what do you do for a living?"

And Rodney would answer, "I get guys for your sister . . . Why don't you come with me into the men's room and I'll show you how small you really are."

When I was with Rodney at the Aladdin, that was *my* job. I yelled it from the back of the room every night. The tourists would turn around and glare at me. It was terrific. I can only report that, god*damn*, I felt so fucking cool.

Years later, in 1981, at some point after I had released (started giving away and trying to sell at my shows) *Goin' Ape*, my second album, I heard someone use the expression, "Normal people are people you don't know that well."

I thought, "Wow. That's great. I *love* it. I'm going to use that for the name of my third comedy album."

I was finished recording and editing the new album, and was about to press it, when there was an article in *People* magazine about Rodney Dangerfield. In the last paragraph was a quote from Rodney:

"It's like Joe Ancis says . . . the only normal people are ones you don't know that well."

My heart sunk.

I had met Joe a few times with Rodney, so I called Rodney, got Joe's address, and sent him a postcard that said, "Joe, I was going to name my next album 'Normal People Are People You Don't Know That Well,' an expression I heard a while back. Then I saw Rodney's *People* article, where he attributed the quote to you. Is it yours? And if it is, can I use it? If not, just tell me to go fuck myself and I'll forget about it."

Joe wrote back, "Yes! It is an original quote! You can use it! And fuck you anyway! Good Luck, Joe Ancis."

So I go to pick up the girls for our Florida flight, and as we're putting their suitcases in my car and Rodney's telling us what we should and shouldn't do, I'm just grinning from ear to ear. I mean, aside from his jokes, he was a man of very few words. And here he was, being Daddy and arranging my job as our director as best he could.

"Tips, big tips. Yeah, when you're with me, big tips, always big tips. Big tips."

It was the purest entertainment ever. Rodney wasn't being funny, he was just being Rodney. It was the cadence, the phrases uttered with such effort, the weight of the years pulling on his every word. It had always mesmerized me, and now I had two weeks of daily bombardments in store. It was sheer joy.

I said, "Boss, you realize I'm going to laugh every time you open your mouth, right?"

And he said, "Whatever."

We flew without incident. It was my first time in first class. And in 1980, first class was just that. They waited on you hand and foot, they cut the steak in the aisle, the amenities seemed to flow just endlessly. Of course, I'm sure the fact I had spent the last fifteen years as a very poor college kid, then a very poor musician, and then a very poor comic, underscored the proceedings.

I rented a car, checked the girls into their Bahia Mar hotel rooms and me into the motel right next door, on the marina, with my room opening to the pool.

And then I know I lay on my bed for what seemed like a very long time, staring at the ceiling in disbelief.

I may have been laughing.

At the time, my studio was still in the attic of my parents' home. Many nights, I'd be up late editing my audiotapes, directly above my mother's bedroom. As quiet as I'd try to be, I'm sure whatever noise I made was annoying. But I was hell-bent, even though I had no idea what for.

Often, late at night, my mother would get up while I was working, go into the bathroom and *slam* the door, both on her way in and on her way out, to let me know I was keeping her up. My stomach would knot up, but I'd plow on . . .

So I'm standing there in this Florida motel, with the windows and my room door open to let the sweet Florida breezes flow through, the wind catches the door and it *slams* shut.

And as sure as Pavlov stepped in dog shit, my stomach immediately knotted up.

Somehow, not very logically, that hit me in a very sweet way.

The next day I was waiting for Rodney at the Fort Lauderdale airport baggage claim when here he came, in his usual frenzy, wired to the gills, wearing a short-sleeve flowers and flamingoes and herons shirt, glad to see I was there.

I've told people the following, about collecting Rodney's luggage, many times, but I've always felt that very few believed me . . .

Rodney said, "Okay, I got about seven pieces."

His luggage came, five or so pieces, but then there were two differ-ent-sized, obviously well-traveled cardboard boxes tied up with twine. Actually, it was closer to string than twine.

He pointed and said, "There, that one . . . and that one . . ."

I did a double take as I saw what he was pointing at.

The ratty cardboard boxes housed his toaster oven and his huge salad bowl with his various utensils.

He didn't like to eat at restaurants and make a commotion, and he didn't trust the hotel's room service to make what he wanted the way he wanted it—his chicken à la lettuce—as he was always on some kind of diet, and always trying to quit smoking, both of which made him nuts. So he brought his own kitchen and made his food himself.

I remember I thought it was a *Twilight Zone* episode as a baggage handler loaded Rodney's suitcases and boxes onto a luggage cart and people stared in disbelief.

Rodney was, of course, unfazed. I led us out to where I had parked, the baggage guy loaded it all into the car, and Rodney handed him what seemed like four or five twenties.

"Tips, big tips. Yeah, when you're with me, big tips, always big tips. Big tips."

Rodney hadn't done *Caddyshack* yet, but he had done a good many Miller Lite beer commercials that aired every two minutes on various TV shows, so many people recognized him and said hello and told him how great he was, and I was so glad to see how very personable he was with all of them. It was obvious he was touched and pleased with his new notoriety.

On the way to the hotel he said, "You know, I did lots of Ed Sullivan's and then years of Dean Martin's shows and more than fifty Carson's, but people have never recognized me anywhere near as much as they have since these Miller Lite spots."

When we got to the Bahia Mar they were all ready for Rodney, greeting him like royalty.

After the bellman dropped off the assorted belongings in his room, I said, "I'll unpack this stuff and set it up, Boss, just gimme a toot."

He broke out the cocaine, we did a few lines, and I proceeded to put one small end table on top of the other and then put his oven on top so it'd be at a good level for easy access.

He said, "Not bad. You're earning your keep, you know?"

We spent time at the ocean and poolside with his daughter and her friend and, after a few days, his son Brian, who's a few years older than Melanie, joined the gang. We swam, went for walks, drank a lot, smoked pot, did a little coke. Just hung out, very low key.

One night, we were out on the balcony of Rodney's room smoking a joint when there was a knock on the door. Rodney opened it and it was Melanie.

She walked in, and then smelling the weed she took a few loud sniffs. *Sniff! Sniff!* And said, *"Da-ddddy . . ."*

He said, "For Christ sakes, don't *bug* me, Melanie."

After she left, I said, "You do realize that was exactly backwards? Your daughter catching *you* smoking pot?"

He said, "Whatever."

Rodney loved to smoke pot. But it made quitting smoking cigarettes really hard for him.

He said to me so many times, "Quitting smoking, that's a rough one, you know. My whole life, it's been smoke a joint, smoke a straight, smoke a joint, smoke a straight. It's tough to kick it, you know?"

I loved to make him laugh, and I could do it pretty easily. As funny as he was, he was totally unschooled in the world of regular stupid jokes and I always had them at my disposal. I knew them all and he'd heard very few, so when I applied them he was always a bit impressed.

One day we were walking along Fort Lauderdale beach and the place was packed with college kids, tourists, old locals, middle-aged folks. A real hodgepodge.

We looked over and on the beach there was a muscle-bound guy in a bathing suit doing push-ups.

I said, "Look, Boss. Somebody stole his partner."

Rodney said, "You really are fucking funny, aren't you?"

I smiled, trying not to take too much credit for such a well-worn joke.

People would recognize him—which, as I said, he liked—which we all like, and many would ask him to pose with them for a picture. After a few people had taken their shots, he'd turn to me and say, "I'm gonna be in a lot of basements."

But, like anybody, sometimes they'd get to him.

One woman, fully dressed in the broiling hot Florida sun, recognized Rodney, came up to him on the beach, and said, "Can you tell me where there's entertainment?"

He said, "Jesus Christ, buy a *paper*, lady. What the fuck's wrong with you?"

One of the funniest things he ever said to me was one afternoon when we were walking down the sidewalk near the intersection of Las Olas Boulevard and A1A, the corner that houses Fort Lauderdale's world-famous Elbow Room, in the heart of the spring break crowd. Everywhere you turned, there were countless beautiful girls in bikinis, each skimpier than the next.

Matter-of-factly and unceremoniously, he turned to me and said, "Don't you wish you could just fuck anybody you wanted?"

By Thursday I was as horny as he had just exclaimed he was. Poor Rodney was in his father role, so as easy as it might have been for him as a celebrity, he couldn't go trolling for babes at the hotel bar, and calling on the services of a professional really wouldn't have flown, though by now I was sure it wouldn't have fazed Melanie, or any of them, even a little.

But me? I was a free bird.

It was about six o'clock, and I told him, "I can't take it, Boss. I'm going to get laid tonight. I'm not coming back until I find myself a girl."

He said, "Oh, really? Well, good luck with that."

I dressed as decently as I could—I still wonder what the hell clothes I had as a pauper in 1980—walked up A1A to the aforementioned Elbow Room, and sat on a barstool, determined to drink beer until there was a woman drinking with me.

I, of course, have no idea exactly how it happened, but a few hours later a woman—a very attractive woman from Long Island—who was alone in Florida for her last hurrah before she was to get married, took a shine to me. We both got very bombed, and sure enough, here we were on our way back to the Bahia Mar.

I told her, "Before we go to my room, I want you to meet my friend." She said, "Sure."

We went into the Bahia Mar's main building, and the girl at the desk by now knew me, so she gave me a passkey so we could take the elevator to the penthouse.

I knocked on the door and, a bit sobered up from our half-mile walk, I can still remember trying to determine who was more shocked: my new girl pal, when Rodney Dangerfield answered the door, or Rodney, seeing I had succeeded in my quest.

He smiled and invited us in. And then it was my turn to be shocked. He had company. Louis Nye, one of the classic "Men On the Street" from *The Steve Allen Show,* whose partners in crime had been Tom Poston, Don Knotts, Dayton Allen, and Bill Dana. We stayed long enough for my friend and I to down a few more drinks and mingle a bit with these two very gracious celebrities.

Rodney walked us to the door and smiled at me very knowingly, still not quite sure if I had actually pulled it off. Looking back, I have to imagine my flirt game most likely had an edge, knowing where I was and who I was with and whatever. Or, maybe, as they say, I simply "got lucky."

There's an excellent chance my temporary sweetheart still walks among us, and that either she or someone she knows will read this book. She was a New Yorker, a Long Islander no less, somewhere between twenty-five and thirty-five years old in 1980, and pretty wild, wouldn't you say? That makes her an excellent candidate to have become a Stern fan. She was spending Easter in Fort Lauderdale a few weeks before her wedding. And even if I wasn't memorable, which I most certainly want to believe I was, she had a one-night fling and met Rodney Dangerfield. Engaged or no, she *had* to have shared that story with somebody, yes? There can't be too many people who fill that exact bill. Where are you?

The Fort Lauderdale Comic Strip, the sister club to the Comic Strip in New York City, had opened that spring, and the comedians all wanted to work it. Lauderdale was a wild town, plus it'd be wonderful to be down south in the winter months, let alone during the craziness that was spring break.

We were in town for the week leading up to Easter Sunday, when a good percentage of colleges had their spring breaks. I had passed the audition that qualified me to work the Comic Strip in the city, but hadn't had the clout to get booked in the Lauderdale club yet. I hadn't even been there.

I knew there were three good comics working that week, and the three guys who were booked for the next week, who were also good, were already in town to wallow in the rampant festivities and whatever else. So if we went there, we'd be running into Paul Reiser, Larry Miller, Dennis Wolfberg, Glenn Hirsch, Bob Nelson, and Peter Bales, as well as Richie Tienken, who owned both of the clubs.

Friday night, Rodney had made arrangements for us all to go see Louis Nye's one-man show, and I said, "Hey, after Louis's show, why don't we head over to the Comic Strip? It's close, it's an offshoot of the club in New York, and I know there'll be some great guys working tonight."

He said, "Well, we'll ask Louis what he'd like to do."

Louis's show was great. Afterwards we went backstage to see him and he was thrilled Rodney had made it. When Rodney asked him if he wanted to head over to a comedy club, he was all into it.

We all piled into the rental car, me driving, Rodney riding shotgun, and Brian, Melanie, Debbie, and Louis packed into the backseat. I promptly got lost and the next thing I knew we were in bumper-to-bumper traffic, barely crawling on A1A, which ran along the beach, in the thick of thousands of college kids. Back then, A1A was a two-way street. I still thank my lucky stars nobody looked in and recognized Rodney. My God, who *knows* what would have gone down. *Yow.*

Eventually, with of course no GPS or cell phone, I somehow got us to the club. The show hadn't started yet, so all of the comics were in the bar area. I walked through the door, followed by Rodney Dangerfield—which more than got their attention—and then, right behind Rodney, the *piéce de résistance*, Louis Nye.

Paul Reiser was standing the closest as we entered.

He said, "You arranged this?"

Richie Tienken is still in love with me for dragging Rodney to the club that night. After that, any time Rodney was in south Florida, he'd of course find his way there, like an approval-seeking moth to a laughing and applauding flame.

We sat in the very back of the room, and we all really enjoyed every second of the show. Louis loved Bob Nelson's act so much that he actually got up and danced while Bob was killing. Yeah, he danced. I was watching Rodney Dangerfield watch Louis Nye do the shimmy as Bob Nelson was doing his classic football routine. "Surreal" is not a strong enough word.

Peter Bales was MC, and after the last regular act, he asked Rodney if he'd come to the stage for a guest set. Rodney went up to the insanely wild applause of a disbelieving full house and destroyed the place for fifteen minutes. They comped our bill and we left the showroom pretty drunk, smiling from ear to ear.

We were mulling about in the bar before we took off, the guys still not quite able to wrap their heads around the whole thing, as they chatted up Rodney and Louis, as well as the rest of us. Wanting to cement my relationship with my fellow comedians, I said, "You guys should come over and hang at the pool on Easter Sunday. Let me see what I can arrange."

The next day, I said to Melanie and Debbie, who had really enjoyed meeting and hanging with the comics, that the hotel had grills on the beach right across the bridge and that it'd be fun if we threw a barbecue on Sunday and invited all of them. Then I went to the store and bought everything we'd need and put it in the small refrigerator in my room. What didn't fit went in the sink, covered with hotel ice. Then I called the guys at the comedy condo and told them the party was on. The hardest thing to believe about this story is that there was a phone entrusted to the comics in the place they were being housed. That was soon to end for all time.

A bit of comedy club history . . .

The term "comedy condo" came into existence with the creation of the Fort Lauderdale Comic Strip. When the club first opened, the three owners—Richie Tienken, Bob Wachs, and John McGowan—bought a condo in a high-rise building near the beach where the comics would stay. Within a month, the comics had been such loud, drunk, and annoying neighbors that they were ousted. Then the owners bought a duplex, half for them and half for the comics. Duplex or no, the term "comedy condo" stuck, and has been applied to every place comedians have stayed since: houses, waitresses' apartments, wherever.

Later that day, Rodney said to me, "Hey, Melanie's thinking she'd like to have a barbecue tomorrow, and thought maybe you could invite those comics from the club."

I said, "Okay."

"Well, we're gonna need a bunch of stuff."

"I bought it already, we're all set."

"And you gotta call the comics."

"I did already, they're all coming."

Realizing I had orchestrated the entire soirée, he shook his head in disbelief and said, "You're a pisser, you know that?"

All of the guys came to the Bahia Mar about noon on Easter Sunday. I still have the greatest picture of the entire group, including Melanie, Debbie, and Brian, in my motel room just after they got there . . . minus me. I took it.

We cooked and drank and ate and cooked and smoked some pot and ate and drank and it was all just too perfect. The girls were thrilled, so Rodney was thrilled, and I was over the moon.

When we were stuffed full of all things grillable, us fellas found our way to a circle of seats near the pool and somehow situated almost directly in front of a three-piece reggae band. In the group were Rodney, me, Reiser, Miller, Wolfberg, Hirsch, Nelson, and Bales. I also remember Rodney's cousin, Lenny, who's a dentist, was sitting between me and Rodney.

This was a group to die for. You didn't open your mouth unless you had something pretty damn funny to say. And with this group, the banter was beyond priceless.

Rodney was in shorts, his knees were far apart, and he was kind of staring down at the cement. We were very close to the pool, so none of us could miss Rodney's son Brian's entrance. He came walking down the far side of the pool, about five foot ten and no more than 120 pounds, naked but for his bathing suit, with a very long and very wild Jewfro, some of which was being held in close by a bright red Willie Nelson–style bandana he had tied around his forehead. He was right out of an R. Crumb comic. His arms were flailing as he took long, gawky Flakey Foont–type steps. He got to the corner of the pool and took a hard left, his very kinky locks dancing in the breeze.

Rodney watched his entire approach, then turned to us and said, "How the fuck can I be happy?"

We were very close to the band, which was very loud and very annoying, and rather than simply getting up and moving, we were taking turns making comments about the situation. Everybody was being pretty damn funny, and I'll include myself. It felt great to know I was right in step with these guys, all already incredibly accomplished acts.

Sensing it was kind of his turn to speak, Rodney's cousin looked at the band, then turned to us and said, "We should ask them to play 'Far Far Away.'"

Rodney looked over at him and said, "You're lucky I know your family."

A while later, Rodney had gone to his room, and we saw Louis Nye sitting at a table by himself.

I said, "Hey, let's go get Louis going."

And almost all of the guys said, "No, we don't want to bother him. No, let's leave him alone. He doesn't want to talk to us."

I said, "You guys are nuts. Come on."

I walked over and sat across from Louis, and I swear all I said was, "Man, *The Steve Allen Show* must have been great fun."

Louis proceeded to wax on and on for a few hours, telling us so many wonderful stories about his times in show business, with Steve Allen as well as a million other people. Stuff I'd kill to be able to remember.

To this day, everybody who was there remembers it so, so fondly.

On Monday, I had to drive us to Miami Airport in time to return the car and get to the gate. It was pouring rain as we left Fort Lauderdale; it was also spring break and the day after Easter. We were at a standstill on the road leading out of town and Rodney, who'd have been in a panic even if we were already at the gate waiting to board, was freaking out.

I'm sitting there driving in stop-and-go traffic in the pelting rain, he's riding shotgun and he gets out the cocaine, puts it on his lap, and snorts a bunch of it. Which of course made him even antsier and crazier.

He looked over at me driving, assessed the situation, and said, "Let's switch."

In the pouring rain we did a Chinese fire drill. We each jumped out and we switched places. So now he was in the driver's seat and I was sitting shotgun.

He said, "It's better to drive, right? Driving's better?"

He was so petrified that perhaps I had the more socially preferred place in the car, that the guy driving was cooler than the guy who wasn't.

Trust me, I couldn't make this up. As he sat behind the wheel I think he might have actually felt a bit better.

I know we had both been stoned and drunk when we left Lauderdale. When we finally got to Miami Airport, he took a wrong turn and, worried we'd miss our flight, corrected it by making a death-defying U-turn in the pouring rain that still scares me as I type this.

When we got to Las Vegas, as we walked along the American Airlines corridor, the (recorded) announcements were being made by comedian Henny "King of the One Liners" Youngman.

Rodney said, "You hear that? That was my idea. I told them, it's *Vegas*. *Celebrities* should be making the announcements. And they went for it."

Something very eye-opening and jaw-dropping happened when we got to the Aladdin. Looking back, it shouldn't have surprised me even a little, but at the time, it broke my heart.

When we got out of the limo (please know what a huge fucking deal this still was to me), the first thing Rodney did was go straight to the showroom box office to see how his ticket sales were going.

At that point, in my mind, once you reached the echelon Rodney had, I (obviously erroneously) figured that you'd no longer need to be concerned with ticket sales, with box offices, with how your show was selling. That once you were a star, people were very fortunate to get a chance to see you perform, and so on.

This was a very rude awakening.

I realized, "Holy shit. It never ends. It will never end."

It hasn't and it won't.

When we walked into his suite he said, "Put on the TV. No comedy, black and white if you can find it."

We were there waiting when the luggage and the tied-up boxes got to his room.

Rodney said, "I know, a little coke and you'll set up house."

We did a few lines, I cracked open one of the many bottles of booze that made up the full bar they had provided, and then I set up Rodney's toaster oven et al.

I can't believe my priorities. I took a few pictures of the bar and all the booze they provided for Rodney . . . but not of his outfits.

One of the all-time most iconic things I ever laid eyes on—his closet was filled with about eight black suits, each with a white shirt and a red tie—and somehow I didn't deem it worthy of one of my cardboard camera's twenty pictures.

I can still see them.

One afternoon, we were sitting at the dining room table of his suite as he read his mail. Lots of people, not just comedians, sent Rodney jokes, and I convinced him to let me look at the jokes people had sent him after he looked at them first. Maybe one he rejected would hit me different, or might be easily switched. He knew I knew my stuff, so he figured, sure. Plus, sometimes they'd inspire me, or whatever. So we sat there, he read what they sent him, I read the ones he was tossing and pitched a joke here and there. It was like I died and went to Comedy Heaven.

So he hands me a joke and I say, "What are you doing? This is a *great* one! This is the ultimate 'she's so fat and she's so ugly' joke rolled into one."

He said, "You really think so?"

I said, "Well, hell yeah. I wouldn't fuck around."

That night, at the height of the "she's so fat" and "she's so ugly" part of his act, he said, "This girl was fat and ugly, I'll tell you, fat and ugly. Yeah, she's got a hairdresser for each armpit."

Nothing. There was no crowd response, like he hadn't said anything or he hadn't finished the joke.

I could feel he was seething. I think he may have thought I had sandbagged him, which of course I hadn't.

It's a great joke on paper, structurally, but I guess it's a little too much for an audience to process all at once.

It took some doing, but I finally did convince him I'd really thought the joke would kill. We had accomplished quite a bit working like that, so I got a pass.

When I was with him those two weeks, he really did stress himself over trying to quit smoking and lose weight. He was crazed by those two things, totally crazed. And I felt bad, because it was so funny. So fucking funny. So repetitious and so futile.

One night between shows we each had a salad in the coffee shop.

He said, "You want a piece of cake?"

"Nah."

"Come on, have a piece of cake. It's good cake."

"No. I don't want a piece of cake."

He called over the waiter and said, "Bring him a piece of chocolate cake."

The waiter brought me a huge piece of cake and Rodney proceeded to reach over with his fork and eat the entire piece of cake himself, off of the plate that was sitting in front of me.

I said, "You of course realize if you eat a piece of cake off of my plate, *you* still get the calories, right?"

"Whatever."

One night . . . well, most nights, but one night in particular, in the beginning of the week, I was in Rodney's room when there was a knock on the door. It was his favorite hooker, Angie.

We all had a few laughs for a few minutes, but then I very calculatedly, dejectedly said, "Okay, well . . . I guess I'll go now. I-I'll see you tomorrow, Boss." Then I dragged myself out of the room like my dog had just died.

Twenty minutes later the phone rang. I answered.

Rodney said, "Okay, she'll be down there in five minutes. Have fun, it's all paid for."

"What? What're you talking about?"

"Don't play dumb. I saw the look on your fucking face. You made me feel like a piece of shit. You knew what you were doing, I bet I'd have done the same thing. Fuck her, whatever, have a party, I'll see you tomorrow."

Three words in I was already smiling and could feel my dick starting to throb.

She showed up, we had a lot of laughs, I played my guitar and sang her a few of my songs. And then, I must say, thanks to the week of looking at the women in their bikinis poolside and the whores and the college girls, thanks to the whole scene, with but the one lucky escapade, I think I outdid myself. And so did Angie.

She said, "If you want to do that again, it's on me."

No offense to Rodney, but I'm sure Angie had spent most of her energies in bed or on her knees night after night with horny old men with close-to-limp dicks. And then here's this thirty-two-year-old with a reasonably hard body who could pound nails with his hard-on. And she wanted more.

You don't have to believe it. But everything in this book is 100 percent Gospel.

Richie Minervini's version of the story I just told you is that Rodney paid Angie extra to tell me I was so good that she'd give me the next one on the house, to fuck with me. One of the most creative things, if not the only creative thing, Richie ever wrote.

To complicate matters, I showed this chapter to Richie, and he said the other version was that I was in Rodney's Las Vegas room when two hookers showed up.

I said, "Wow. Thanks, Boss."

And Rodney said, "Thanks for what? They're both for me. They eat each other, and when I get aroused, I join in."

After that night, Rodney would occasionally wax poetic about how Angie had the perfect mouth. Now that's bonding.

As I said, Rodney was co-headlining the Aladdin with the very popular singer-songwriter and Academy Award–winner Paul Williams. Paul was incredibly moved by Rodney's decision—actually the only decision that made sense—for Rodney to open the show and Paul and his orchestra to close.

Rodney said, "Of *course*. The comic opens, the music goes on last. Of course, basic show business."

It would be crazy to have a comic, one lone voice, follow an orchestra. I guess that happens plenty now, but at the time, it was how it should have been, how it was going to be, and Paul was very happy.

Paul felt so indebted to Rodney that he let him take his private jet back to Los Angeles that Friday so Rodney could shoot his reaction shots for *Caddyshack* and fly back in time for their show.

As if that wasn't enough, Paul later insisted that Rodney and I join him and his wife Katie at their Las Vegas home for Sunday afternoon dinner.

When we got to their house, they were ready for us. A magnificent spread of appetizers, and the cook had all kinds of wonderful food cooking in the oven and on the stove. The place smelled like a magnificent mix of gourmet chow and marijuana.

Rodney broke out a huge mound of cocaine, and the festivities kicked in. Within no time at all, we were all sailing.

Every few minutes, Rodney would sing a line from Paul's huge hit "Rainbow Connection." "There's no getting o-ver that *rainnn*-bowww . . ." Finally, he said, "How do you come up with these songs, Paul? How do you write these songs?"

As a songwriter (I still wasn't sure I was never-to-be), and high as I was, I was all ears.

Paul said, "They're just out in the air, Rodney. I just pluck them out of the air . . . they're just out there."

Rodney took a huge *snnoorrtt* and then leaned way back on the couch. Gesturing upwards with his arms, he said, "They're just out there, huh? They're just out there? There's nooo getting o-ver that *raaiinn*-boww . . . That's fucking *beautiful*, Paul . . . So they're just out there, eh?"

We snorted and smoked pot and drank and ate and then did it all over again. An afternoon I'll never forget.

Decades later, when I asked Paul Williams if he remembered it, he said, "*An afternoon getting fucked up with Rodney Dangerfield? Are you kidding?*"

I had a brutal faux pas that afternoon. Paul and I were standing in a kitchen doorway, screamingly high and baring our souls.

He said, "You have that light behind your eyes, Jackie. You're gonna be a star. A big star. Are your folks still alive?"

I said, "Yeah."

He said, "My one regret is that my father didn't live long enough to see me succeed. But I've been so very fortunate. Have you ever heard of Johnny Hart?"

I said, "Fuck yeah, he does the comic strip *B.C.* I love that."

Paul said, "Well, he's my best friend, and we're going to do a movie of his other comic strip, *The Wizard of Id*. I'm going to play the king."

My head in a stratospheric spin, I said, "Oh, it's going to be an animated movie?"

Paul said, "No, live action."

And then, looking down at five-foot-nothing Paul, I said, "You can't do that as a live action movie. All of those characters are so short and stumpy . . ."

I didn't realize what I was saying until I was saying it. I felt like such a dick. But Paul was so beyond cool, he just smacked me and then smiled at me and put me completely at ease.

A few years later, I was working at the Funny Bone in Knoxville, Tennessee. It was so long ago that *Crook & Chase*, which went on to be a big national show on many country channels, was still a local show in Knoxville. I was booked to promote my week at the comedy club, and I was in the green room as they interviewed the guest before me, Paul Williams.

Charlie Chase said, "Paul, you've written *so many* big songs. Tell me, have you ever written any songs that *weren't* a big hit?"

Paul said, "Oh, sure. Of course."

"Like what?"

"Brown Christmas."

One night after both of Rodney's shows, a bit of craps, and a lot of drinking and whatever else we could ingest, even though it was already late, he said, "Let's take a walk over to the MGM and see if there's anything going on."

Back then, the MGM Grand was next to the Aladdin on the Vegas Strip. It was the week after Easter 1980, at the height of a gasoline shortage, so business in Vegas was way, way off. Not to mention it was very, very late—or very, very early. The MGM was close to barren and we sat around for a long time with the one of the maître d's who was an old pal of Rodney's, just the three of us.

The maître d' kept calling Rodney "Roger Danglefoot," which made me laugh harder every time, mainly because it was making Rodney crazy.

Walking back along the Vegas Strip, it was chilly as the sun was just starting to peak at us.

We were almost to the Aladdin when Rodney said, "You gotta take a leak? I gotta take a leak."

I'm a beer drinker, so I said, "Sure, I can always piss."

Instead of waiting a few short minutes until we were in the lobby of the Aladdin, we hung a sharp left which took us in back of the hotel. Soon, we were standing next to two of the most gigantic Dumpsters I'd ever seen. They were each literally the size of a small McDonald's, at a right angle to each other. Rodney unzipped and started peeing on one of them, and at ninety degrees to him, about twenty feet away, I started peeing on the other.

As our streams doused the bottoms of these huge bins, Rodney turned to me, cock in hand, and said, "Welcome to the Big Time."

I smiled as broadly as anyone could, shook my head, and said, "Do you know how many people I'm gonna tell this story to?"

He said, "Go ahead. Have a party."

1983

A CALL FROM HOWARD STERN, PART ONE

In January 1979, frustrated that Nixon look-alike Richard M. Dixon wouldn't pay any of us more than five bucks and a few beers for performing at his White House Inn variety showcase in Hicksville, New York, my new pal Richie Minervini and I produced Long Island's first all stand-up comedy show Tuesday nights at Cinnamon, a bar-restaurant in Huntington. The club was owned by Roger Pinto and Michael Cooney. Michael is heavyweight boxer Gerry Cooney's brother, Gerry was very prominent at the time, he stopped by often, and Cinnamon was a very popular spot.

I provided the sound system, Richie MC'd, I closed the show with a long set of dirty jokes and raucous songs, and each week we hired a few local comics to fill it out. The audiences loved us and it was immediately a huge success.

To help promote the show, I created the still-in-operation joke line, "Use Your Finger! (516) 922-WINE," and started going by the name Jackie "922-WINE" Martling. Word spread like wildfire and almost immediately we packed them in. Most weeks I'd do over an hour, because the laughs and the energy were incredible. After a year of solo gigs, playing songs, and telling jokes to three scattered tables, being in front of those full houses was like dying and going to pig heaven. Guzzle a beer and do another ten minutes . . . Guzzle a beer and do another ten minutes . . . I never wanted to get off.

Comics began gladly coming out by car or train from New York City to work for us, because they'd actually get paid forty or fifty bucks, as compared to five dollars a set in town. Not to mention how responsive the crowds were, the free drinks, and how mesmerized the ladies were by the funny fellas (female comics were scarce back then) and this (to them) brand new form of entertainment. The comedy boom had yet to kick in—we certainly helped it along—and there were still very few road gigs, so the comedians lined up to work for us. Our night was such a hit that within a year, Richie and two partners opened the first full-time comedy venue on Long Island, the East Side Comedy Club, in Huntington Station, the next town over.

I recorded every Cinnamon show and always listened to it the next day, over and over, to see what was working really well, write some ad-libs, whatever. When you're in the heat of your set, things are moving so fast—at least the way I work—that you don't have time to grasp and devour all the responses. Factor in two six-packs and sometimes listening back, you're basically hearing it for the first time.

One day, after we had been doing the show for a few months, I was really pleased, as I was playing my set from the night before.

I said to my girlfriend, "Listen to this. Jesus Christ, they laugh their asses off at every joke. I should make a comedy record."

With no hesitation, she said, "So make a comedy record."

One night, around that same time, Dave Hawthorne, Eddie Murphy, Eddie's best friend Clint, and I drove out to do Hal Ennis's Comedy Caravan at the Jade Fountain on Route 17 in Paramus, New Jersey. We were on a big bill with three or four other comics and I was hosting the show. It was the first road gig Eddie and I did together. I got up and did fifteen minutes to open the show and then introduced the first act. I walked off stage and over to the side of the room where the guys were sitting.

Eddie said, "Jack, they laughed every time you opened your mouth."

Hawthorne said, "That's the idea, Eddie."

I realized the only thing keeping me from having an album was not making one. My act was working really well. I just needed to capture it and get it out there.

I had spent a few years as a gofer at the Workshoppe Recording Studios in Douglaston and had learned it was relatively easy to get a record made. It was as simple as baking a cake. You gather the ingredients, send them to a pressing plant, and *bingo!* You need a tape of the content, the art for the jacket, the labels, and a few shekels. I had no money, but huge balls, and a huge surge of adrenaline shot through me as I made the conscious decision to go for it, to put my nose to the grindstone and proceed to do whatever the fuck I had to do to produce my very own comedy album.

I decided my 1961 eighth-grade class picture, where I'm sitting on the floor in the front row flipping the bird, would be the cover. I wrote "What Did You Expect?" under the photo, tacked it on the sloped wall of my attic office at eye level, and took to telling everybody they were looking at the cover of my first comedy album. It, of course, met with quite the array of reactions.

Then I went to work transferring my Cinnamon shows from the cassette player to the reel-to-reel tape deck my pal Butch Mehrtens had won cheating at cards in Vietnam, mixing (combining) my voice on the left track with the audience on the right track, riding the laughs a bit, and then taking the razor blade to any garbage I didn't want in there. I culled from three or four of the hottest nights, and pretty soon I had two twenty-minute hunks, side one and side two of my first comedy LP.

To pay for my folly, I borrowed a hundred bucks from each of fifteen friends and relatives and anybody I could talk into it and gave them stock in the record.

When I was working in Denver in 1973, I had come up with "the Colorado Number System," where we gave numbers to common expressions and used the numbers as shortcuts, like in the prison joke.

It's Harry's first day in prison, they all go into the cafeteria, and after they eat, a guy stands up and says, "Two hundred and eighty-five," and everybody laughs.

A few minutes later, another guy stands up and says, "Five hundred and seven," and everybody laughs again.

Harry turns to the guy next to him and says, "What's going on?"

The guy says, "We've all been in here a long time, and we all know all the jokes, so we numbered them. Now, we just get up and say the number, everybody thinks about the joke, and they laugh."

Harry says, "Can I try it?"

The guy says, "Sure."

Harry stands up and says, "Three hundred and ninety-two," and nobody laughs.

Harry sits back down and says to the other guy, "What happened?"

The guy says, "Well, some people can tell a joke, and some people can't."

A fan of my old band, the Off Hour Rockers, worked at a printing plant, and at my request, he printed a thousand huge copies of "the Colorado Number System." It's over two hundred numbers, it's ridiculous, and, not too understandably, I've always been very proud of it. The sheets were so big that folded into six panels, they'd just fit into a record sleeve. I painstakingly folded them, and then shipped them, the master tape, the class picture and a few other pictures, the text for the back cover, and the labels and a money order to a record manufacturer in Nashville.

A few weeks later, *voilà*. *What Did You Expect?* my first homegrown comedy album, arrived at the Port Authority. Picking up those first thousand LPs remains one of my proudest memories. I immediately sent a copy to anyone and everyone. What I got in return included:

1. A set of sipping glasses and a sweater from the good folks at Jack Daniel's.
2. A letter from Lanier Electronics that literally said, "We don't know what you're doing, but you seem to have energy. Please use this letter to purchase any of our products at a 50% discount." They had created the first microcassette recorders that were a godsend for comedians.
3. An order from Adam & Eve, a lingerie/sex gadget mail-order outlet in North Carolina that had decided to include my album in their catalog. In later years, they'd make nice-sized purchases of all three of my albums in three formats: records, cassettes, and eight-track cartridges. Today, Adam & Eve is a huge adult toy company in Los Angeles.

4. A nice letter and a penciled cartoon of me picking my nose with a hook, I have to believe due to the joke on the record of Captain Hook wiping with the wrong hand, from Don Martin, the delightfully off-center *Mad* magazine artist.

5. An equally nice letter from William M. Gaines, the publisher of *Mad* magazine. As a longtime fan of *Mad*, man, that was a thrill.

My album was pretty impressive to many people. It seems nobody realized (or comprehended) that it had been entirely self-produced. Conceptualized, written, performed, recorded, edited, designed, packaged, and paid for by me. And that anybody with a tape recorder could have their own album.

As a matter of fact, it couldn't have been more low rent. The master tapes were mono. In layman's terms, mono is the absence of stereo. If an album is in stereo, you'd be able to discern a drink rattling on the left and a sneeze on the right. On my album, if a herd of horses had run through the audience during the taping, it would have sounded like they were dancing in front of me.

One Friday night, at the East Side, I handed a copy of the record to Jerry Seinfeld.

The next night in the kitchen he said, "Jackie, I listened to your album."

I said, "Really?"

He said, "Yeah. I lied on my bed and listened to both sides. That was a great night, huh?"

I said, "That was the best of a few nights I edited together, Jerry."

He looked at me with an air of surprise and said, "You can do that?"

It was November 1979, and to this day, I have no idea if he meant, "You mean that can be done?" Or he was impressed I had the skills to accomplish that.

I was so damn proud of my record. I took piles of them to every show and sold them afterwards. I usually had a few sales, it was a big kick autographing them, and the extra twenty or thirty bucks was always nice. At first, the other comedians goofed on me for doing it, but less and less as they watched exiting audience members gladly handing over their five-dollar bills and me going home with a lot more money than them.

One night at the Fort Lauderdale Comic Strip, I gave a copy to a very hot waitress who had a shiny new bright red Corvette. I hopped in her car and she gave me a ride to the Brickyard, where we all usually went drinking after the show. A few hours later, when we came out, the passenger window of her car was smashed and thieves had taken everything.

Mike Reynolds, the juggling comic, said, "Wait a minute."

He reached in, and from under the pile of broken glass on the passenger seat, he pulled out the Jackie Martling record that the thief obviously wasn't interested in. Everybody's a fucking critic.

In spring 1980, I was recording at the East Side for my second record. Eddie Murphy was on the show, too.

He came up to me and said, "Jackie, you're making another record? I want to have a record. Can you help me make a record?"

I said, "Sorry, man, I'm too busy."

Yipes. A heartbeat later, he was on *Saturday Night Live* and then the moon.

In late 1980 I released that second record, *Goin' Ape*, which featured another classic cover. I had bartered with Lillian's Costume Shop in Mineola: a plug on the album jacket for the loan of a gorilla suit. My buddy Burf and I smuggled it into the Bronx Zoo in a few paper bags, I put it on, and he took pictures of me running around the zoo in a full gorilla costume for the album until we got tossed out, which happened pretty fast.

Most of the pictures didn't come out, which still greatly saddens me. What a tale they would have told. It was September and there were lots of classes of school children there, walking in tandem. Until we were bounced out by a guard with no sense of humor, I was jumping from behind trees to scare the kids. I'm sure to this day, there are people who try to tell their friends that one day in grade school, they were at the Bronx Zoo and an ape jumped out from behind a tree.

I sent both LPs to everybody and his brother and their companies. And my joke recordings, (516) 922-WINE, were now on six phone lines. When somebody called (516) 922-9463 and it was engaged, it rolled over to the next line, and then the next, and I was getting hundreds of calls a day. I was ever so slowly gaining steam.

By spring 1981, I was fairly well established as a local comedian and comedy producer, creating and working in lots of small-time shows, much like at Cinnamon, in bars and restaurants all over the tristate area. Nancy Sirianni, an Oyster Bay girl I had known for a few years, approached me about us working together. She felt stagnant in her job as studio manager at Kingdom Sound, a high-profile recording studio in Syosset. She wanted the opportunity to grow and somehow saw a lot of potential in what I was up to. I was thrilled and flattered by her interest. She was smart and talented and creative and beautiful and full of energy. I said sure, and she joined Off Hour Rockers Inc.

When Nancy came aboard, I was producing—among a smattering of weekday shows that seemed to come and go—the weekend comedy shows I had started at the Brokerage Pub in Merrick. We'd drive there together when I was in town, and at the end of the night, I'd drop her at her apartment. We had both recently become free agents and were spending a lot of time together and I could tell I was starting to grow on her. We both did our best to keep some distance, since we were working together and both knew if we started anything, it could get icky.

But I'd been crazy about this very pretty girl nine years my junior since the Tuesday afternoon I officially met her. She'd been sitting in the sun outside Rumrunner, a rock and roll club in Oyster Bay, the first time my partner and I pulled up in Tweetie, our 1955 bright yellow Cadillac hearse, to unload and set up for that night. Nancy and I had already been somewhat familiar, as back then it was a very small town and everybody had some awareness of everybody else. She was the head waitress and a very close friend of the girl I was going out with. A while back, the two of them had come to see us play one night at the Lobster House in Bayville. But even if I had been available, she was too young and too cute. I immediately dismissed her as being out of my league.

So on our way to and from whatever shows we were producing, we'd yak on and on as we drove, about anything and everything. I was still smarting from having been cheated on and dumped, so she saw a lot of the tender and sensitive side of me. And she loved my songs.

She told me that the night she had seen our two-man band, original songs, and dirty jokes, she told my girlfriend on the way out, "Those guys are assholes but I loved their music."

One thing I had mentioned to her a few times in our travels was that, in the band, we drank a lot of Jack Daniel's, but that I had left those days behind when I moved to comedy. Hey, I drank way too much beer, I certainly didn't need the craziness of hard liquor. You really paid for it when you messed with that stuff. I know I specifically told her I hadn't done shots of Jack in a few years. And she said she was in very much the same place, that her shot days were in the past, too.

She's a very sexy woman and it was getting tougher and tougher to resist the inevitable. Sometimes I'd kiss her goodnight, and then we'd both pull away and say, "No, no, this isn't a good idea," etc.

Friday night of Labor Day weekend, 1981, we were standing at the bar after the show at the Brokerage. I had a few beers in me and she looked *so*, so great . . .

I sheepishly said, "You want a shot of Jack Daniel's?"

And she smiled and said, "*Umm* . . . yeah."

The conversation in the thought bubbles was, "You want to fuck tonight?"

"Hell yes."

We downed enough shots that the pictures from that night show us all in a Johnny Pile—comics, club owners, strangers. We went back to her apartment and had what Nancy claims was "the worst sex she's ever had." She left for the Hamptons the next morning and when she got back, she came to my house and stayed twenty years.

A few weeks later, the owners of Barrymore's, a rock and roll bar in Levittown, Long Island, were being forced to shut down due to the neighbors' complaints about the loud music. They decided to try something different and tracked down the comedian who had the dirty joke line.

Nancy and I went and looked at the club, told the owners what they should do to make it work as a comedy club, such as where to put the stage and the speakers, and soon Governor's Comedy Shop opened its doors. We booked the acts, supervised the advertising, and ran the shows. We were the producers from soup to nuts. My deal was I could take off and do a road gig one week a month. I'd host the shows the other three weeks and occasionally headline.

We promoted the hell out of the club. I pumped it on the joke line, it got plugged on my very popular daily phone messages for Bob

Buchmann and Peri Appollo's WBAB morning-drive show out of Babylon. We also had a nice-sized weekly ad in *Newsday*, Long Island's biggest paper. Since we got a piece of the action, we were making decent money, especially relative to what lower-echelon comics were making. Very quickly, I was pretty much synonymous with Governor's and it was a nice home base. Plus, I was working on the road when I could, which was more and more, and since my name was getting around a bit, my price was creeping up. The reality of having a twinge of success hit home when I was able to not only buy a brand new car for the first time in my life, but exactly the one I wanted, a 1983 Volvo station wagon. (No need to reread that sentence . . . Yes, that was the car I wanted.) We were rolling.

In early 1982, I recorded my third LP, *Normal People Are People You Don't Know That Well*, at Governor's. More jobs were coming in. (516) 922-WINE had topped out at ten phone lines and we were getting over five thousand calls a day from all over the fucking world.

By 1982, the comedy boom was starting to catch hold and clubs slowly started to spring up here and there around the country. Fortunately, my albums impressed lots of out-of-state club owners. Unfortunately, just as many of them refused to book the filthy bastard on those records, so that about evened itself out.

In August 1982, Harry Monocrusos, the owner of Garvin's Laugh Inn, a comedy club I was working in Washington, DC, told me about a disc jockey who had just been fired from local station DC-101 and was taking a job at WNBC-AM in New York City.

Harry said, "There's this wild man Howard Stern who used to do live broadcasts in his underwear on Friday mornings from here at Garvin's. He got fired because after a plane crashed into the Fourteenth Street Bridge, he pretended to call Air Florida and ask if the bridge was going to be a permanent stop. You should look him up, you guys are like peas in a pod."

Following the protocol I had initiated right after picking up my thousand copies of that first LP, we would mail an extensive promotional package to any interesting people I met in my travels, as well as to anyone that was suggested to me, just as Harry had suggested Howard Stern. In those days, anyone I came in contact with, directly or indirectly, or was given a lead to that in any way seemed like a potentially viable route to anywhere, got all of our stuff.

So, when I got home from my weekend gig in Washington, Nancy and I did what we had always done. We blindly sent our package to Howard Stern, care of WNBC-AM.

In 1982, well over four hundred people or companies were sent my three LPs and the matching cassettes and a promo folder with 8 x 10s, flyers, and joke line stickers. It was very hard to gauge just how much good it was doing, and you have to believe me when I tell you that the cost of the contents and sending them was staggering to us at the time. But since we both believed it to be a great idea, and a necessary one, and having been a couple and business partners long enough that we had already begun to agree on less and less, we kept it up.

Nancy was wonderfully organized in those days. Long before computers made everything much easier and more nauseating, the contact information of anybody or any company we had targeted went on a card and was snapped into our business Rolodex. So when she threw a surprise birthday roast for me at Governor's that January, she invited many of the people in the business Rolodex, and one of them had been Howard Stern. The roast was to take place a few weeks before my birthday, which made the surprise come very close to working.

Unfortunately, one day there was a returned invitation in the mail and, not having any idea what it was, I opened it, and that was that. Surprise wrecked. Damn. I'm not sure if I ever told Nancy about that. Very ironically, the invite that came back had been sent to Brian Battles, the first guy who ever put me on the radio, on his Saturday morning show on WBAB, which had led to my daily slot with Bob Buchmann. And Brian had worked with Howard and the delightful Meg Griffin at what was all of their first radio jobs, at WRNW, in Briarcliff Manor, just north of the city.

On a bleak Tuesday in February 1983, I walked up the two flights to our office in my mother's attic, the first JokeLand, which housed my audio studio, our fledgling Off Hour Rockers Inc. and the joke line(s). I was almost thirty-five years old, and had been working my balls off on the outskirts of show business for a long, long time, waiting patiently for someone to notice.

Nancy said, "That disc jockey Howard Stern just called. He wants you to come be a guest on his show this afternoon." She gave me Howard's number at WNBC.

I called and he got right on.

He said, "Jackie?"

I said, "That's me. Nice to hear from you."

Howard said, "Thanks for getting right back to me. I'm sorry I missed your roast. Me and Fred, a guy who works with me, listened to your albums, and we think you're a pisser. Man, you know every joke in the world."

"Thanks. Yeah, Harry told me you were leaving Washington to come to New York to WNBC and that I should try to hook up with you. I was hoping those records would get to you."

"Well, they did. I got them a while back, but it's taken us some time to get established here. The reason I'm calling is we're holding a listener talent contest over the telephone today, and I was wondering if you'd like to come to the studio and join us on the air and be one of the judges."

"Sure."

"Great. It'll be fun, and I can plug your comedy shows. We go on the air at four. Get here around four-thirty to five. Thirty Rockefeller Plaza, second floor. Your name will be at the door."

"I'll be there."

Of *course* I'd be there.

I looked around the office, high above the skirmishes that were my parents' marriage. A few tape recorders, the ten answering machines for the joke line, joke lists, pictures, posters, and phone numbers all over the slanted claustrophobic walls that made the room a long teepee. And a typewriter and a row of loose-leafs. An insult to the expression "small time."

But I still had unbridled optimism. Hell, I had been marking time at the Workshoppe Recording Studios for five bucks a day in 1978 when I quit to put all of my energies into performing. All I left with was the knowledge that anybody can make an album and how to do it myself. So pulling in a thousand bucks or so a week as a comedy producer of sorts, I'd already come a long way.

Governor's ran Wednesdays through Sundays and I mainly worked in my studio the rest of the time. I didn't play the New York City game of running from club to club, doing a set here and a set there, seven to fifteen minutes at a clip, for five dollars, fifteen dollars, a hamburger here, a Budweiser there.

I had, at my new friend and fellow comic Peter Bales' insistence, done a few sets at the Comic Strip on Second Avenue until I "passed," which meant I was qualified to perform there, which opened up the opportunity to get started in the ranks of the "city comics."

But no. It was a decision I had made early on that my time would be better invested doing things my way. I had no desire to live and work in New York City then. In retrospect, I guess I'm a bit sorry it took me so long to get there. But I love the North Shore of Long Island, and after seven long years in East Lansing, Michigan, I guess I had kind of decided that once I got back there I'd stay.

From the time I graduated from Michigan State as a mechanical engineer in 1971, I had longed for the day that I would be accomplished enough as a musician or in some permutation of show business to make a living at it back east, and after grabbing the slightest hold here with our new duo in 1973, I just wasn't going anywhere. When I gravitated to comedy in 1979, I still wasn't budging. Bowels no move.

I could look at Jerry Seinfeld and Paul Reiser and kick myself in the balls for not taking that route. But then, there would have been no albums and no Howard Stern phone call.

Pretty ballsy to mention myself in the same breath as Seinfeld and Reiser? Maybe. But, hey, you're reading the ramblings of Howard Stern's former head writer. That must mean something to someone on some level. Not to me, of course. But it's easy to type stuff like that, because nobody can see me sitting here, no one can see the flop sweat rolling down my back and the insecurity raging rampant in every cell of my body.

As Holden Caulfield said, "Goodbye King Kong, hello Eddie Arcaro."

But I do have a reasonably big ego. Which certainly came in handy for the fifteen full-time years I was constantly attacked and belittled on the *Stern Show*. What's a reasonably big ego? I swear, I had countless dreams where I was one of the Beatles, or one of the Marx Brothers. Big deal, you say? Listen to this: In those dreams, I wasn't Paul, or Harpo, but Jackie, the fifth Beatle, or Jackie, the fifth (sixth?) Marx Brother, fitting in perfectly, like that was the way it had always been. Waking from one of those dreams was more disappointing than *Godfather III*.

Though we were making money, and having a great time along the way, my career was improving gradually at best, and this was a rush, to be invited to come be on the air on WNBC-AM in Fun City. Of course, at the time I couldn't tell you what happened on Howard's radio show, or anybody's radio show for that matter. The first and last time I had heard of Howard was from Harry, who had told me to look him up. I was an old hippie from the sixties who never listened to the radio, except maybe WCBS-FM when I was cruising with a buzz on and was feeling especially nostalgic. If I wasn't listening to tapes of my jokes and shows and my own music, I was listening to one of my zillions of homemade cassette compilations of old favorites and unknown artists I knew and, however minutely, supported.

1983

A CALL FROM HOWARD STERN, PART TWO

But I knew one thing for sure: 30 Rockefeller Plaza was a good leap in the right direction from Governor's Comedy Shop in Levittown. And I also knew the value of having your name or your club talked about or even just mentioned on the radio, let alone a major-league station like WNBC-AM.

Not to say I was feeling at all encouraged about what this appearance was going to do for me in the long run. There was no reason to expect this to be any more than a one-shot deal. It was definitely going to be somewhat exciting, and most likely a lot of fun, but it was certainly no career move. The thought of it blossoming into anything further never ever entered my mind. All that was clear was I had to make the decision whether or not to go to New York City on a Tuesday afternoon to be on WNBC, which was a simple call. Hell, mother fucking yeah. Hey, I wasn't even working that night.

So, I put no stock in this trip, in this glorious invitation. I was really ramped up at the prospect of going there, but, like I said, there wasn't even a glint of, "Hey, this could lead to something." Not anymore than I thought anything could. Trust me, when you live your life day to day hoping everything will lead to something, it'd be redundant to say to yourself, "No, really, this could lead to something." Or worse, you'd realize you've been bullshitting yourself all along.

I hadn't had a lot of interaction with celebrities, though I'd had more than the average person. I was awestruck to be going to 30 Rock, and to WNBC, but I wasn't the least bit intimidated knowing I was going to meet Howard Stern, not only because he wasn't the media giant he is now, but because I was totally unaware of anything to do with radio, or just about anything at all, for that matter. I don't think I read a single newspaper in the seventies. Luckily, nothing happened.

With absolutely no idea what to expect, I jumped in my Volvo, smiling and teasing myself that I was thrilled to be in a car that I knew could make the trip, and headed for the Long Island Expressway. I didn't travel to New York City a lot, let alone late in the afternoon on a rainy weekday. Years later, I'd learn that three drops of rain usually mean you should tack an hour onto your commute. Luckily, I left in plenty of time, as the trip took what seemed close to forever. No cell phones, no passengers, just me and some music and lots of time to daydream about what may be in store.

I pulled into the parking garage directly across Forty-Ninth Street from one of the entrances to 30 Rockefeller Plaza and made my way to the revolving doors with a definite spring in my step. Walking into that lobby for the first time was a huge rush. Truthfully, it was a rush every time. Huge photos of Johnny Carson and all of the heroes of NBC-TV and WNBC-AM were everywhere. I hadn't expected it, but my heart was pounding as I got on the elevator to head to the second floor.

I stepped out of the elevator, spoke to the receptionist, and had a seat in what seemed an oddly quiet reception area. As soon as there was a commercial break, Boy Lee came and fetched me and brought me to the studio. Boy Lee was Howard's producer before Boy Gary Dell'Abate, the infamous Flavva Flooey Baba Booey.

We walked in and there they were. Howard Stern, Robin Quivers, and Fred Norris. Howard was wearing a blue work shirt and had a big Afro. Next to his chair were a snare drum and a cymbal, and I vividly remember that when he stood up to greet me, he kept standing up. No one had bothered to mention to me he was ten feet tall.

Howard smiled and shook my hand, as did Robin and Fred. She was African-American and very pretty. Fred was pretty tall, too, and thin and blond and Nordic. A Viking. They couldn't have been nicer or warmer. And somehow, they all seemed smart right away, though I have no idea why that struck me so strongly. Maybe simply because they were working here, at the top. At any rate, it felt great from the onset.

They sat me across from Fred and Robin. Howard was to my left, ninety degrees to us, facing a big window, the engineer looking back at him, controlling the show from behind the glass. I was jazzed but not nervous. It just seemed like it was going to be a hoot.

When he got back on the air, Howard announced that he had a special guest in the studio, one of New York's top comedians, Jackie "922-WINE" Martling. He plugged the shows at Governor's Comedy Shop in Levittown and the joke line, and for the next few hours, he continued to plug them again and again. I was thrilled. Without knowing anything about him or his show, it was very obvious that this was big-time radio, that there were more people hearing my name in one breath than I had reached in my years of barroom shows and dial-a-joke stickers and homegrown records and 922-WINE and whatever other shenanigans I had been up to for as long as I could remember.

Pretty quickly, they realized I laughed loud and a lot, though I'm sure Fred and Howard already knew that from listening to my records. Years later, Howard claimed they never actually listened to them, that they were simply impressed that I had albums and that's why he called. Then he rescinded and said they had played my cassettes in the car. Then he reversed himself again. I'd be annoyed if I didn't love pulling that reversal crap on people so much myself. FlaFlu Gummy's still trying to figure out how old I am, after endless years of lies. Well, fibs.

Helen Keller could see Howard and Robin had a sweet chemistry.

After he'd say something goofy, or say anything at all, he'd hit the snare drum, and then say something else and then hit the snare drum and the cymbal, and/or all of the combinations. Or he'd clap his hands. Robin would constantly laugh at his silliness. He'd talk to her or a caller and punctuate his comments with a bang on the drum or a whack at the cymbal. Or he'd clap his hands. He'd ask me something, I'd answer, and he'd bang the drum. Or the cymbal. Or both. Or he'd clap his hands. The show was kinetic, it kept moving. I immediately fell in step, instantly feeling like I fit nicely into their radio world.

I remember Fred going out of his way to see I was comfortable. I liked him right away, and I can't explain why, but I innately knew how funny he was from the moment I met him. Very often, you just know, maybe it's a comic thing. God knows how right I was. Fred's one of the funniest and fastest comic minds I've ever encountered, and I've met my share.

The show was loose and really fun and I was loving every second of it. It wasn't but a few minutes before everything else melted away and it became just the four of us in that room, laughing and being silly and forgetting that a huge chunk of the tristate area was listening in to our antics. It quickly became surreal. It's easy to Monday morning quarterback here, but it was magic. Not having had enough experience in radio at the time, I don't think I had any idea exactly how well we all clicked. We were still clicking that exact way the last day I was on the air a bit more than eighteen years later.

As much as I was enjoying it, I had no way of knowing their take on me or my contribution. They were laughing and having the time of their lives, but, hey, that was their job. I'm pretty sure I wouldn't have dared to let myself hope I could come back again. I'm not reeking of humility here, but why would I have let myself go there? What was I bringing to the table? I had no idea, so I just relaxed and had the time of my life along with them.

Soon another guest joined us, Willis Demalt, an executive from Electra Records. We had our second celebrity judge, so Howard had Boy Lee line up people on the phone for the talent contest.

I clearly remember one guy had pulled off the New Jersey Turnpike and was standing at an open phone in the rain singing "Strangers in the Night" or some Frank Sinatra classic. Everybody who performed in the contest was worse than the other, and I helped Howard and the gang heap on the abuse. And I was screaming. It was funny as hell and it was outrageous and, though I had no idea at the time, it was so exactly what the show was all about.

I thought to myself, "This guy is great. They're *all* great. How lucky are they? This is their work, their *job*. God *damn*."

Needless to say, the time flew. Suddenly it was eight o'clock, and we turned into a pumpkin. The show was over. It had been a roller-coaster ride. The longer I had sat there the more I had embraced it, the more hooked I was.

I stood up to leave, and was thanking everybody and saying my goodbyes, when Howard said, "You're a lot of fun. We really liked having you on the show. You want to come back next week? Come back next Tuesday?"

I'm usually pretty tuned in to where I am and what I'm doing, but I'd be lying if I didn't say that caught me way off guard. Wow. Son of a bitch. Did I want to come back?

I have no idea what I said besides yes.

Howard talked to me a bit about how on the show in DC, they had something they called a Think Tank once a week, or once in a while, where they had extra people in the studio for the show who all chimed in here and there and made it more of a fiesta. He said he had been toying with the idea of creating that again on WNBC, and that maybe he'd want me as part of that.

I'm sure that for our entire exchange, I laughed and did whatever a happy Jackie does, which could have been anything. I thanked him and them again and again and floated out of there.

I called home and Nancy said it was so much fun hearing me on the radio and that it sounded like we were having a blast. I assured her we were. Thanks to the on-air mentions, the joke line machines had gone nuts. Nancy had called the people from Governor's and told them to run over to the club to field the calls when she heard it being plugged on the radio.

When I told her they wanted me to come back again the following week, she howled. We didn't know where it could lead, but it was huge compared to just one shot.

The comedy club was jammed all weekend, and everybody wanted to hear all about my radio appearance. I was ecstatic. We didn't know it, but we were about to take a giant step.

The next week, there I was again, in my chair at WNBC, ready for action at 4:00 p.m. That day they had as a second guest Looney Skip Rooney from *The Uncle Floyd Show*. I had done Floyd's UHF TV show years before and of course remembered Skip. He was a nut, wearing a plaid hat and constantly honking his ridiculously loud English taxi horns. He was way over the top, but you had to love him. Christ, he made me look like I was embalmed. And I'm no shrinking violet, you know?

That second week, Howard plugged the joke line and Governor's so much it even embarrassed me (yes, I know, that's the hardest thing to believe yet). And he kept referring to me as "one of New York's top comedians," which had me cringing, as I most certainly wasn't even in that ballpark.

Once again, Fred repeatedly made sure I was comfy and Robin was as sweet as pie. It was another splendid time, from start to finish. None of the luster was gone, it was as great as it had been the first time. And you know what? My last day as a cast member on *The Howard Stern Show*, in March 2001, was equally as exciting and fun, as it has been every time I've gone back on as a guest. I loved it then and I still love it. Again, the four of us clicked. We just did. It was instant, it couldn't not be. It's the emperor's new clothes. It can't be denied.

When the show was over, they all said, "Great having you on again. See you next week."

Was I in? Was this going to be an ongoing thing?

Howard said, "We really like what you add to the show. Why not plan on coming in every Tuesday?"

I said I most certainly would, except for any weeks I was on the road.

And he said, "Fine, we'll take you when we can get you."

Whoa. Not too shabby. Wowie kee-flowie said Flibbity Jibbit. I wasn't getting paid, I was working for the plugs, but that was *huge.*

And then, at some point later that week, Howard called me up.

He said, "Jackie, we've got a problem."

My heart sank. I knew it had all been way too good to be true. Hey, what the fuck, it had been spectacular while it lasted. I had done my best and that's all anyone could expect, right? My God, does someone not like me? Did I say something I shouldn't have? We've all had those near-death experiences (okay, a bit of exaggeration), those few seconds when hundreds of thoughts and scenarios zip through your mind.

Howard said, "I can't plug your dirty joke line anymore. WNBC got complaints. Sorry, man. Do you still want to come in on Tuesdays?"

Was he kidding? The hook was set. Dial-a-joke shmile-a-joke, hell, yes, I still wanted to come in.

I said, "Hey, I understand. You can totally forget about plugging the joke line, it wouldn't serve me to clean it up and it's probably too late to put that toothpaste back in the tube anyway. Hey, the Governor's plugs are priceless. And I love doing the show. Yes, yes, yes, I still want to come in on Tuesdays."

He said, "That's terrific. See you then."

So Tuesday's steady guest on *The Howard Stern Show* was no longer Jackie "922-WINE" Martling; it was now the much more normal-sounding "Jackie Martling."

After the show on the third or fourth week, Howard pulled me aside before I left and said, "I'd really like to have a piece of business I can do with you, some kind of bit that we could do with you each week."

I told him, "Sometimes at the end of my shows, I have the audience try to stump me. They raise their hands, I pick somebody, they stand up and give me a subject, and I do my best to give them a joke about it. I cheat a bit, I'll back up the category to open up the umbrella, like if they say, 'Garlic,' I'll say, 'Okay, Italian foods,' or I'll just tell an Italian joke, because it's really hard to pull off. But it's always fun."

He said, "Okay, that sounds perfect. We'll call it Stump the Comedian. But not long jokes, just two-line jokes. The callers will say the first line, and then you can do the punch line. You know every fucking joke, let them try to get one past you."

The next week, he announced we were going to be playing Stump the Comedian in a later segment so people could start calling in with their jokes. We did a bunch for a few weeks, but the callers' jokes weren't too stellar.

After the second or third time we did it, Howard said, "Why don't you bring in some great two-line jokes and we'll have Fred call in from another room?"

I said, "Sure," and the next week I brought a few pages of the foulest and most offensive jokes we could get away with on the radio. Howard announced the segment was coming up, and when it was game time he took a call or two and then picked up Fred's call.

Fred used a very weird voice that was difficult to distinguish as a man or a woman. It was whiny and funny as hell. He'd ask his jokes and Howard and I would take turns knowing the answers.

What goes, "Click, click, click, did I get it? Click, click, click, did I get it?"
That's Ray Charles doing a Rubik's Cube.

After however many weeks, Howard suggested I bring in some of my comedy pals to join us on Tuesdays. So I put the word out. To this day, it boggles my mind that a lot of them turned me down.

I'd call a comic and say, "You want to do *The Howard Stern Show* with me on Tuesday?"

And I'd hear, "What's it pay?"

I'd just say never mind. I mean, come on. If a performer didn't inherently know the value of being heard on the radio, especially the 50,000-watt flagship NBC station in New York City, when it was almost unheard of to have a comedian on a radio show, how was I going to be able to explain it?

Every once in a while, I'll see somebody from way back when and they'll say, "I can't believe I turned down going on *The Howard Stern Show* with you back in the WNBC days."

Here's a beauty. For a traveling comic, there was no greater place to work than the Fort Lauderdale Comic Strip, even though we had to work seven nights a week for a pittance. Hey, the club was where we wanted to be anyway. That place will continually pop up in this memoir.

As if it wasn't fun enough, the manager was off on Sunday nights and it became a free-for-all. We'd get very drunk, get stoned, do each other's acts, it was almost like a night off. Very often, there were only ten or twenty people in the crowd, and after we had killed four hundred fifty people at each of two shows the night before, I guess we felt we deserved a bit of R&R.

Kelley Rodgers, a very funny comedian who's still a good friend, would sometimes go on stage as a brash and very annoying Catskill comic he called Jackie Phlegmstein. The character was hysterical. And I fell in love with that ridiculous name.

One time after Fred had called in from another room with his Stump the Comedian jokes, I said, "I love when Mrs. Phlegmstein calls in," or something to that effect, to give her a name. But no one made much note of it.

After one of the next times Fred called in from another room with his Stump the Comedian jokes, Robin said, "Is that a man or a woman?"

And I said, "It's an old lady, it's Mrs. Phlegmstein."

And slowly but surely it became carved in stone that our caller was a Jewish grandmother named Mrs. Phlegmstein. I'm sure Kelley wasn't too thrilled that I had lifted the name from him, even though he really didn't employ it for anything.

And much later, one day the subject of Mrs. Phlegmstein's name came up, and someone said, "Where'd she get the name 'Mrs. Phlegmstein?'"

I said, "I named her."

And Robin said, "Right. *You* named her. Sure."

So on one hand I was being blamed for stealing the name, yet on the other hand I wasn't getting the credit for bringing it to the fold.

You gotta love it all.

A year or so later, Rick Dees, a Los Angeles air personality, hired me to send him recorded jokes for his very popular local and syndicated radio shows. He suggested he credit them to Jackie "Joke Man" Martling, a guy from New York who knows all the jokes, and I said sure, that sounded great to me. I had Howard start plugging me that way, and just like that I was back to having a dopey middle name. (That's the *Cliffs-Notes* version . . . full story to follow.)

I had taken to playing "Stump" at a lot of my shows, the two-line version, and people loved it. So it became a staple in my act. After Rick anointed me, the game quickly morphed into "Stump The Joke Man," and I play it at the end of every one of my stand-up shows to this day.

After I had been doing Tuesdays at WNBC for a little over a year, I left Governor's Comedy Shop, so I struck a deal with Mark Magnusson at Rascals Comedy Club in West Orange. I'd plug the Tuesday audition night on *The Howard Stern Show* and then come over and host the show, and they'd pay me well for both doing the show and for the plugs. Simple commerce, great fun. The audiences loved hearing me in the afternoon and then seeing me on stage in person a few hours later, and we did great business on what would otherwise have been an off night.

One auditioner was filthy dirty and came back week after week. He was so foul, yowie. So I started introducing him as "Reverend Bobby Levy," which he goes by to this day.

I continued my Tuesdays on *The Howard Stern Show*, working for plugs, until September 1985. I had a week of shows at the Virginia Beach Comedy Club, and as usual, I drove down. When I pulled into the parking lot on a Tuesday afternoon, the owner, Ricky Cheeks, was standing on the landing at the top of the stairs.

He said, "Jackie, you have to call home right away."

Nancy never ever called me when I was on the road. There was rarely a phone available for the comics, it was too expensive, there was always too much to relate once you got started, and forget about it if we started to fight, which we excelled at. And we'd been together way too long for the, "Hi, sweetie. Goodnight, honey." So we just got used to me being out in the ozone for the duration. Unless . . .

So I thought, "Oh, no. Somebody died. This can't be good."

I called home and Nancy answered right away.

She said, "Are you sitting down?"

Now I was sure the entire family had died in a house fire. *Fock.*

I said, "Yeah, I'm sitting down. Hit me with it."

"Howard Stern just got fired by WNBC."

I don't want to sound cold or uncaring, but my first reaction was, "Is that all?"

It was a huge deal, and it really stunk for Howard and the gang, and the repercussions would certainly ring in my life as well, but I was braced for, "You're never going to see your parents alive again." So I felt a bit of relief at the news, as catastrophic as it was.

But soon it sank in how much it sucked. Howard's show was zooming in popularity and those assholes at WNBC had tossed it. It was hard to believe, because even if they didn't like what he was doing, he was kicking ass. It seemed like a very stupid business move. And I loved going to 30 Rock, and my weekly appearances were great for my head and my gigs and the club. The whole situation was just the pits.

I called to offer my condolences, but only got as far as leaving a message, with no way of knowing if it'd get to them. I didn't expect it to, as it was arriving in the middle of a shitstorm. I mean, this was a huge deal.

As much as I would have liked to, there was certainly nothing I could do. I know now that by the time I called they were long gone from the halls of WNBC.

I was sure, as was everybody, that Howard would rise again, and soon, and of course he did. Yes, he did, didn't he? And not too long after another station hired him, he reinstated my Tuesdays, *ahhh*. Not too long after that, the show went to morning drive, I became a salaried employee, and the rocket ship took off for Pluto.

So, thanks to the package we sent him, one of the so, so many Nancy and I had mailed out, I had been invited to join Howard Stern and his gang on the air for one of their shows, and we had struck pay dirt. Suddenly our system made sense.

I always say, "Meeting Howard Stern was the turning point in my career. Of course, when you're going in circles, everything is a turning point." That joke is about as close as I ever come to applying my 1971 Michigan State mechanical engineering degree.

Hooking up with Howard was a classic case of, "The harder you work, the luckier you get."

And the equally well-worn, "If you throw enough shit against the wall, some of it has to stick."

My shit stuck to *The Howard Stern Show.*

1983

BLANK A DOODLE DOO

One afternoon in late 1983, CBS-TV News came in to tape a piece on Howard during one of my Tuesday appearances on the show.

It always seems that whenever the news or any cameras roll, the funny stops. But I was very lucky that day. I hadn't said three funny things in our version of the Match Game, with Howard as the host Gene Rayguns, since I had joined the show on a weekly basis months earlier. They usually had me playing a character and I never seemed to be able to get in step. I was long overdue.

That day, I was playing Michael Jackson when the CBS crew joined us mid-game. In the Match Game, there's always a blank space among the words in a title or a familiar phrase, and the panelists have to fill in the blank with what they think is the most obvious answer, to try to match as many of the other panelists as they can.

The Howard Stern Show's version of the Match Game always begged for a word that was very easily construed to be vulgar, such as "Pandora's _____ ," or "a _____ and bull story."

That day, the clue was "blank-a-doodle-doo." Of course, everybody wrote down "cock," and Gene (Howard) would beat it to death.

"Brett Summers [Robin Quivers], what do you have?"

Robin would answer to the tune of, "I've got cock, Gene. Of course."

She'd hold up her paper and say, "Right here in my hand, I've got cock." And so on . . . There'd be that kind of banter with each person who was playing.

Gene asked me, "Michael Jackson, what do you have?"

I held up my card and said, "No women."

And Howard, in what was maybe the first display of how seamlessly our minds are connected, immediately said, "No women, a dude will do. Very funny, but unfortunately not a match."

Our laughter trailed off as the CBS-TV news piece wiped to the next hunk.

We reenacted the Stern show version of the Match Game in Howard Stern's *Private Parts*, the feature film based on Howard's life. In the Match Game scene in the film, I was playing myself and the clue was "blank willow."

Gene said, "Jackie Martling, what have you got?"

I had written the word "pussy" very sloppily on my card and said as I held it up, "I've got pussy. Only I wrote it sloppy, Gene. I've got a sloppy pussy."

1983

STUMP THE JOKE MAN

People still come up to me and say, "Jackie, I've been listening to Howard since WNBC. I remember when you used to do the show on Tuesday afternoons and play Stump the Comedian." Here's the longer version of how that bit came to be . . .

Though he'll occasionally deny it, when Howard first listened to my records, he'd been impressed with how many jokes I knew. That was why he called me. He figured I might be a great person to have in the studio. Good laugh, good energy, and a huge body of stupid knowledge.

After a few weeks of me guesting on Tuesdays, he said it'd be great if I had a piece of business, something they could do with me on the air. I told him that lots of times at my gigs, I'd play a game where people gave me a subject, and if they stumped me—that is, if I couldn't tell a joke on that subject—I'd give them one of my albums.

I'd always wanted to be able to do that. I honestly haven't the foggiest idea why, where that desire had created itself. I do know one night I was watching *The Tonight Show with Johnny Carson* when Morey Amsterdam was one of his guests.

Morey was sitting there, and Johnny said, "They say you have a joke about everything."

Morey said, "Yep. Give me a subject."

"Birds."

"Why do hummingbirds hum?"

"Why?"

"Because they don't know the words."

And the house came down. And for some strange and, as I said, unknown reason, I said to myself, I guess figuring I knew enough jokes, "Damn, I could do that."

Actually, I knew I didn't know enough jokes, but was thinking I could and might aspire to that. And with dirty jokes.

By the way, I now know that before the show Morey surely said to Johnny, "When we get out there, ask me for a joke about birds."

The result of their false spontaneity delighted millions. No harm, no foul. It was simple, delightful entertainment.

But I wanted to be able to really do it, which is about as silly a goal as anyone could pursue. I thought it was a fun challenge.

Many years later, during a commercial break on his syndicated television show *Comedy Tonight*, Bill Boggs asked me what subject he should ask me to tell a joke about, and I said, "Cows."

When we came back on the air, we were sitting in the audience, and Bill said, "Jackie, you have jokes about everything. Give us a joke about cows."

And I said, "What do you get when you cross a cow with a masochist?"

"What?"

"Cream that whips itself."

Bill roared. The crowd laughed.

And I sat there feeling like a rip-off artist. Calm down, Jackie, it was show business, and in reality we had just done a hunk of a script, for Christ's sakes.

But you know what?

Even as I write about the incident, I feel like a rip-off artist all over again. It was like Mickey Mantle dropping the baseball into the center-field bleachers from a helicopter.

So now I'm Mickey Mantle? Boy, you sit at this typewriter, and it's Walter Mitty, get the fuck out of my way.

Hey, it was a more colorful way to express it than "shooting rats in a trap."

The more I played the game at my stand-up gigs, the better I got at it.

I'd fudge a bit. If a person yelled, "Paul Newman's dressing," I'd say, "Okay, Paul Newman's Dressing . . . uhh, salad." Then tell a lettuce joke or a salad joke. By backing it out like that, I'd widen the umbrella and I very rarely got stumped.

A guitar-playing comedian named Keven Sullivan had started having audiences try to stump him before me, but he did it with songs. They'd yell an artist and he'd play a hunk of a song by whomever they requested. The similarity between us was the more that we played our respective games, the smoother the game got, as we'd hear the same requests again and again (such as anal sex for me, Springsteen for him), and each time they do, you bark the same spontaneous ad-lib(s) that you say every night, and impress the piss out of the audience. It was almost like comedy.

One of my favorite examples of the always-at-your-disposal ad-lib was at Governor's Comedy Shop in 1981.

I asked a guy his name and he said, "Jay."

I said, "Second letter?"

And the house came down.

It was four years later I asked a guy his name and once again the answer was "Jay."

But when it finally happened, I ad-libbed "Second letter?" And the house came down again.

After that, I said, "Folks, I hope you enjoyed that. I only get to use that joke every four years or so."

They, of course, had no idea what the fuck I was talking about. Occasionally you play to an audience of one.

So Howard said, "Okay, Jackie, we'll let them try to stump you on the air, but just two-line jokes. I'll let them ask you the questions and we'll see if you know the answers. We'll call it Stump the Comedian. And maybe you can call some of your comedian friends and see if they'll come in with you on Tuesdays, you know, a couple of different guys each week."

It sounded great, and it was. It wound up being my signature contribution to the show when it was on WNBC.

Stump the Comedian died out after a year or so, as Howard tired of it. But, fortunately, he didn't tire of me, so even though the game went out the window, I obviously stayed.

Occasionally over the years, a caller would ask if he could try to stump me, but it was about fifty-fifty they'd be met with the click of Howard hanging up.

I kept the game in my act. I liked the two-line version. It was snappier. After being reborn as "The Joke Man" by Rick Dees, I thought "Stump The Joke Man" had a great ring to it. So that became the official name of the game. We made T-shirts that said "I Stumped Jackie The Joke Man," and I sell and use them as prizes in my stage show to this day. At one point in the nineties, Off Hour Rockers Inc. was selling Stump tees in seven colors and six sizes, as well as extra-large sweatshirts in white and heather. People constantly show up at my shows in that dopey attire and it always makes me smile. I French kiss the folks who show up with a copy of one of my first LPs.

The game, fun from the start, evolved over the years into a great, great bit. In 1998, Mark Magnusson, the owner of Rascals Comedy Club in West Orange, New Jersey, who'd had comedians at his club five nights a week since 1981, told me the only thing he still watched on his stage was Stump The Joke Man. Always different, always wild.

I nearly always end my stage act with Stump The Joke Man. At least fifteen minutes' worth, a half hour or even more if the energy is up and the place is really cooking. It's very spontaneous and displays the depth of my knowledge in this ridiculous arena.

Truth be told, anybody can memorize and then go up and tell sixty minutes of jokes, but after that, to stand there and know almost all of the jokes asked of you at random gives the audience a much better idea of just how many stupid fucking jokes The Joke Man knows.

Here's how the game goes at one of my live shows:

"Now we're going to play a round of Stump The Joke Man.

"It's an easy game. All you need to play is a two-line joke. A simple, set-'em-up, knock-'em-down joke . . .

"What's it mean when two lesbians make love?
It doesn't mean dick."

"You raise your hand, and when I call on you, you stand up and give me the first line of a two-line joke. If I know the answer, you're a dick. And the whole crowd will call you a dick.

"Let's try it. You're a . . ."

And the entire crowd yells, "DICK!"

"Now, if I don't know the answer, and it's a good joke . . . it's got to be decent, at least a little bit funny . . . you win a beautiful three-color 'I Stumped Jackie The Joke Man' T-shirt, with (516) 922-WINE on the back.

"But don't get too excited, you wash it once and you won't be able to get it on over your foot.

"Yeah, this is some cheap shit. And I don't understand it, we pay those girls over there four cents an hour . . . I have all the five sizes, small, medium, large, extra-large, and fucking Rosie O'Donnell . . . And I have to tell you right here: stumping me with a joke is the only way to get one of these shirts. Unless of course you want to buy one. Join the elite group.

"If it's a great joke, and the crowd loves it, and it's something I can use, I'll give you a Joke-In-The-Box, a sweatshirt, a video, a few CDs . . .

"You walk out of here thinking you're a hero. The stuff costs me three bucks. I use your joke the rest of my life and make a fortune.

"Look . . . the Jewish guys are scratching their heads, saying, 'Can he do that?'

"He can, and he does.

"Now, the kicker to the game: If you're a girl, a babe, a chick, a honey, a guidette . . . you come on stage and tell your joke. If you have *any tits at all*, you win. No, no, you don't have to show them, you just have to *have* them. If you've got bumps up here bigger than your kneecaps, you win. And if you don't, shave your ass and walk on your hands, I don't care, I just want a few girls on the stage so we can play the game and have some fun.

"Does that sound good? Okay, let's turn on the house lights, guys raise your hands, girls, don't wait to be asked, just come right up. We'll play for a while, and then we'll all go drinking and driving."

Here's what may well have been the most epic round of Stump The Joke Man ever . . .

Summer 1993, I was invited to perform at Montreal's prestigious Just For Laughs Comedy Festival, to appear in the late-night nasty show. Each comic on the bill was only allotted a little more than twenty minutes, but since they requested it, I somehow managed to do a healthy wad of filthy jokes and also play Stump. It was short but very sweet both nights. The second night I was moved to perform last on the show because no one wanted to follow the energy Stump creates.

The girls who came on stage for Stump The Joke Man the second night, as with most nights, were right out of central casting. A Jewish girl, a tall girl, a black girl, an Italian girl, a girl with huge knockers, and an Asian. The mix is always perfect.

So I work my way down the row of girls, meeting them, teasing them, embarrassing them, everything obviously in good fun. I ad-libbed like crazy, which as I said is for the most part repeating well-worn workhorse lines that never miss.

"Look at that hairdo. I can't believe before you left the house you looked in the mirror and said, 'That's good.' Tell me that bathroom wasn't fucking foggy."

"You're a housewife? How many houses?"

"You go to college? So you only have class during the day? Scholarship or full o' shit?"

"You're shaking. You want to hold me in the bathroom?"

After the get-to-know-the-girls segment, I played the game with about ten guys. Much less than usual, but I was pressed for time. I could only hit them with a minimum of insults and slurs.

"You work construction? What are you building? Obviously not a career."

"Okay, you. What's your name, over there? What's your name over here?"

I mowed down the guys one after the other, knowing every punch line to every one of their jokes, at some point abandoning asking their names and just having them scream the setups so I could fire back the answer in a heartbeat. Not one guy stumped me, or even slowed me up. I was at the top of my game, a master (monster?) in full control.

Now, it's time for the line of ladies. One after the other, I listen to their joke setups and then break their hearts with the punch line to the one they were sure would get me.

They poke me in the stomach, they smack me, they yelp, and it's exactly the way it's supposed to be. Totally unplanned, crazy fun, as I'm winning big time.

After all the jokes in my act that bashed women and every ethnic and minority group and then all the bashing and insulting of the girls on the stage, the last contestant on that second night in Montreal, with a packed house of five hundred that was maybe the hottest crowd I ever worked, and that I had worked to a fever pitch, is the Asian girl.

I brought her to center stage, and after a few more very cheap shots, I asked her for the setup to her joke.

Her accent and her speech pattern made what she said *just* hard enough to understand, just foreign enough, to help the situation incredibly, but not impede her riddle.

She said, *juuust* within range of comprehension, "What do anniversary, toilet, and clitoris have in common?"

My God, I had no idea. And it wasn't one of those times where I had heard the joke and knew it, but just couldn't recall it at that moment for some reason, which was how I usually got stumped when I lost.

I stormed back and forth across the stage like a tiger waiting for a slab of raw horsemeat. The place was more than electric. What a fantastic setup. Had I known the joke, I would have pranced the same way, building the tension of this situation only to spurt out the punch line and be the hero.

But not this time.

I mumbled the setup a few times, and finally said, "Tell me, lady."

Very understandably, she said, "Men miss them all."

The crowd exploded, and the place shook with laughter and applause. The perfect finale. Put in my place, handed my comeuppance, defeated by the last girl, an Asian woman, with not only a clever joke but a man-bashing joke. She deflated the pompous know-it-all, and it was one of the greatest comedy moments I have ever witnessed, let alone been part of.

I thanked the crowd and the festival, grabbed my bag of T-shirts, handed one to each of the girls on stage, blew kisses to the audience, gave the show back to the MC, and left the stage. Fellow stand-up Nick DiPaolo thanked the crowd and said goodnight, and as he joined me in the wings, the crowd was still tumultuous. Yikes.

After the show, Charles Joffe, of Rollins-Joffe, who were the management team for Woody Allen and David Letterman, among many others, came up to me and said, "Jackie, that was *unbelievable.* But how often do you get girls to come on stage?"

I told him very honestly, "They come up every night. It's never not wild. This was a great one, Charles, but they always come up, and it always works."

He shook my hand and said he'd never seen anything like it. Needless to say, I never wanted to leave that room.

1983

THE FIRST NOTE

Since the first time I joined Howard and the gang on the air in February 1983, I had been appearing on *The Howard Stern Show* on WNBC-AM every Tuesday afternoon unless I was on the road doing stand-up. The show was from 4:00 p.m. until 8:00 p.m. and I'd sit in from about 5:00 p.m. until the end, playing "Stump the Comedian," and joining in whatever else was on that day's agenda.

In those days, I'd bring in the dirtiest and most offensive two-line jokes we could get away with for Fred Norris to use when he called in from another room as the Jewish grandmother Mrs. Phlegmstein during Stump the Comedian, a few pages of insults in case Howard wanted to have rank-out contests with the listeners, and perhaps a few pages of silliness for Mama Looka Boo Boo Day, the African-American helicopter traffic reporter. That was the extent of my writing for the show.

Occasionally, Al Rosenberg, a very talented radio personality who also worked with WNBC's other big gun, Don Imus, would sit in as Lou Ferrigno, the deaf body builder/actor who played the Hulk. Al is a scream and his Lou impression was hysterical. He'd feign hearing things wrong and his comments and reactions were always funny.

One day after I'd been there a few weeks, it was just before 7:00 p.m. and we were going to have to stop an hour early because there was a New

York Knicks game coming on WNBC. Howard was reading a Coca-Cola ad—that's how long ago it was, he still had mainstream advertisers like Coca-Cola—and he said, "So always make sure you have plenty of Coca-Cola and snacks on hand for the game."

Al was sitting next to me. When Howard said "snacks," it hit me that his Lou Ferrigno character could have heard it wrong, as "snatch."

In a heartbeat, I grabbed a scrap of paper and a pen—I can still remember I had to scurry since the show was very nearly over and I was packed up to go—I wrote: "snacks . . . snatch?" I put it down in front of Al and then underlined "snacks" and then "snatch?" as he looked on. And Al Rosenberg's mind works like lightning.

He immediately mumbled in his Lou voice, "*What did you say,* Howard?"

Howard said, "What was that, Lou?"

Al said, "Make sure you have lots of Coca-Cola and *what?*"

Howard caught on right away and said, "Make sure you have lots of Coca-Cola and *snacks.*"

Al said, "*Snatch?* Boy, you're dirty, Howard."

Howard said, "I said *snacks,* Lou."

Al said, "*See?* You're disgusting, Howard."

By now we were all howling. It was perfect double-entendre comedy. All I could think of were the thousands of guys who weren't (yet) fans of the show, who had tuned in to WNBC to hear the game and had stumbled onto this wildly funny and filthy interchange.

As best I can recall, that was the first time I passed a note and started something like that. What it generated was so great that I must have been inspired to pass more notes.

I have no idea to this day whether Howard or Robin or Fred or anybody even knew that I keyed Al into that. But it didn't matter, just like it went on to never matter. We were all just trying to do a funny, funny show, with everybody doing all they could. Whatever you could throw into the mix, you did.

To this day, once in a while, somebody will tell me they were listening to WNBC that day and they almost drove off the road. That was some wild, wild radio in 1983, even for *The Howard Stern Show.*

1984

THE COINING
OF THE JOKE MAN

Since the creation of my joke line "Use Your Finger! (516) 922-WINE" in 1979, I had changed the jokes every single day, seven days a week. Really. By 1982, it had grown from one to two to four to six to ten lines, each terminating in a PhoneMate answering machine, with the same one-minute message on each machine's tape . . . jokes, with information on where I was performing sandwiched in.

The jokes were changed each day around noon. Nancy and I would make about a dozen answering machine tape copies of each day's offering (a few extra in case one busted) a week or two in advance. And then, quite unbelievably, come hell or high water, one of us would drive to East Norwich from Bayville—about four miles away—run up to my parents' attic (the first JokeLand), take out the tapes, clean the machines, and put in the replacement tapes with the new jokes. It was an unspoken ritual. Like laundry, or actually more like milking the cows, it just had to be done, and we accepted it.

As I type this, and see how ridiculous it was, I feel even *more* insane, because even though now the PhoneMate one-minute machines have been replaced with a Dictaphone digital machine and I program it over the phone, I feel the pressure to put on new jokes because I've been rotating the ones that are loaded on there now to the number one spot for a couple of weeks.

Though now there's ten or fifteen minutes of jokes on each line, all of which can be accessed by any caller at any time.

[Author's note: I wrote this chapter many years ago. (516) 922-WINE slowly reversed paths. It's 2017, and now it's just one line, the original 516-922-9463, and it's the second phone line in my home. I just can't seem to let it go. At this point it's been operating nonstop for thirty-eight years.

Nowadays when someone says to me, "Hey, I used to call your joke line all the time," I say, "Dial it now." They'll dial their cell phone and freak when they hear, the same as in 1979, "Hello, this is Jackie The Joke Man, and you know how much I love it when you Use Your Finger and dial 5-1-6 9-2-2 W-I-N-E!" And I get a big kick out of that every time. Though I only change the content from live show to live show, I'm always on the case. Some things never change.]

So . . .

One day, in 1984, my good friend Bill Haberman said to me, "Jackie, we were working in Jersey on Saturday and I heard your joke line on the radio."

I said, "That's great. What jokes did you hear?"

And when he told me, I said, "Bill, that's not possible. That was on 922-WINE a couple of weeks ago."

He said, "Do you really think I don't know when I hear your voice? And that I don't know what jokes I heard?"

A few weeks later, my sister Kathy said to me, "Jackie, we heard 922-WINE on the radio in Wisconsin."

I said, "Are you sure?"

She said, "Of course I'm sure. All of a sudden, your voice was blasting jokes and Jessie [my goddaughter, two at the time] turned, looked at me, pointed at the radio, and said, 'Uncle Ha-Ha.'"

My sister proceeded to tell me what one of the jokes was, and once again I said, "Are you sure that's what you heard? That was on 922-WINE weeks ago."

And she said, "Come on. I know your jokes as well as you do."

A little background here . . .

When I started the line, in January of 1979, I put very filthy jokes on it. The worst I had. After a few days, a guy from the phone company called and told me to clean it up. So I cleaned it up a bit.

The next day he called back and actually said, "You'll have to clean it up a little more, Jackie." He addressed me by name, like he was familiar with me. It must have been a fun water cooler topic at what I would imagine to be the very mundane phone company offices.

So I cleaned it up a bit more. To this day, that was the last time I ever heard from them regarding any kind of censorship.

It was 1979, and it was a very transitional time for the country. Cable TV had just started. Now you could be sitting in the living room with your mother when a suddenly there's a bare set of boobs on HBO.

So things were loosening up. And as things loosened up, I kept (516) 922-WINE in step, gradually making it dirtier and dirtier.

One day the phone rang, and it was the very prominent Los Angeles disc jockey Rick Dees.

Seems since the onset, he had been turned on to (516) 922-WINE by a girl who was a phone nut. In those days long-distance calls were very expensive, many people used phone calling cards—and some people lifted the numbers and passed them around, using them to call all over the world. A sort of club, they were also always the first ones to know about weird, offbeat numbers, such as my joke line. This girl had told zillions of people all over the world about my (free) lines, and her being from Los Angeles, Rick Dees had been one of them.

He said, "Jackie, I've been calling your line for years, recording the jokes, and playing them on my local show here in LA and on my nationally syndicated Top Forty Countdown show. Sometimes I tell my local listeners that 516-922-9463 is Tom Selleck's home phone number."

Bingo.

My friend Bill had been listening to Z-100 in Jersey, and on Saturday morning they'd run Rick's syndicated show with my jokes on it. And Kathy had heard Rick's syndicated show on some station in the Midwest. His syndicated shows were taped in advance, thus the lag in time from when the jokes had been on my 922-WINE machines and when my gang had heard them.

Rick went on, "I love your stuff, but I've always had to edit out anything that's too dirty, and it's gotten to the point where there's nothing on the line clean enough for me to use."

Ah, how I had grown.

He said, "Could you make some answering machine messages clean enough for me? Twenty spots a month? With the little voices in the background and everything? I'll pay you. I always say that the jokes are told by a crazy dentist from Encino. My listeners love it."

I told him I'd be glad to do it, knowing the exposure was terrific and we could, of course, use the money. But I also told him the dentist thing not only was a little dippy, but didn't benefit me at all. In addition to getting paid, which wasn't much, I wanted being on his shows to help me somehow. He said he'd go back to the drawing board and call me the next day.

Sure enough, the next day he called and said, "How's this: you're Jackie 'The Joke Man' Martling, a crazy guy who knows every joke in the world, who supplies us with them every day from all the way out in New York?"

He had a deal. And I had a new middle name. It was dumb, downright hokey, but it certainly explained who I was and what I did.

So, for a short while, I was "The Joke Man" on both Howard Stern's and Rick Dees' radio shows, the only common denominator these two ever had or ever will have. Unless Westinghouse buys California.

(That was a dated gag I chose to leave in. Westinghouse owned CBS for about ten minutes. One day in 1995, after Westinghouse bought CBS, David Letterman, who was also on CBS, came on the Stern Show, *and to celebrate his new employer, he and his people brought Howard a gift. They rolled a huge Westinghouse refrigerator into our teenie radio studio at 600 Madison Avenue. It was very funny.)*

1986

DON'T EDIT

As *The Howard Stern Show* began to really take shape and things started getting carved in stone, we all became aware that we were part of a wonderful entity. We never discussed it, as I'm sure we were superstitious. It just kept getting bigger and bigger.

After one of our many noontime Scores parties (Scores was a Manhattan gentleman's club . . . a strip joint), so early in the game that we were all walking from Sixtieth Street and First Avenue back to the studio at Fifty-Eighth and Madison, Howard put his hand on my shoulder and said, "Bringing you on full time was the single best business decision I've ever made."

Creating live commercials on the spot for Roselli Movers, with Mrs. Roselli carrying the furniture on her hairy back; outing Gary's breath as one of the Wonders of the Modern World; Robin Quivers coming clean about a vivid sex dream she had about me . . . the formative years of the Greatest Show On Earth are packed with endless color and cackles.

One of the highest compliments people used to pay Howard and us back in the mid-eighties was they enjoyed the live commercials as much as the show. Hell, the live commercials were *part* of the show. We'd develop characters and themes on the fly that were damn near as good as anything Madison Avenue ever conjured up. You couldn't hear the names Snapple, Dial-A-Mattress, P. C. Richards, the Beanstalk, Car Cash, and Jan & Craig's Window Factory, as well as Roselli Movers, without thinking "Howard Stern."

One day not too long after I had joined the show full-time, Howard, Fred, and I were sitting in Howard's office writing. Unless Howard had something pressing to do, we wrote after the show nearly every day. But only bits and song parodies. The bulk of the show was Howard waxing on and on, totally unscripted, on the fly, day after day.

Howard would be sitting at his desk with pen and paper. If we didn't have one already, Fred and I would toss ideas, and after we settled on what we were going to write, we'd toss lines, Howard writing down what he liked and adding whatever.

The beautiful and famous and quirky Cher had taken up with a guy from Queens who worked in a bagel shop, and we of course found it ripe for a song parody. Back in the early days, we did a lot of them. The first song parody Fred and I wrote together was about Mary Beth White-head, who was one of the first surrogate mothers, to the Crosby, Stills & Nash song "Teach Your Children." They still play it on the show, a classic among *The Howard Stern Show* classics.

We pretty quickly decided on a parody to "I Got You, Babe," the six-ties Sonny & Cher love song. It was maybe their first and probably their biggest hit. It was such a cherry situation that the parody just about wrote itself. As we were working on the middle section of the song, I laughed to myself and shook my head.

Howard said, "What?"

I said, "No, no, it's too stupid."

He said, and this was something I never forgot and always, always adhered to, as long as I was working on his show, "*Nothing* is too stupid. Tell me what you've got. Always give me what you've got, let *me* edit."

Many years later, I did just that one morning, and he almost fell off his chair. Robin was doing a horrible news story about these despicable guys in Texas who had tied up a black man, attached a rope to him, tied the other end of the rope to their car, and dragged him to his death.

I wrote a note, Howard looked at it on his monitor, gasped, said, "We'll be right back," and went to commercial.

He looked over and said, "How the fuck does your mind work?"

The note said simply, "Polish waterskiing."

Hey, he was the one who told me, "Don't edit. *I'll* edit."

So as we were sitting there, I told him and Fred the idiocy that was running around in my brain. They screamed, in it went, and it was the highlight of the ridiculous parody. Fred sang the song, from the point of view of Rob Camilletti, Cher's bagel-maker boyfriend.

The real words to the end of the middle section, which builds to these two lines and then modulates (changes pitch) up a step, are "And when I'm sad, you're a clown . . . and if I'm scared, you're always arow-ow-ow-ound . . ."

We replaced those words with, "I see London . . . I see France . . . I saw Cher, in her under pa-a-a-ants."

To this day, when I hear that song, I pee. It's that kind of incredibly stupid crap, alongside the filthy, rude stuff, that makes the show so unique and fun. It's just fucking comedy. Funny, that's all, just funny.

By most everybody's yardstick, another of our classics.

1986

THE FIRST ATTEMPT TO SYNDICATE
THE HOWARD STERN SHOW

We'd only been on morning drive at 92.3 K-Rock for a few months when Toyota signed Howard to do a nationally syndicated radio show. I write this in retrospect, as I had no idea the deal had taken place at the time.

The show was recorded on Saturdays. They must have had a somewhat decent budget, because they had a pretty major guest each week—for the few months it lasted.

I wasn't a part of that show.

When we first went to mornings, Howard had said to me, "Great news. Don's company [Howard's agent was Don Buchwald & Associates] has agreed to represent you."

I said, "Thanks, man, but no thanks."

That decision was to impact my entire run with the Stern organization. I'm sure it affects me to this day.

To me it was simple. Don Buchwald represented Howard, his sidekick Robin Quivers, and Howard's right-hand man, producer and impression-ist Fred Norris. So when it came time to be paid, I'd be the fourth bird in line for a worm—what fell off Howard was going to Robin, what fell of Robin was going to Fred—and what was going to be left for me? I know this is a gross oversimplification, but it explains my thinking (which I'm sure is often grossly oversimplified).

So one reason I wasn't included in the syndicated show was that Buchwald had of course made the deal, and I wasn't part of his stable.

But I think a major factor was that Toyota wanted a studio audience of thirty or forty. And the setup of the radio show had evolved. My job had been expanded, to three then four then five days a week, I was madly passing Howard notes throughout every show, and as yet, that wasn't very well known (many people still have no idea that I was doing anything but laughing, breaking balls, and getting my balls broke). And I don't think Howard wanted the audience and the media, who were certain to be invited to the shows, to see that.

Howard told me it was due to budget constraints.

Once in a while, I'd meet a celebrity who'd say they'd done *The Howard Stern Show*, and I wouldn't remember them. Then I'd realize they'd done the Saturday Toyota show.

To kick off the syndicated show, Toyota threw a big press party at the renowned and now sadly gone and certainly missed Elaine's.

When it was time for him to say a few words, Howard started off with a bunch of the great but very distasteful jokes Fred and I had written that morning about Len Bias, the basketball player who had just OD'd on cocaine.

"What's black on the outside and white on the inside?
Len Bias's nose."

I guess Howard felt bad that he was killing with jokes I had written—even though it was my job—so he took me aside, put his arm around me, and said, "As soon as we get a bigger budget, I'll bring you on board."

It wasn't to be, as the show was canceled after a short time, I guess because not enough markets signed up for it. I like to think it was because Howard wasn't as funny without me and the show had fewer sparks without my dopey laugh. Of course, that's all speculation. *My* speculation. And whose book is it? Heh, heh.

As I said, we'd only been on mornings for a few months, and I'd only been a regular member of the show since we went to mornings. I'd met Howard's parents, but I hadn't yet met his sister Ellen. It seems Ellen hadn't been able to listen to his afternoon shows, but now that he was on mornings, she could listen on her way to work.

A woman with a big, friendly smile came up to me at Elaine's and said, "Hi! I'm Howard's sister, Ellen. Since the radio show's on in the morning now, I can listen. And I said to my brother, 'Howie! When did you get so *witty?*' and he said, 'That's not me, that's *Jackie.*' And [pointing at me] *you're* Jackie! It's so nice to meet you!"

Needless to say, I liked Ellen a lot from Jump Street. Of course, as I occasionally saw the family and got to know them, I soon realized Ellen and her husband Peter were about as sweet and kind as any two people can be.

One week, their guest on the syndicated show was Elton John. Fred wrote a terrific set of lyrics and they gave them to Elton when he arrived at the taping.

I think it was to start the show, but nevertheless, at some point, Elton sat at the piano with Fred's lyrics in front of him and created a song on the fly. Any Stern fan knows it.

It begins, "There's a man . . . Who has a small penis . . ."

Which was incredibly wild for 1986. The entire song is genius, words, music, and performance. A huge home run. It's been played countless times on the show over the years.

Fred always created (maybe he still does) a montage to start the morning show. It always had some kind of theme, some connecting link. He'd play a *Stern Show* potpourri, an audio stew of our radio bits, sound bites, sound effects, and often conclude with a song parody or a song that had been performed on the show. It was always brilliant. I lobbied more than once (to no avail) for Fred's opening to be repeated mid-show, as most listeners weren't listening right at 6:00 a.m.

Howard had a dump switch under his mixing board that he could get at fairly easily. We were on a seven-second delay, which means the show was seven seconds behind real time. If somebody slipped and cursed or something very inappropriate was said, he could hit the switch, the show would jump to real time, and then the delay would slowly *strettcchh* the show until we were once again seven seconds behind so the dump switch would be ready for the next mishap. Many radio shows have the same thing.

One morning, in the late eighties, Fred ended the opening montage with that Elton John song, which I've never tired of.

As the show started and the microphones went on, for no apparent reason, I said, "Howard, I think that's the best thing Fred ever wrote. I love that song. Man, that's great, Fred."

Howard kind of muttered, "Yeah?" He leaned over and didn't say anything for a few seconds.

I said to myself, "No . . ."

In those early years, Nancy recorded almost every show on cassette, so she was often up for the beginning, and then if she was tired, she'd go back to bed until the tape had to be changed.

During the first commercial break, I called home and asked her if she had heard the opening of the show, right after the montage. She said she had.

I said, "Did you hear me say to Howard that I think that Elton John song that played at the end of the montage was the best thing Fred ever wrote, and then tell Fred how great I think it is?"

She said, "No, I didn't hear that."

Howard had dumped me telling the listeners—the ones who were listening at six in the morning—that Fred had written that song. I guess if they didn't hear that, they'd continue to assume Howard wrote it, or that Elton John or his people had written a song about Howard and he'd brought it with him . . . but either way, the credit wasn't going where it belonged.

Man, that was an eye-opener. And though I always was, I had no right to ever be shocked by anything along those lines after that.

1986

TWO FORTY-FIVE

By fall of 1986, I had settled in as a full-time member of *The Howard Stern Show*. Initially hired as a salaried writer for two days a week in February of 1986 when the show went from afternoons on K-Rock to morning drive, my job had expanded to three days a week to four to full-time in a bit less than three months. The hours notwithstanding, I was enjoying the show, and for the most part, everybody was enjoying me. We all had our roles, it was all new. Howard was breaking ground where there hadn't even been ground before and the show was on fire.

I was writing a lot of really good lines, which had of course accounted for my jump to full-time, but that role was still far, far in the background. The listeners knew there was a comedian sitting there, a laughing hyena who was part of the ensemble, but my written contributions were definitely, for the most part, hush-hush. Part of the reason nobody was aware of how much I was writing, aside from it not being written about and talked about too much, was that as much and as quickly as the show grew, it was an incredibly smooth operation from the moment of inception.

I consistently wrote my notes in very big, very clear capital letters. Howard was always able to read my writing—even hastily scratched notes that I got up there in a flash—and he always worked them in, whether in part, verbatim, or in his own interpretation, so seamlessly that anyone would be hard-pressed to know what was from the papers in front of him or what was just rolling from his frighteningly agile imagination and stunningly creative mind.

Everywhere I went, people were talking about how witty Howard Stern was. How funny, how quick. And I always agreed with them. But I also knew that since joining forces with him, I had something to do with it. Some days more than others. But all the years I sat there, I always had something to do with how funny the show was. Hey, it was my job, and I knew it, but I had created this note-passing gig, it was working out big-time, and though I couldn't say I was actually frustrated, I wouldn't have minded the word slipping out a bit here and there.

One day during the news, Robin read a story about how a few of Ronald Reagan's cabinet members hadn't fared well on a rock and roll oldies quiz, and that she wanted to give the quiz to Howard.

She started asking the questions, and always wanting the boss to fare well, Fred and I were helping a bit. Of course, Howard knew the names of the Rolling Stones, but some of the questions were a bit tougher, and it was good that we had three minds jumping on them.

So Robin asked, "What were some of the hits of Gary 'U. S.' Bonds?"

Howard immediately responded with one of Gary's major hits, "This Little Girl," which was from his era.

Fred, being cryptic (what a shock, eh?), said, off mike, "What time is it?"

Fred said that because Gary "U. S." Bonds had a monster hit in the early sixties with "Quarter to Three." That song was from my era. *Every* era was Fred's era.

Seeing a wide-open hole to run a practical joke through, with my ever-faithful Sharpie, I wrote on one of my trusty 8 x 11 sheets of paper "2:45" and put it up in front of Howard.

And Howard said, "Two forty-five?"

Robin squealed with laughter. Fred and I were screaming.

Fred yelled, "No! *No!*"

Meanwhile, Howard had begun to laugh as hard as us, pretty quickly realizing something ridiculous had gone down.

He barked above the din, "What's so funny?"

Robin finally calmed down enough to sputter, "It's 'Quarter to Three!'"

In a cover-up that would have embarrassed Nixon, Howard started saying, "Well, I call it 'Two Forty-Five.' I talk digital."

But it was too far gone.

He railed at me, "You *idiot!* If you're gonna cheat, at least make it so . . . Ah, never mind. What's the next story, Robin?"

So in my mind, anyone who was listening and paying any attention at all that morning knew I had passed Howard a note that read "2:45," that I was writing for him, and was now aware I was in on the creation of some of this phenomena that was about to engulf the country, the media, the comedy community, the censors, and the very fortunate soon-to-be-millions of commuters nationwide who were lucky enough to be within earshot.

Little did I know that, in the years to follow, most of the people who would sit right next to me, guests who would watch me write notes and put them up in front of Howard for entire segments of the show, would have no idea what in the world I was doing or why I was there.

Needless to say, it wasn't a headline the following day.

Another time early on that I thought the cat had jumped out of the bag was the first time we had the rock legend Leslie West on the show.

Man, I was excited that he was coming in.

Gary Gargantuan Gums had come in one morning and said, "Howitt, there's a guy on the phone says he's Leslie West, the guy from Mountain."

Howard took the call, and after hearing his voice and his attitude, I immediately looked at Fred and said, to Fred and to Howard and who-ever else might have been listening, "This is him. Somehow I'm sure this is Leslie West."

And it had been. It turned out he was Howard's biggest fan, never missing a word of the morning show. Howard was, of course, flattered and asked him to come in and be a guest as soon as he could.

I realize the terms "legend" and "rock legend" get tossed about a lot, but to the gang on the show and to me, Leslie was and is truly a rock legend. Two notes of "Mississippi Queen" and you know what you're listening to. I had seen the three-hundred pound Leslie West in a full-blown Sgt. Pepper outfit when his killer band the Vagrants opened for the Young Rascals at the Singer Bowl in 1967 and when Mountain headlined Michigan State University's mini-Woodstock in 1970. Plus, he was the personal hero of Larry Wickett, the lead guitar player in my college band, so to have him joining us on the show was huge for me.

Plus, I was fairly new to the show, and hadn't met the tiniest bit of the gazillion people I was to meet in the next fifteen years, so just his celebrity had me jazzed.

Leslie had recently been in the film *The Money Pit*, and for his role, he had cleaned himself up and even gotten a brand new set of choppers. Here was this scruffy rock and roller with this broad bright-white piano-keys smile. And Leslie's bouts with drugs and whatever else were as legendary as his musical prowess.

I wrote a note and put it up: "Leslie's got a very addictive personality, Robin. He just spent ten thousand dollars on teeth, and now he wants more teeth."

Leslie had seen me write something and then put it in front of Howard, and then listened as Howard read it and now I was screaming.

He said, "So that's how it works. Jackie's writing the stuff. Jackie writes the funny stuff you say."

And Robin said, "Not all of it, Leslie."

We all laughed and it went on to be a terrific show, with Leslie being very forthcoming about his life and his many foibles.

I remember that day so well. For many reasons, I was beside myself. Not just being on what was rapidly becoming an iconic radio show, but meeting and hanging out with a rock and roll hero of mine, plus thinking the entire world had heard Leslie out our writing system to everybody within earshot.

Once again, if anybody caught what he said, I certainly never heard about it. And once again, it wasn't a headline the following day.

The truth is, I really didn't care. I was so damn thrilled to be doing what I was doing, thrilled to actually have a job and an income. Life was way too great for my writing being undercover to matter. Howard knew precisely what I was contributing, and that was what mattered.

I laughed a lot on *The Howard Stern Show*. Contrary to what many people think, I didn't only laugh when Howard said something I wrote. I laughed when something was funny. Which was often. I usually howled at what I wrote because I thought it was funny. If I hadn't thought that, I wouldn't have passed it.

But I also laughed very hard at a lot of things Fred wrote, a lot of things that Howard said on his own, or that Robin or anyone said that was funny.

And unlike Robin, who would giggle if Howard read a death notice in Japanese, I was an accurate gauge . . . I always laughed as hard as a line was funny.

Many times, I'd came home from work and Nancy would say, "The best thing you wrote today was yada-yada." And I'd have to say, "*Fuck*, I didn't write that, Fred wrote it." Or "Shit, Howard said that on his own."

I was an equal-opportunity audience.

1992

DOM AND BRUCE WITNESS THE NOTE SYSTEM

It was always interesting who picked up on what I was doing during the show and who didn't.

One day, Dom DeLuise and Bruce Jenner were booked, and it was especially entertaining because of the A-B situation.

Whenever a guest was a star with a certain degree of stature, they were never made to wait to come on the air. So when Dom DeLuise got to K-Rock, Gary rushed him into the studio. It turned out that almost right away, we went to commercial.

And of course, in the maybe three or five minutes Dom was there, I had passed a bunch of notes. This was in the old studio, and before we were on E!, so I was still churning out the notes and flipping them with my left hand up and over and onto the easel in front of Howard. There was definitely a rhythm to it. I'd write a note, flip it up there, he'd read it—usually sooner rather than later—and I'd howl.

After those few minutes, Howard said, "We'll be right back." Dom turned to me and said, "This is fantastic, this arrangement. You and Howard, you passing those notes. That's just great. What a team."

I thanked him profusely and told him it was great to hear that from such a well-respected, funny guy like himself. It made my week.

The next guest was Bruce Jenner. Bruce came in, sat with us for a very long segment, and I was tossing jokes (and insults . . . he was a great target) like a madman.

After Bruce had witnessed that same rhythmic ballet, for at least forty-five minutes, Howard said, "We'll be right back."

Bruce turned to me and said, "What are those papers you keep putting up there?"

I said, "I have to keep letting Howard know what time it is."

And he said, "That's what I thought."

1987

THE SUPER BOWL FINGER

In 1987, the guys from *The Howard Stern Show* were having a Super Bowl party at Howard's new civilian pal Neil Drake's house in Queens.

We were all there. Howard, Fred Norris, Gary Flualooie, Howard's limo driver Ronnie Mund, John and Tim Curtin from Howard's band Pig Vomit, Neil, and former WNBC coworker Tony O. Howard's special guest was the two-time Super Bowl champion New York Giant Leonard Marshall. Neil had a huge TV (back in the days when hardly anyone else did) in his living room, and we had tons of booze and weed and food. Neil booked a few of the ugliest hookers that ever peddled their wares, and we dug into everything pretty quickly.

As we're getting rolling, Tony O. pulled down his pants and mooned us. He had "Giants" written on one cheek and "Suck" written on the other. He bent over so the "Giants Suck" was blazing across Neil's living room.

Ronnie said, "Hold on, let me get my camera . . ."

If you're paying attention, you just read we had a *two-time Super Bowl–winning Giant* at our party! And this interloper was flashing this incredible diss?

Right here I have to briefly veer off the story . . .

By coincidence, years ago, I was at the New York Friars Club when someone spun me around and said, "Joke Man, give me a hug."

It was an elderly gentleman (even compared to me), and as too many people know, I'm easy, so without a care I hugged him. I pulled back and it was Bill Dana. I was so thrilled he knew who I was. He's a show business legend. He created Don Adams's *Get Smart* character, was one of Steve Allen's regulars on his ground-breaking television show in the late fifties, and his "José Jiménez" character, nationally known for his many *Ed Sullivan Show* appearances, sold millions of LPs in the early sixties.

Excited to have this new mutual fan and friend, I Googled him and read that he had written one of *TV Guide*'s "Top Ten Sitcom Episodes of All Time." He wrote the episode of *All in the Family* where, due to a newspaper contest, Sammy Davis Jr. winds up having dinner at Archie's home. It's local news, there's press outside the door, and as Sammy's leaving they all want a picture of Sammy and Archie. Archie's of course already a bit bent out of shape that an African-American dined at his home and then gets noticeably uncomfortable at the thought of them being in a picture together.

Sammy says to the photographers, "On *three*, man . . ."

Sammy counts, "One, two," and on "three," he turns and plants a big kiss on Archie's cheek as the flashbulbs all pop.

The picture winds up on the front page of all the local papers. Just so damn clever.

So I had seen the episode and loved it.

when we last left you . . .

Ronnie came back, he was standing there with his camera ready, Tony O.'s pants were down to his ankles, he's just bending way over and pulling his cheeks apart so the "Giants Suck" would be perfectly displayed . . .

Channeling Sammy, I said to Ronnie, "On *three*, man . . ."

I counted, "One, two," and on "three," I stuck the pointer finger of my left hand way up Tony's ass. I didn't tap the rim, I passed it on the way through. I'm pretty sure I did a very quick circle around the perimeter to make sure it was properly aligned, and then *innnn* it went.

Ronnie snapped the photo and a legendary Stern story was born.

The very next time we took to the airwaves, the story had evolved. I don't know if I ever got to explain where I stole the "one, two, three" idea—which had made the picture possible—but the first thing they insisted was that I had been eating barbecued ribs in sauce, and then invaded Tony, and then, without missing a beat, went back to my plate of ribs.

Playing along, I said, "The barbecue sauce was great lube."

I staunchly denied, and still do, their version of the incident, that I didn't go wash my hands after I skewered Tony, that I had dug right back into my food. The truth? I have no idea. Is it possible? *Ummm...*

(We never saw Tony again until years later, when he was a guest on a 1991 Channel 9 Super Bowl party. We were all naked in towels ready for our massages and Howard recounted the whole sordid tale to a huge new crop of fans.)

After Neil's Super Bowl party had gone on a while, it was obvious nobody was going for the hookers, even though they'd already been compensated and were downstairs in the den ready for action. Being who I am, I figured, what the hell, and went downstairs to see the ladies.

Again, they were no fiesta for the eyes, even though I was bombed. So I may have had them rub my back a bit, but I mainly talked to them and had a few laughs and then came back upstairs. To this day, I don't think anybody believes I didn't at least get myself a blow job. But no... not this time. Nowhere near worth it.

That was so damn long ago. I think I may have even passed a lie detector test that I didn't do anything with them.

For years, Leonard Marshall came to my comedy shows whenever I was in Boca Raton, and that damn story never got old. Hey, it never will.

1988

QUENTIN THE STUTTERER

One of the cruelest yet funniest bits of business that Fred My-God-Is-He-Funny Norris and I ever pulled was on the first Stern pay-per-view, "Howard Stern's Negligee and Underpants Party."

Long before "Stuttering John" Melendez became a household name by assaulting people from every walk of life with his unique talent of stammering out the totally unfathomable questions Fred and I wrote for him while being almost always oblivious to their impact, there was Quentin the Stutterer.

Quentin's brand of stutter was not to be believed. He'd be rolling along fine and then stop dead on a word. Like his speech had hit a brick wall. Cakes could have baked during the pauses. Smack me with a fish, my friend, but *that's* entertainment.

We got Howard to talk Quentin into introducing the pay-per-view. Quentin was pretty frightened, but he only had to read the intro, not memorize it, and we gave him the script a week in advance, so he got to practice it over and over and work out any spots that might pose a problem.

Of course, we knew what would be tough words and phrases for him, so for the most part, we avoided them. It turns out the toughest thing for a stutterer to say, for whatever psychological reason I won't go into because I'm saving that for the sequel, is their own name.

The night of the live pay-per-view, even though he was well prepared, Quentin told me and Fred how unbelievably nervous he was. But he was all decked out in one of those T-shirts that are supposed to look like a tuxedo and we assured him how great he looked and he managed to get himself primed and ready, able to leap tall buildings in a single . . . bound.

When it was showtime, and I mean when the producer said, "Thirty seconds until air," Fred and I took back the script from Quentin and handed him a rewrite of the introduction he was to read. It was now full of all the hardest words any stutterer had ever hurdled and ran broken-field through and around, including multiple mentions of his name, which as I have informed you is customarily the very toughest task for a person of his circumstance.

It was brutal.

"Hi, I'm . . . . Quentin the Stutterer. That's right . . . . Quentin the Stutterer . . . ."

That much alone took somewhere around twenty minutes.

To me that story is *The Howard Stern Show* personified. Having a stuttering announcer is wild enough. But having a stuttering announcer and setting him up to stammer even beyond his own worst nightmare of the situation is just too fucking funny. We always seemed to keep the show's funny quotient just ahead of the bad taste. You just can't scream at us or about us while you're laughing. Some people do, but they're full of shit, and we weren't doing the show for them.

To put what we did to Quentin in perspective, on that same pay-per-view, I competed against the guy who beat me on *Star Search*. In my underpants. Humiliation reigned across the board that night, at least for some of us.

"The Wack Pack" is how *The Howard Stern Show* refers to all the crazies who closely orbit the show. I came up with the name the Wack Pack and was always proud of it. Quentin the Stutterer was a charter member, I'm fairly sure a card-carrying member, before we even named it. The people who floated in and out of that batch on the fringe of humanity were and are responsible for a lot of what made and makes the show click.

I always befriended them, often a bit too much, and when they weren't using it to skewer me, they appreciated it. And now, as I drift further and further from being a cast member, I've probably meandered frighteningly close to becoming a Wack Packer, if I haven't already. Now that's comedy come full circle. And as I said, I love it all.

1988

STERNAK THE IMPROBABLE

My favorite thing to write for the *Stern Show* was Sternak the Improbable, our parody of Johnny Carson's Carnac the Magnificent. It took me a while to convince Howard to try the bit, and when I had finally sold him on it, the pressure was on me. But it almost always was a killer.

In case you don't know the routine, Carson's Carnac would walk out from behind the curtain wearing a huge turban and a very garish sultan's robe, then trip on the lip of the stage, eventually taking his seat as sitar music swelled behind him. He'd hold a series of sealed envelopes up to his head one at a time, give the answer to the question contained in the envelope, rip open the envelope, and then blow into it so he could get at the contents. Then he'd reach in, take out the piece of paper, and read the question he'd already answered, with Ed McMahon playing straight man, chuckling incessantly and absorbing the many very colorful Carnac insults that peppered the proceedings.

We parodied the bit very closely. Just like Carnac, Sternak would sprinkle the goings-on with horrible insults he would toss at me, the crew, and whoever was there. The material could be about anything as long as a good percentage of the listeners would know what the hell he was talking about. Sometimes, I'd throw in stuff that was way too inside, but that was always hysterical. At least to us.

116

I wrote the entire Sternak every time, the questions and the answers and the insults, with a few Fred Norris contributions here and there, so I was in the hot seat for every joke and every line. Howard and Robin of course often tortured me with their usual antics of feigning they didn't understand the joke, or a line I knew was stellar wasn't any good, etc. But for the most part, it was always great. Just like Johnny, Howard sold the hell out of it even when the jokes weren't home runs. And when it was really off course, he'd naturally go after me even more, which was (is?) always funny.

One time, Robin really sandbagged the bit when I wasn't in the right head for being sandbagged. When she ran into the studio from her little enclave after the bit while we were in commercial, cackling her wicked giggle (or giggling her wicked cackle), I wasn't laughing. I had worked really hard on the material, it was great, and she had steered it into the toilet. I was really pissed off and actually called her a cunt. She giggled at that, too, so I repeated myself, a healthy bit louder, at which point she exited, stage left. The truth is, she hadn't done anything she didn't always do; just for any of a zillion possible reasons it hit me very wrong that day and man, was I seething. That was the only time I think I was ever really mad at her, and it lasted about five minutes.

The Sternaks are fun to go back and listen to because very often the answers involved a current news event, movie, or TV show, so they're somewhat time-stamped and thus, besides being really funny, they can be a bit nostalgic. And this was of course long before Howard made the move to uncensored satellite radio, so we were still dealing with dancing in and around and past the scornful ears of the FCC (Federal Communications Commission), which of course made writing it a challenge and its success very rewarding.

Occasionally, Howard would invite our old pal, the aforementioned and incredibly talented Al Rosenberg, to join us for the bit, to play the Ed McMahon role. As I said, Ed McMahon was talk show host Johnny Carson's sidekick and Ed would laugh at everything Johnny said that was even remotely intended to be funny. Al Rosenberg's "Ed McMadd" would laugh—no, he'd *guffaw*, too loud and too long—at everything Howard said, whether it was intended to be funny or not. His boisterous laugh was way over the top and Sternak's sidekick was a riot.

A few years after Johnny Carson left *The Tonight Show*, HBO flew Nancy and me to Los Angeles to the second season premiere of *Sex and the City*. While we were in LA, we went to a friend's party where there were a lot of Hollywood writers and actors and it was a gas. We met Mike Reiss and Hank Azaria from *The Simpsons*, plus a whole potpourri of people who were, for the most part, as glad to meet us as we were to meet them. I say "we" because, by then, due to her many on-air calls and the trappings of being my wife, Nancy was a well-known entity on the radio show. It was a really great time.

One of the guys we met was Tony DeSena, who came over and introduced himself and said, "Jackie, I have a story for you I know you'll love."

Tony had been a writer on *The Tonight Show with Johnny Carson* the last few years before Johnny left, right up until he was done, and had maintained his relationship with Johnny. They'd do lunch occasionally, share a phone call here and there, like that. Tony was a big Howard Stern fan, and Johnny knew it.

Tony said to me, "A while back Johnny called me up and said, 'What's this I hear, Ed was on *The Howard Stern Show*?' I guess people who knew Johnny heard, 'Joining us today is Ed McMadd,' and weren't listening closely. And I said, 'No, Johnny, that's a guy named Al Rosenberg, who plays an Ed McMahon character they call Ed *McMadd*. They do a version of Carnac that's as dirty and offensive as they can make it and get away with it on the radio. And sometimes when they do it, they bring in Al to play Ed.

"Johnny said, 'Oh, really.'

"He took a beat, and said, 'Is it funny?'

"And I said, 'It can get very funny. A comic named Jackie Martling writes them and he can hit home runs. The best one the other day was, the answer is *Eyes Wide Shut* [the movie had just hit the theaters at that time]...

"... and the question was, 'How would a black man tell you his name is Wide Shut?'

"Johnny dropped the phone he laughed so hard. He was still laughing when we hung up. I thought you'd like to hear that."

Like it? I had a hard-on for about a week.

My great-grandfather Franklin Hall, Sagamore Hill, Oyster Bay, NY, 1902

My mother, Dorothy
Poole, Mineola, NY, 1938

My mother and father, Dorothy Poole and John C. Martling, New York, NY, 1946

With Pop,
East Norwich,
NY, 1949

On my grandmother
Dorothy Hall's lap, with
"double cousin" Lenny
Martling and my brother
Bobby at her feet,
East Norwich, NY, 1953

The Martling cousins:
Pete and me on the
couch, Lenny and Bobby
on the floor, 1955

With Lenny and Bobby, my first puppet stage, East Norwich, NY, 1956

COME TO A MAGIC SHOW!
with 11 tricks, a movie, games, & refreshments

1. Cut the Lady In Half   6. Magic Wedding Ring
2. Oriental Card Trick   7. Magic Slate
3. Talking Dice   8. Key Chest
4. Whispering Colors   9. Magic Flower Pots
5. Chain of India   10. Vanishing Box
     11. Mystery Chamber
     Time: 1:45 p.m.
Date: January   , 1959
Place: Corner of Whitney Ave. & Oyster Bay Rd., EN
Show, 15¢; Games, 5¢; Refreshments, 5¢
All Welcome! Bring Friends!

My first show business flyer, East Norwich, NY, 1959

Close-up of my 8th grade class photo, East Norwich, NY, 1961

Pole vaulting in my back yard, East Norwich, NY, 1962

The Sonics… Paul Cicarelli, Chris Bates, me, and Louie DeGennaro, Oyster Bay, NY, 1963

The Sonics… Chris Bates, me, and Carl Dincesen, Oyster Bay, NY, 1965

With my mother
Dot, Tobay Beach,
NY, 1965

That's me!
Spring Break,
Ft. Lauderdale,
FL, 1967

The John C. Martlings:
Pop (John), Kathy (Katie),
Bobby, me, Mom (Dot),
and Jimmy, East Norwich,
NY, 1968

With my pal
Zippy The Chimp,
Freeport, NY,
1971

Rocking at Michigan
State University,
East Lansing, MI, 1971
(photo by Gary Lazar)

With "Tweetie" and Chris Bates, Mill Neck, NY, 1974 (photo by Andrea Green)

With Chris Bates, *The Off Hour Rockers*, Huntington, NY, 1976

With Herby Werner and Chris Bates, *The Off Hour Rockers*, Neptune Pub, East Meadow, NY, 1976

A sticker advertising my joke line, active since 1979

1. CI CLUB

TITLE: ALL THE CRAP

?	#	clue		?	#	clue
1	CI	CLUB INTRO		19	F	FAT
2	PP	PERSONAL PROBLEMS		20	SK	SKINNY
3	OC	OTHER COMIX		21	PL	POLISH
4	SM	SMILE!		22	HB	HEBREWS
5	NS	NEWS		23	CA	CATHOLIX
6	DR	DRINKS		24	N	NEGROES
7	T	TOASTS		25	CH	CHINESE
8	Ti	TITIES 8		26	C	CONFUCIUS
9	SP	SPONSORS		27	i	ITALIAN
10	Y	JOKES		28	I	INDIAN
11	LL	LITTLE OLD LADY		29	IIS	QUEERS
12	J	DIRTY JOHNNY		30	HP	HIPPIES
13	QK	QUICKIES		31	d	DRUNKS
14	A	ANIMALS		32	G	
15	VA	VIRGINIA		33	Z	ZIPPER
16	HK	HECKLERS		34	OO	OLDER OWNERS
17	RK	RANKS			BP	BACHELOR PARTY
87		UGLY GIRLS 18			XP	FUNNY EXPRESSIONS
?	#	clue		?	#	clue 37 - parodies

My joke filing system, 1979

The first JokeLand, East Norwich, NY, 1979

Pencil sketch from
Mad magazine's
Don Martin, 1979

JACKIE —
THANKS FOR THE RECORDS...YES, I FOUND A LOT
OF FUNNY STUFF THERE. GOOD LUCK —
DON MARTIN.

An *Off Hour Rockers Comedy Production*, Reinhardt's, Bayville, NY, 1979

Many of the wacky cast of characters in my jokes as drawn by the very talented late, great Linda Romano, Long Island, NY, 1979

With Dave Hawthorne and Bob Woods, *The Rolling Clones*, in King Broder's office, Hicksville, NY, 1979

Top: Bob Nelson, Larry Miller, Peter Bales. *Bottom:* Melanie Roy, Brian Roy, Melanie's girlfriend Debbie, Paul Reiser, Dennis Wolfberg, and Glenn Hirsch, Bahia Mar, Ft. Lauderdale, FL, 1980

With Rodney
Dangerfield,
Dangerfield's,
New York, NY,
1980

With Eddie Murphy and Rob Bartlett, on stage at *East Side Comedy Club*,
Huntington, NY, 1980

My first three LPs: *What Did You Expect?*, *Goin' Ape!*, and
normal people are people you don't know that well, 1979–1981

Top: Joe Mullin, Joe Bolster. *Bottom:* Jon Hayman, David Sayh,
Jenny Jones, and me, The Comic Strip, Ft. Lauderdale, FL, 1981

On stage at *East Side Comedy Club*, Huntington, NY, 1982

Use Your Finger! (516) 922-WINE! the first *JokeLand*, with Nancy Sirianni, East Norwich NY, 1983

On stage at *Club Bene*,
South Amboy, NJ, 1988
(photo by Steven Hersh)

With Sam Kinison,
Westbury Music Fair,
Westbury, NY, 1988

With the Jackie
puppet, New York,
NY, 1989

With my brothers Bobby and Jimmy, and Pop, East Norwich, NY, 1990

With the legendary Henny Youngman, K-Rock Comedy Riot, NY, NY, 1992 (photo by Godlis)

Lunch with Steve Grillo, New York, NY, 1993

At *K-Rock* with Fred Norris, New York, NY, 1994

With Steve Schirippa, *Riviera Hotel*, Las Vegas, NV, 1994

The premiere of *Private Parts,* with Fred and Alison Norris, Rory Rosegarten, and Nancy Sirianni, New York, NY, 1997

With Keith Richards and Les Paul, *iridium,* New York, NY, 2000

On stage with Les Paul, *iridium*, New York, NY, 2003

Jackie Ratcliffe and me on stage hosting a marijuana benefit concert, Austin, TX, 2007

With Willie Nelson, Austin, TX, 2007

With my sister Katie Dunn, nephew Brendan Dunn, and niece Jessica Dunn, Crystal Springs, NJ, 2008

With Billy West and Ian Karr, *Jackie's Joke Hunt 127*, SiriusXM, New York, NY, 2009

With Jena Axelrod and Ian Karr, *Jackie's Joke Hunt 118*, SiriusXM, New York, NY, 2009

The Jetty, Long Island Sound, Bayville, NY, 2009

The night I met my honey, Barbara Klein, *The Brokerage*,
Bellmore, NY, 2015

With Barbara Klein; Katie, Brendan, and Jessica Dunn; and Kevin Kelly—the world's greatest gang, *JokeLand*, Bayville, NY, 2016

With Dan Falato and Artie Lange, Hoboken, NJ, 2017

Oglio Records joke CD collection, as of 2017

1990

THE CHANNEL 9 SHOW

The Channel 9 show, the first regularly televised attempt at television by *The Howard Stern Show*, accounted for two of the craziest and most creative years in my life.

Five hours of radio, give or take, five days a week, and somehow, with a skeleton crew of incredibly energetic cohorts and whatever juices we had left, we put up a sixty-minute television show on Saturday night about thirty-five times a year for two long, exhausting, draining, and wonderful years.

The story I always tell first is about the time we had Siamese twins booked. To be politically correct, let's call them the conjoined twins, although I'd bet Eng and Chang Bunker, the Siamese guys connected at the chest who were the origin of the term, would appreciate being remembered.

It is of the utmost importance that you realize the show was violently understaffed. We were constantly working on a shoestring budget and writing and producing the shows in a nonstop time crunch. That will make it easier for you to believe that major facts could slip through the cracks and create wonderfully glaring situations later.

Such as with the booking of the conjoined twins. (It pains me to type that. I love the term "Siamese twins," it's so exotic.) Just before we called their agent (my God, they had an agent), our booker and a few of the crew had seen who they thought were these twins on a television show and thought it would be a good idea. They were attached on the side of their heads above the ear and faced forward and, aside from the obvious, were perfectly normal.

We writers immediately decided the way to go was to play "I've Got A Secret" and have the celebrity panel wear blindfolds. We would have Robin Quivers be a panelist and we'd try to book Arlene Francis and Dorothy Kilgallen, two of the original panelists from the classic television game show *What's My Line?* when it originally ran in the late fifties.

When we got the twins' resume, we couldn't believe it. One of them had a high bowling average, the other was a nurse—it went on and on. The reading of their resume would have been great television. Man, were we screaming.

We figured the resume had to be at least a bit tongue-in-cheek, so that we could have a little fun with them.

Certainly one of my all-time low jokes was for Howard to have a regular carpenter's crosscut saw behind the podium so after their secret had been guessed he could pull it out and say, "I have an idea . . ."

We had the saw there. It actually got that far.

On the fateful day, the twins arrived at the station, and a few minutes later our stalwart, priceless producer Dan Forman came flying into the studio to fetch me.

I can't say enough about Dan's energy, his talent, his dedication to the show and every show he's ever worked on or with, or how thoroughly we enjoyed breaking his balls. He is not the World's Most Handsome Fella and after we got ahold of a few of his Channel 9 news 8 x 10 show business glossies, we started putting him and/or them on camera every chance we got. But we'll get back to that later.

Out of breath, Dan ran up to me and said as only he could, "*Ahhh*, Jackie, you're the head writer, *ahhh*, I need a judgment call, *ahhh*, I need a judgment call. The twins are too sad. *Ahhh*, they'll bum everybody out. *Ahhh*, it's a different set of twins than Kevin [McMahon] saw on TV . . . *Ahhh* . . . the twins are too sad. *Ahhh* . . ."

I knew we were in big trouble, because short of writing sketches and writing lines for Howard on the fly on the air and coming up with ideas and lines for live commercials and what to do with guests and how to fuck with Dan, I was never consulted about anything. So, obviously, something was way askew and either they wanted to spread out the blame for something or they were stuck with a very weird situation that needed an outside yet show-based opinion.

Dan said, "*Ahhh*... Go up and have a look. I think it's an instant tune-out. *Ahhh*... no one, not even our audience, will be able to handle them. *Ahhh*... the image is too much. *Ahhh,* a tune-out... it's a tune-out..."

I'm a good sport. Hell, I was flattered I'd been asked. I'd go up there and come back with my two cents.

I bounded up to the second floor and turned into the large room that was our Channel 9 offices. As I strolled in, I saw them on the left, one standing and the other on a stool on wheels facing her. The one on the stool was smaller and more deformed. They were connected at the left side of their foreheads facing each other. The one standing was kind of "in charge," so when she needed to address you, she'd turn and the other one on the stool would spin around accordingly.

I just said a quick "Hello," and then went about my business, mumbling, "Where is my pencil?" All the time sneaking peaks at the Co-Joinettes.

It had really only taken that initial glance for me to agree with Dan. It was too sad. Nothing funny here. Scrap their appearance and let's make do.

I left the room and before I even reached the top of the stairs, that old, "Holy Christ are you a fucking asshole" light bulb lit up. A cold chill went up my neck.

Flop sweat.

"I'm a dick" sweat.

It hit me like a ton of bricks that these girls had spent their entire lives watching as people came into the room where they were and mumbling nonsense like "Where's my pencil?" as they stole glances at their incredible misfortune. What a glaring putz I was.

I reported back to Dan in total agreement. The twins would be way over the line for television on this or any planet. Years later of course Howard and others would claim we should've gone through with it, but it was the only possible decision at the time.

By the grace of God and three other white men (a Redd Foxx quote), we had a beauty pageant winner booked on the show who was a lesbian. We used her as our contestant in "I've Got A Secret" with her lesbianism being her secret, and that alone was enough to almost polish off Arlene and Dorothy. I can't begin to imagine the effect the attached babes would have had on them. I think it's just as well we never found out.

Dan Forman was wonderful to work with and for and I'm sure he still is. He'd get so wound up, so crazed. Fred and I could never get enough of him.

The first time we met Dan was when he walked into our initial meeting with Bob Woodruff and David Somebody, two other guys from Channel 9. As I said, we all liked him a lot, right away. He's a true soldier, and nothing scares him except the thought of ever standing still for five minutes. The man runs around like he has a lit flare in his ass, flame-end first. With Dan, you can either be amazed and respect his relentless energy or think he's truly an . . . I withheld judgment until I was sure.

There are countless stories of the Channel 9 days, the great episodes that went down as Dan developed into one of the people I most admire and respect on this same planet that should never televise my conjoined pals. I concurrently developed an intense love affair with breaking his balls.

As I said earlier, the day that Fred and I saw Dan's Channel 9 promo photo was a highlight of my comedy career. We lit up like candles. We had panned Comedy Gold, our very own Alfred E. Neuman. If this sounds the least bit cruel, it's because it was unrelentingly cruel. But funny, really *really* fucking funny.

Whenever we could we'd get that picture on the show. We stapled three of them together to make the angel for our tree on the "Christmas Bowling Show." We had sweatshirts made with that photo on it. I still treasure mine, though Dan and his glasses are fading like network television.

But the best was when I had one of the segment producers, Kevin McMahon, mount Dan's promo picture on cardboard, cut it out, mount it on a stick like a fan, and mail it with the show briefing to mob rat Henry Hill, a scheduled guest who was very secretly stowed away somewhere deep in the Witness Protection Program. Howard started to interview

Henry via satellite and Henry said he was in disguise. Then he held up the fan with Dan's face covering his. I thought I'd piss my pants. Dan E. Neuman's finest hour.

Dan worked *so* hard on the Channel 9 show, and we were impossible, like school kids with a substitute teacher. And the harder he worked, the more we broke his balls.

A couple of times a week, we'd talk to the guys at Channel 9 on speakerphone from our K-Rock boardroom. Howard, me, Fred, and Gary FaFlooie on our end, and Dan, Kevin, producer John Lollos, and a few others on their end in Secaucus, New Jersey.

Dan would get wild every call. Finally, I drew a few lightning bolts on a piece of paper and when Dan started really firing away, barking like a rabid starving dog, I'd hold the drawing of the lightning bolts by the phone and waggle it up and down so it looked like sparks were flying out of the phone. If he stopped to take a breath, which he rarely did, and it was quiet on our end because we were holding our sides and our mouths and bursting, in his best Dan Forman impression (and who does it better than him?), he'd say, *"Ahhh . . . ahhh . . .* I know you guys are goofing on me . . ."

Then we'd all make our own version of the Dan Forman face and make snarling Dan noises and it would be absolutely hysterical. Christ, I hope someday those calls are re-created for a movie.

Eventually, we'd have to calm down. Howard would take the floor and give Dan a hundred things to get accomplished in forty-eight hours.

At the end of one call, after Howard had given Dan this incredibly long laundry list of tasks and said, "Get on it," Dan said, "Okay," and I swear, before he hung up the phone, just before it hit the cradle, faintly in the distance, we heard Dan yelp to his assistant, *"Kaarrinn!"* Never a second to waste. He's just priceless.

Dan and I still have dinner every once in a while and it is one of my real joys in life. I hope to always know him and his wife Robin and their kids. To put it simply, they're good people. Knowing Dan makes me feel better about myself. And as long as I have breath in my body, I will never, ever stop breaking his balls.

Dan, if you're reading this, just because I know how uncomfortable it makes you, I have to say, "I love you."

1990

THE JESSICA HAHN BATHTUB INCIDENT, PART ONE

In August 1986, Infinity Broadcasting decided to take a chance on syndicating *The Howard Stern Show*. It had been suggested by Andy Bloom, the program director of WYSP in Philadelphia and after some consideration they had determined it was well worth a try, even though up to that time morning radio had always been local.

We all went through the roof when they told us. The rumors had been circulating for a while, but nobody had any idea if they held any water. And now it was a reality. If it was successful, it would be *huge*.

The Howard Stern Show's first syndication was to WYSP-FM in Philadelphia and WJFK-FM in Washington, DC, in August 1986. And it worked big-time. It took a while—and no shortage of over-the-top radio antics—but Howard eventually took over the number one spot in Philly in May 1990. Right away, Howard decided to throw a huge funeral for John DeBella, the morning personality we had knocked out of first place. It was to be an outdoor rally, on Thursday, May 10, in Rittenhouse Square in the heart of downtown Philadelphia, within spitting distance of DeBella's WMMR radio studio.

For years, "sex kitten" Jessica Hahn, of Babylon, Long Island, had been in the headlines. She had gone public about her episodes with the infamous Reverend Jim Bakker and another well-known religious leader, which had led to the downfall of Bakker's PTL ministry. It was a huge scandal and had brought Jessica into the limelight, where, thanks in part to our good friend lawyer Dominic Barbara's getting her a spread in *Playboy* magazine, she had managed to stay.

Howard had befriended Jessica early on and she loved him and loved the radio show. A Long Island girl, she had been hiding from the media after the Bakker incidents hit the news, but was more than thrilled when she got a call from Howard.

Howard invited Jessica, by now an old friend of the show, to be our guest at the Philadelphia rally, and, to add a bit of spice to what was to doubtless be a wild trip anyway, to ride on the very elegant bus with all of us from New York to Philly. We left after our regular radio show at noon on Wednesday, May 9, 1990.

And it was a hoot. Not really over the top, not by anybody's standards, but great fun. We drank, got stoned, played poker, flirted with a half-naked Jessica, and laughed our asses off. Me, Howard, Robin Quivers, Fred Norris, Gary "Big Teef" Dell'Abate, "Stuttering" John Melendez, Billy West, Dominic Barbara . . . the *Stern Show* gang. As we used to say, "the Stern Family and Stuttering John."

After three hours of assorted shenanigans, we arrived in the City of Brotherly Love around 3:00 p.m., just managing to dodge commuter traffic. Everybody was exhausted, having gone nonstop since 6:00 a.m., but we were jazzed as hell as we checked in to the Omni Hotel.

The *Stern Show* had made it to the top of the ratings heap in a city we were syndicating to, something that was unheard of at the time. Buzzed and now free of the confines of the bus, we created quite a commotion in the hotel lobby as we each stepped up to get our room keys. The rest of us had rooms scattered all over the different floors, but Jessica's suite was right next to Howard's.

After we had settled in, we all went to Howard's suite to hang out and eventually have dinner. Howard was always thoroughly entertained watching me order from room service, as it was quite dependably like I hadn't eaten in a month. Always the same drill: shrimp cocktail, Caesar salad, medium-rare steak, chocolate cake and ice cream, a few bloody Marys . . . A *fiesta grande*. Everybody else overdid it, too, and we gorged ourselves. And some of us—*umm*, mainly me—had kept drinking since we first boarded the bus back in New York.

Done stuffing ourselves, we were all sitting there boozing it up and goofing around when Howard decided to call Jessica and ask her to come over and take a bath in his suite. Normally I'd write, "and she agreed, because it helps the joke," but this was real life.

Needless to say, whatever it was, she agreed. And it helps the story. Fuck, it *creates* the story.

The stand-alone bathtub was incredibly ornate, with gold faucets and huge gold lion's claw feet. We drew a bath, and when it was full, for whatever reason, we wrestled Stuttering John into the tub, clothes and all. As high as most of us were, it's a miracle nobody got hurt in the scuffle.

Like it happened two seconds ago, I can still see it . . . the water immediately went black. It looked like a swamp, thanks to Charlie Brown's pal Stuttering Pig Pen. After he climbed out we had to drain the tub and swipe it and start over. Seriously.

We drew another bath, went back and sat in the living room, and continued fucking with each other. We could have sold tickets to the show whenever Fred and Billy and I started in on Gary Flapgums and John. Hey, in the spirit of full disclosure, I hardly went unscathed. It was as brutal and wondrous as a room of smart, funny, and potentially vicious pricks can get. It was like—well, it *was*—*The Howard Stern Show*.

And then Jessica arrived, wearing but a pink negligee under an open bathrobe. She was her bubbly self, rambling on and flirting with Howard and standing there long enough that we all got a good look at everything she had to offer.

Then she went back to the bathroom. It was a good hike, as it was a huge suite and the bathroom was a good fifty feet away. Presumably, she got naked and climbed into the tub.

After a few minutes, she yelled, "Howard, come get in with me."

We all looked at him, of course realizing the absurdity of the situation.

He said to us, "I can't do that. My wife would kill me. One of you guys, come on, get in with me."

Nobody even considered it.

"Come on, Fred. Gary? Come on, Billy . . ."

I was hammered, I was always fun and loose, and I thought to myself, in my drunken stupor—although I still think the logic holds up fairly well—that if I leave my underpants and my jeans on, how bad a foul will it be? My wife knows how crazy the show is, and of course knows how crazy I am, and I assumed it'd be obvious that I was taking one for the team.

So I got up and said, "Come on, let's go."

Howard and I went into the bathroom and there was the beaming Jessica, sitting up in the tub, in the negligee that was so sheer she may as well have been stark naked. Howard stripped to his underpants, and as per my plan, I stripped to my underpants and jeans. Howard got in the tub in front of her, facing her, and I climbed in behind her.

As fancy as the tub was, it wasn't much bigger than a regular hotel room bathtub, so the three of us were jammed in, somehow sharing this very small space. I scrubbed her back and to this day have no idea what was going on in front. But I know it wasn't much, if anything.

We were in the tub all of two minutes. And I might even be exaggerating. Then Howard and I hopped out, dried off, and went back to the living room, all of us howling at the absurdity of it all. I know I kept drinking and then found my way down to the hotel bar and drank some more, finally turning in so I could get up at 5:30 a.m. to do the radio show.

The craziest part of this is that getting in the bath with Jessica hadn't struck me like it had been a big deal. It was just Howard and me being our goofy selves. It had happened and then I'd dismissed it. I'd been doing wacky stuff like that for forty years and therefore paid it very little mind. When I arrived at the hotel bar, I don't think I even mentioned it to the people I started drinking with: listeners, our people from both the New York and Philadelphia crews, and hotel guests. You know, that's probably the hardest thing to believe about this story.

In retrospect, how I didn't realize that Howard's sole reason for getting in the tub had been for the air and that it would be embellished fivefold in the retelling, I can't explain. I'd been on the show for a long time and I knew everything was for the air and that everything made it to the air. I guess I just wasn't thinking. It certainly wasn't the first time.

Our short-lived bath with Jessica couldn't have been less titillating or less sexual. I had joined him and her because I thought it would be fun and funny, which it was. All the years I was on *The Howard Stern Show*, if there was one word they all quoted me saying more than any other, it was "*Fun!* Come on, it's *fun!*"

This situation falls in the cracks of my logic, because since I maintain I didn't do anything too heinous, it shouldn't matter if Howard talked about it on the radio. But somehow I thought that he'd keep it under his hat, with just the group in his suite sharing the experience, following some kind of unspoken Man's Code.

I know how preposterous that sounds, but I've been looking for an explanation for why I was oblivious to what the repercussions of the three of us in a tub would be for twenty years. What can I say, sometimes on the roads of my thoughts the bridge is out.

The plan for the big Philadelphia celebration show was to do the first two hours of the live broadcast from inside the hotel and then move out to Rittenhouse Square for DJ John DeBella's funeral. After turning in crazy late, my alarm went off at the crack of night. Hungover as hell, after very little sleep—which I can't say was terribly rare—I sat up and looked around, quickly assessing where I was and then, as it all came into focus, jumping out of bed to get dressed and get my ass down to what was going to be a red-letter day. Oh, *boy*, was it going to be a red-letter day.

When I got to my seat next to Howard—when we were on location Robin was usually on his left and I was on his right—he was chomping at the bit to get on the air. When the show started, he immediately began describing the events of the day before, quickly hopping past the bus trip and the ball breaking at dinner and getting right to Howard and Jackie and Jessica in the bathtub, making it sound like Sodom and Gomorrah could have picked up a few pointers from our *ménage à porcelain*.

As he began, it immediately hit me how blind I had been to realizing that this of course was going to be the day's big story. For Christ's sakes, two men and a woman in a bathtub. What the fuck had I been thinking? There's that word again.

I swear I knew better. It had taken some time, but years before, I had learned that everything was fodder for the show. When we first went to mornings, many times I had driven in from Bayville, parked in my garage, walked across town, come up the elevator, grabbed a cup of coffee, joined the guys in the office, and, them being the first humans I had been in contact with since my stop at the local deli an hour earlier, began to spout off, often bitching about my wife.

And ten minutes later, no sooner did the microphones go live, when, "Robin, you should have heard Jackie ranting about Sirianni. He started before he even sat down." (Howard always loved the fact that I referred to my wife Nancy Sirianni as Sirianni.)

Most mornings, Nancy was listening. And if she wasn't, one of her dear tattletale girlfriends surely was. So I'd arrive home that day wondering how much Nancy had heard or been told. Looking back, it seems fairly harmless, but our relationship was always on the brink of something, so anything could easily ignite a shitstorm.

Hey, no foul whatsoever. That's the show I was on and I knew it. Anything goes. That had been apparent since the day I walked into the studio at WNBC back in 1983. Sometimes I'd forget it, but I knew it. Unfortunately, it took more times than it should have for me to learn to stifle a bit there, Edith. I'm embarrassed how often that had to occur before I knew to put a lid on my morning rants and anything I preferred to not be shared with the tristate area. And now, not only had I not heeded what I knew, but the dish was entertaining another two entire major American cities.

So millions of people got a first person play-by-play of what was, in the version they were hearing, tantamount to a full-scale orgy. The Philadelphia Threesome. That's Howard's genius, making a mountain out of a molehill. Me, even though I was amazed that I hadn't had the forethought to know that this would take place, I thought very little of it. Because although Howard made sure not to mention it, I had been what I still would claim very close to fully clothed for the incident. All I'd have to do is fill Nancy in on that one very pivotal detail, and it would be like nothing happened.

Many times in my life, I've been wrong, but maybe never, ever as wrong as this time. Not wrong in my actions; wrong about the outcome.

It was one of the classic *Stern* shows of all time, with the entire cast on stage for a funeral that included a skimpily dressed Jessica Hahn, another famous-for-no-apparent-reason Joey Buttafuoco as the executioner who hung John DeBella, Scott the Engineer as DeBella's corpse, and assorted Stern Wack Packers to round out what was an incredibly joyous event for the fifteen thousand listeners who showed up that morning.

The huge crowd cheered and chanted and was so loud it made it out over John DeBella's live radio show on the other side of Rittenhouse Square. It was as festive an occasion as I've ever been a part of, a love fest, a huge gang assembled for the singular reason that they loved *The Howard Stern Show*. No fights, no ugly incidents, no injuries, nothing but, yes, fun. The cast, our guests, the crew, the listeners, the cops, curious bystanders—all caught up in an amazing display of unity.

Me? I was euphoric. I had been performing in Philadelphia and its suburbs since 1979, at the Comedy Works, the Comedy Factory Outlet, Bananas, and Andy Scarpati's multiple Comedy Cabarets, as well as many other area shows that had come and gone. Aside from Fort Lauderdale and the free-for-all that was the Comic Strip down there, it was my favorite city to work. And for years, I had heard from the Philly folks I worked with and for how unassailable John DeBella and WMMR were, how his stronghold couldn't even be scratched. Throw in that I knew John from back in his WLIR days on Long Island where he had been a lot more than a little bit pompous and this bordered on surreal. Howard hadn't merely bitten into his audience, he had taken it, knocked him off his throne. It was *spectacular*.

When we got done with the show, feeling like a million bucks, I called home, as I always did after the show. I hoped Nancy had been listening, because it had been, as I said, a great one. The recounting of the bath with Jessica had been hours earlier, and, honest to God, wasn't even in my thoughts.

Nancy answered. And she was on fire.

Many of her friends had been listening, so the first dribs of what had gone on the night before were Howard's version filtered—let's change that to *exploded*—by her and my "good pals." She screamed at me and hung up and then wouldn't answer the phone when I called back. And she had turned off the machine.

It caught me a hundred percent off guard. I was beside myself. I never even got close to running my version to her, which I thought totally exonerated me. I called and called, but she wouldn't pick up.

As I dialed, and she didn't answer, over and over, it became more and more apparent that the version of what happened that had been told to her was already so carved in stone to her that a few details like I had my clothes on weren't going to make a dent. Whether I had intended it or not she had been horribly insulted. The mere act of getting in the tub was a slap in her face, a fuck you to our marriage, which it of course, of course, of *course* wasn't.

Even now, people are divided on this incident. Exactly how wrong I was, how Nancy should have reacted, the extent to which it should have been chewed up and spit out, and at what point it could have been or should have been dropped. The debate rages on.

1990

THE JESSICA HAHN BATHTUB INCIDENT, PART TWO

On the way home in the bus, everybody was once again having a riot. I was sitting alone in the front, freaking out. I was 180 degrees from where I had been just twenty-four hours before. Hell, from where I had been an *hour* before.

I replayed it all in my head a thousand times. Over and over. I didn't conjure up a story to tell Nancy because I insisted to myself that, okay, what I did was stupid, maybe *really* stupid, but it was harmless. It absolutely wasn't meant to be the tiniest bit malicious, to hurt my wife. I loved her. I still do. I would never have done it had I imagined it would hurt her. In my heart of hearts, I swear I didn't think what I did was way over any line.

And, a little bombed or not, I had thought about it before I did it. In my addled mind, the logic that keeping on not just my underwear but my *blue jeans* would make it evident that, in all our outrageousness, I cared and was trying to do the right thing.

The entire way home, everybody left me alone. The goofing, though of course not nonexistent, was mercifully kept to a thankful minimum. I was a basket case.

When we got to New York, I tried calling a few more times, but Nancy still wouldn't answer. In a daze, I asked the gang to wish me luck, left the station, walked across the four avenues to my garage, gingerly climbed into my car, and headed home, constantly trying her from my car phone.

Innocent in my mind or not, I was shaking like a leaf when I pulled into our driveway. As much as we fought, and fight we did, holy Christ did we fight, there had never ever been a standoff like this. Nothing in this ballpark had ever occurred.

I walked in the back door with my suitcase and she was crazed. I've known Nancy since 1974 and had never and still have never seen her anything like she was right then.

She was red-faced and so furious that I was worried she might hurt herself, or even worse, me. At one point she whipped around a thick, stuffed, cloth wind-blocking tube that had metal on the ends and almost took my eye out. Being in the kitchen, with all the available weapons of human destruction, I was petrified. She was flailing around, here and there coming at me, and of course not listening to one syllable I said.

When I finally got out a bit of my side of the story, it of course sounded like something I had concocted to save my ass. She had heard what happened, and wasn't ready for me to edit the tale. When the discussion, or rather, the lecture and the berating, would calm down even a little, it would almost immediately zoom right back to fever pitch. I have no concept of how long it was before, after some final vicious verbal attacks, she ran out the door, got in her car, and drove off.

I was beside myself, feeling like I couldn't remember ever feeling in my life. I love Sirianni and though we fought like every couple I know and more, the two of us had never encountered anything like this. This was a plane we had never visited. I was a drunk and a loudmouth, but I was never, ever hurtful.

Not knowing what else to do, I opened my suitcase to unpack. And there on top of everything was Jessica Hahn's still-soggy sheer pink negligee. And I can still remember the jolt that surged through me, vividly enough that it makes me shudder as I'm typing. And please believe me when I write if Nancy had been there when I opened that suitcase, and seen that damp nightie, I would be dead. In her state, had

161

she seen that thing, she would have killed me. I'm certain. Not hurt me, but murdered me.

Then I laughed, or came as close as I could under the circumstances, because I remembered I hadn't really done anything wrong and they all knew I hadn't and Jessica's wet lingerie in my suitcase was an incredible prank. I have to give the boys credit, even if their ball breaking could have ended in my death.

As movie gangster Hyman Roth said, "This is the business we have chosen."

In a panic, not knowing if Nancy would be back any second or never, I grabbed the nightie, ran out back, and tossed it over the fence. No time to think, just ditch it and race the hell back into the house. Getting back in the kitchen before she got back, which of course I was able to do, as our Jackson Avenue backyard was the size of a postage stamp, the adrenaline was surging through my body like a fire hose in a woman's prison. As hard as I tried, I just couldn't get the thought of her being there when I opened the suitcase out of my head. It was making me crazy.

And I was worried about her out driving around in a blind fury. As smart and practical as she usually was, she was so enraged who knows what could happen. I wasn't all that anxious to have her come back in and pick up where she left off, but I of course wanted to know she was safe.

But I wasn't going to call her sister or her mother or any of her girl-friends to find out if she was with them. Because once I was on the phone with them I was sure I wouldn't be able to restrain myself from asking if they had heard the show and communicated with her about it earlier that day and thus had a hand in my demise.

I could tell by the severity of the situation that the story as it was now set in her mind had more than likely been the combination of a bunch of varied descriptions, her melding the worst with the worst. All I'd need is to be on the phone screaming at one of her comrades when she walked back in. Yoiks.

Not that there could have been a good place in our lives for this to have happened, but the timing was so, so bad. It was Thursday, *The Howard Stern Show* was to be on the air on Friday, and then we all had a week's vacation. Nancy and I were leaving on Saturday, flying to Venice for a much-needed vacation and then taking a train to Paris for her sister's wedding. A splendid week in Europe, our first ever.

And now this. Yow. She had said several times in the course of her diatribe that there was no way she was going anywhere with an asshole like me. Not to Europe, not to the post office. I couldn't believe this was happening. Lately we had been at odds, really at odds, more than usual, for a garden variety of reasons, and I know I was counting on the time away from everything to get us close again. And I'm sure she was, too. It was the disaster of disasters.

I called Emily, our therapist, told her the entire sordid tale, and after hearing me out, not weighing in at all on the right or wrong of what had happened, she said the solution was relatively simple.

She said, "You have to get Nancy on that plane. That's all there is to it. Whatever you can do, whatever you have to do, do it. Once you two are on the plane and are on your way away from here, it will melt away, at least enough that you can put it all on hold and have a wonderful trip."

Fortunately, Nancy came back fairly soon. Though I couldn't tell you how long it had been, even though it had seemed like forever, I know it wasn't too long because she said she had just driven around a bit and then came home. Though she had cooled slightly, she was still really hurt and upset. I for the most part stayed away from her, knowing I had time on my side, as we both knew I had to get to sleep after a very long few days and be up at 4:20 a.m. to drive back in for Friday's show.

Between being hungover and shaken to my toes by the whole episode, I don't remember exactly how much time we spent trying to make headway into a somewhat normal discussion. I know that after we had attempted a few times and failed pretty miserably, I just went up and tried to sleep until I had to leave the house for work the next morning.

Of course, when I got to the office, everybody wanted to know what had gone down, but I was keeping to myself and saying nothing. I was scared, scared for my marriage, scared for my wife. In retrospect, to me, it seems like I got the electric chair for jaywalking, but how angry Nancy was, justified or not, was very, very real.

I didn't acknowledge my discovery of the wet lingerie in my suitcase for a long time. It may have been months, I honestly don't remember. Because Nancy wasn't aware of it and I didn't need them to have any more ammo. Luckily that didn't make it to the air for a pretty long while. I know that at least it wasn't until after we had flown across the Big Pond and back.

When we were seated in the studio and just about to go on the air that morning, I said, "Howard, please turn on my microphone."

And he did.

And I apologized to my wife.

The Howard Stern Show has played the following clip hundreds and hundreds of times.

Most listeners think Nancy made me to do it, forced me to apologize. Some probably think she wrote what I was to say. The truth is I was simply heeding Emily's advice: I wanted to do whatever I could to get Nancy on that plane. I figured that if lots of Nancy's pals heard about me and Howard supposedly fiddling in the bathtub with Jessica Hahn and reported back to her, maybe those same shitheads would hear my apology and report back that I was doing all I could to make nice.

The truth? I didn't know *what* to do. I wanted to apologize, but in my mind it seemed like a grand apology was admitting that what I had done was very wrong. And as I said, I think yes, it was wrong, but in the grand scheme, not *very* wrong.

But the objective was Get Sirianni On the Plane to Italy, so when Howard turned on my microphone at 6:00 a.m. on May 11, 1990, this is what I said:

"I just want to apologize to my wife Nancy for the Jessica Hahn bathtub incident. It was stupid, and I'll never do anything like that again. And I love you and I'm very sorry. And I'm very sincere and please don't make a mockery of this. I'm serious. I'm sorry, I'm not trying to bring the show down, I just wanted to apologize. Okay. I'm done, Howard."

It helped. It helped a lot. Nancy hadn't been listening to the show but the word indeed got to her. And when I got home I told her what I had done, and what I had said. For once I spoke very calmly and sweetly and did my very best to make her know how important she was to me, and again, how sorry I was.

I of course also explained to her that we couldn't not be at her sister's wedding and please give me another chance and please listen to my side of the story and that we'd take this to our therapist and fix it when we got back from our trip. I'm not sure exactly what I did and didn't say, but whatever it was, it was the right thing, because we wound up on that plane and we had a spectacular European vacation.

Nobody was or is aware of the only other time Nancy and I went to war, I mean big-time, over something that happened on the air. During my run on the show, which God knows can be challenging for cast members in the best of relationships, the two of us had gazillions of minor skirmishes, to be sure. But this bit actually created a problem that we were never able to fix, at least not yet. And it was over something that was as stupid as anything we'd ever done.

Fred and I were the writers and it was our job to come up with absurd things to do on the show. After all the years of doing that, it was understandably getting tougher and tougher to find new ground.

One thing that made it a little easier was that girls always wanted to meet Howard. The endless stream of women taking their tops off to gain admission had caused it to get very *passé*, and after years of looking at countless fake boobs that mostly looked like the doctor had been on the phone during the surgery, we had moved on from that. With numerous exceptions, of course.

So we were constantly trying to come up with new ridiculous things the ladies would have to do if they wanted to get into the studio. That was what spawned guys farting in girls' faces and countless other demeaning stunts, all of which girls agreed to just to get on the show.

One of my favorite show moments of all time was the colossal baloney toss. Howard and I stepped out into the open space in the studio, and the producer, RotMouth Dell'Abate, brought in a girl who had agreed to have lunch meat thrown at her.

He placed her about six feet from us, and this beautiful girl with a perfect body in a very skimpy bikini turned around, pulled down her bottoms enough to bare her butt, bent over slightly, and we took aim. Howard went first and his baloney slice bounced off one of her cheeks.

With an air of extreme confidence based on absolutely nothing, I said, "Move over, I'll show you how it's done," and let fly my baloney slice.

It flipped end over end and landed spanning the top third of the crack of her ass, and stuck there, taking the shape of the valley like it had been painted on. We screamed.

One thing we proposed so often at the weekly staff meetings that it became a running gag was for a girl to let us roll her up in a rug and then take her up and down the elevator in it. I don't know, maybe they finally did it. We never did it while I was still there, but we always suggested it, because it never failed to make me and King Norris laugh.

The weekly staff meetings were as much fun as the show. Hell, they *were* a show. Everybody, with the exception of Robin, was invited, from the interns on up. Robin was never at the creative meetings, as always, because Howard and Fred and I wanted her to hear or see anything we came up with for the first time when we were on the air.

The meetings were all exactly alike. I'd sit next to Howard and make him laugh while an increasingly frustrated Gary Tooth tried to run ideas by him. Benjy Bronk, a writing intern at the time, would pitch one terrible idea after another and we'd fuck with him, too. It was a sitcom. Week after week I'd keep distracting the boss, nothing would get accomplished, and then we'd go home. I might miss those meetings more than anything.

So one of our very bright ideas was to bring in three girls, one of whom was having her period, and we'd smell their crotches and guess which of them it was. It couldn't have been dopier. It was a joke, and not even a very funny one. Of course, there's nothing to smell. There's hardly a bit there.

After GreenGums (you may have ascertained by now that producer Gary Dell'Abate's name is any combination of syllables that approximate his nickname Baba Booey or allude to his gargantuan caps, foul breath, or barn-size ass) brought out the girls, who even more absurdly were completely dressed in their street clothes, he lined them up and it was time for the sniffing. Fred was working the sound effects and Gary knew who the Tampee was, so the only people left to compete were me and Howard.

We walked around to the open area of the studio and stood in front of the ladies in question. We took turns bending over slightly in front of each of them and making exaggerated sniffing sounds. Then we each took our guess. Who was right, who was wrong, who knows, it was just another completely ridiculous concept we came up with to kill some time.

Nancy had been listening. When I got home, she was for some reason totally bent out of shape by what she referred to as our "smelly cunt" game. What made it even crazier is that we hadn't ever said anything in the course of the goings-on about the supposed smell we were seeking out being offensive.

I couldn't believe it. I didn't know where she was coming from. I still don't. Over the years, she's been angry at me for millions of reasons, and very often justifiably so, but this made no sense to me whatsoever.

Not that it makes me unique, but I'm personally a huge fan of that area, and there's never been anything about it, ever, *ever*, that's been a turnoff to me. And if anybody knew that, she did.

Like an idiot, I tried to defend what we had done as having meant nothing, that it was just silly.

I realize that I had been in the eye of the hurricane that was and is *The Howard Stern Show* for a long, long time and my point of view may have been very jaded. And perhaps it still is. In retrospect, maybe just the thought of smelling for periods, an accomplishable task or not, is horribly insulting to women, and I got it between the eyes for the simple reason we not only used it as a concept, but that there was a better than decent chance it had been my idea. Maybe a lot of women will be totally in step with Nancy and her reaction.

You know what? I hope so. I really do. Looking back at our marriage, as well as my time on the planet, the benefit of perspective has allowed me to see how many times I was way off mark, and for the most part I've had no problem admitting when that was the case, to her or anyone.

Throughout my years on the *The Howard Stern Show*, especially after we reached the stratosphere and existed in a rarefied world, I'm sure I occasionally if not often acted a bit if not way too self-centered. I was moving too fast and drinking too much.

So as far as the Battle of Guess the Bleeder, I'm not saying who was right and who was wrong; I'm just writing a book about my life and it happened smack dab in the middle of my life.

It's nuts what a steel trap my mind is.

That just reminded me that when we'd show up at a bar or a party or anywhere there were a lot of nice-looking girls, my brother Bobby would say, "I feel like I just jumped up and landed smack dab in the middle of Pussy City."

The Time of the Month Contest? Once again, I apologize. I really do. But once again I have to add we were just being outrageous. It was our job description.

In the re-creation of the bathtub incident in the film *Private Parts*, Fred Norris is in the bathtub with Howard and actress Melanie Good. I almost lost my marriage and could have been killed, yet I didn't get to re-create it on the big screen.

When I asked him why, Howard said, "I couldn't have put you in that tub. Nancy would have gone berserk."

Me, I would have rolled those dice.

Nancy Sirianni and I stayed together until November 2000. She lives two doors down from me and we remain the very best of friends.

1992

STERN FANS TO THE RESCUE

Very early on, I started to realize *The Howard Stern Show* was already terrifically popular, that the people really loved Howard, and actually even loved the rest of us, too. But this spontaneous event was the most blatant wake-up call to that fact in my experience, and there were so, so many.

In the fall of 1988, I worked a Wednesday night at Chuckles Comedy Club in Mineola on Long Island, an hour give or take from our radio studio depending on a zillion factors. I usually only worked that club the night before a big holiday, like Thanksgiving or the Fourth of July (I always referred to each of those as "the Wildest Night of the Year" because the kids were home from college, nobody worked the next day, and it was always an all-out night of boozing and debauchery). I usually wouldn't get a hotel room because the club was only twenty minutes from Bayville and I didn't have to go to work the next day, but for whatever reason, I had worked Chuckles on a regular weeknight and stayed at a hotel close by, as it would make no sense to drive home and then backtrack to work just a few hours later.

Robin was always doing her last-minute primping or taking that final whiz before we went on the air, so when we signed on, it was my duty to make damn sure it was at least Howard, Fred, and me. Fred was always there way before me, as, once again, he creates and plays the

169

always spectacular array of songs and bits and sound bites that are the preshow show.

So I had to be at work promptly at six when the microphones came on. I usually got there with ten or fifteen minutes to spare, but sometimes it was twenty seconds to spare, and sometimes I'd leap into my seat just as Howard started to grumble his opening comments. And yeah, occasionally, I was late. But for fifteen years, I did my utmost not to be and very rarely was.

The point here is that a hotel room after Chuckles was an unfamiliar template for a guy who timed his wake-ups to extract the absolute maximum sleep. When you get rudely blasted by your alarm clock five days a week at 4:20 a.m., hit your nine-minute snooze alarm once, shower, shave, dress, make your coffee pit stop at the deli, and zoom down the Long Island Expressway for your forty-minute commute at 5:00 a.m., you get it down to a science. Staying in a place foreign to your routine screws you up good. In my normal scenario, if I took a healthy dump in the morning, I somehow knew how much faster to drive to compensate and get myself to work right on time. Anything out of the normal botched the works.

The unsettling combo of being hungover—the crowds were always stellar at Chuckles, one of my hometown clubs, which tended to make me thirsty, as did bad crowds—and not waking up at home already had me off to a weak start that Thursday morning.

When you were on the Long Island Expressway that early in 1988, it was absolutely astonishing what a difference five minutes made traffic-wise. (I'm sure it still does, but, *yippee*, I have no idea.) As the clock ticked away, hordes more people were merging onto that road to zip into Manhattan with each passing second.

Back then, there were treacherous on-off ramps where the westbound LIE met the Cross Island Parkway. People zooming off to go to Connecticut and the northern crossings to the city and people zooming on from wherever and it was every car for itself.

And just as I am nearing this hell-spot without a moment to lose, I get a flat tire.

Already racing the clock (read: late) and thus driving in the far left westbound lane in fairly thick traffic at 5:45 a.m., my Budweiser head pounding from the night before, I'm petrified as I steer my crippled car over to the very thin right shoulder and manage to get two wheels up onto the curb in the worst of all places, right between the off and on ramps to the Cross Island. The traffic was sailing by so damn close and I quickly realized that not only would this be the world's scariest place to change a tire but it was getting more treacherous with each passing heartbeat.

You have to understand that, hungover or not, late or not, the day after a terrific show for a comedian is Show Business Heaven. Of course, it'll only last until the next shitty or even mediocre show, but comedy is such a rattling thing to do, and it gets you so nuts, that you have to let yourself feel great after a good show. And not much can intrude on that euphoria. However, in an instant, I discovered something that can wipe it out: an early morning flat. One minute I was cruising down the highway on the way to my job on the best radio show on the planet, feeling very funny and very good about myself, and the next minute I was in a death-defying armpit on a major thoroughfare, late for work, with a flat tire, a feeling second only to shitting your pants (not that I ever have).

Like I said, I realized I had to get out of that spot, and time was an issue, so fearlessly (stupidly?) I got up the balls to very slowly drive my Volvo off the curb, across the on-ramp to the LIE, and up over the curb onto the big grassy shoulder, all the while driving on a flat. As a guy who never had a decent car for most of his life, I love reporting that flat tires have been the extent of the car trouble I've had with my seven or eight Volvos.

Feeling as crappy as I thought I ever could, I went for my spare and was missing a part to my jack. Oh, fuck. Unbelievably, I felt even crummier. I called the guaranteed quick fix that was part of my lease, "Volvo On Call," which I quickly began referring to as "Volvo On Hold." After five minutes of sitting there listening to a recording of what a great service it is and never speaking to a human, I hung up. I called Nancy and woke her so I could vent to somebody.

Nancy told me to call the show, which I knew I had to do. I didn't want to, because I was late, and I hated, really hated, to make that call. The few times I was late, it was always the day after a gig.

But this wasn't my fault. The tire didn't know I had a gig. Man, I felt like homemade shit on a stale bun. I had no idea what I was going to do.

I called our hotline and got FlaFla Flooey, known at the time merely as Baba Booey.

He said, "Howard's just going on the air, ah'll tell him you're on the phone."

Howard picked up right away and barely said hello before exploding into a fully expected tirade about my unequaled-anywhere irresponsibility. As soon as I could wedge it in, I told him where I was and what was going on.

I swear I wasn't halfway through my explanation when the cars started screeching off the Expressway, up over the curb onto the shoulder in back of me and in front of me. Within seconds, the Stern fans pulled a Volvo jack out of midair and changed the tire. They wouldn't even let me help, they held me back, out of the way. They put the bad tire and the jack parts back in the car and then stood out in the right-hand lane to block traffic so I could roll over the big curb, back out onto the Expressway, and be on my way.

And just like that, I was cruising along on my way to work, with people all around me rolling down their windows and screaming, "Get to work, Joke Man!" "You're late again, you bum!"

From the time Howard picked my call, it had in all taken less than ten minutes. I was ecstatic. I had gone from way up in the stratosphere to the lowest of the pits and back up on top of the world in a matter of minutes. I don't remember if I stayed on the air the entire time or whether I called back to say, "Here I come," but it was incredible.

Thus, before Howard was anointed King of All Media, he was Prince of Roadside Service.

Suddenly, the New York tristate area had become our own little sandbox, chock-full of friends who could be more accurately described as family. It was downright heartwarming.

Somewhere, there are commuters who for years have been telling that story to their friends and meeting their friends' rolling eyes. You know what? I have to go with their friends. If I hadn't been there, I wouldn't believe it, either.

1994

NEW YEAR'S ROTTEN EVE

In 1994, we needed contestants for our Miss Howard Stern New Year's Eve Pageant special that was to be broadcast "live" from Newark, New Jersey. We'd, of course, be looking for women with offbeat talents, the odder the better.

Howard and his agent Don Buchwald had an idea, and Buchwald asked me to meet with him in his office. I walked in and sat, and after a few pleasantries, he explained that he and Howard were thinking of arranging small pageants in a bunch of different cities to find girls for the show, and that it'd be great if I hosted them.

At the time, I was doing really well with my stand-up act. Of course, I was packing them in and making much more money than I ever had because I was on Howard's spectacular radio show, but that was by design.

I don't remember the details, I just know Don wanted me to head up these talent search/beauty contestant shows in a bunch of Stern markets for very little money. And, of course, any weekend I'd be traveling to, say, Chicago, to host one of these shows, would eliminate me working that weekend for big pay or having a well needed few days off.

As gently as I could relay it, I explained to Don it wouldn't be beneficial to me. And needless to say, he wasn't especially thrilled at me not jumping on the opportunity.

After however long, Buchwald said, "Let me call Howard and see what he thinks."

He made like he was dialing and then put Howard on speakerphone, and the way Howard joined the conversation made it immediately apparent he had been listening to the entire meeting, that we'd been on speakerphone the entire time.

If it hadn't been already, that tied my stomach in knots. Not that I said anything disparaging or that I wouldn't want repeated—I knew better—but who knows what I may have said, even just being stupid, which is what I do. And why not simply have Howard in on the meeting from the onset? I'll go out on a limb here and say nobody wants somebody eavesdropping on them.

Needless to type, I left feeling violated.

As far as my involvement, the concept was never addressed again.

The week we spent at the hotel in Newark rehearsing and preparing the New Year's special was a hoot. Every night when we got back from the theater, much of the ridiculously eclectic gang would congregate in what we quickly started to refer to as the Star Wars Bar. What a cast of characters. Hot, crazy women (I was berserk for Elaina Beasty), John Wayne (his wife Lorena cut it off) Bobbitt, Mark ("*Star Wars*") Hamill, Nicole "the World's Largest Female Body Builder" Bass, Daniel "the KKK Guy" Carver, Fred the Elephant Boy, Marty Klebba (the little person in the *Pirates of the Caribbean* film franchise), Sherman (George Jefferson) Hemsley . . . Wowie.

By the grace of God, I was still drinking.

The opening of the New Year's show featured the stage floor opening and a platform slowly rising in the open space, Howard sitting on a toilet on the platform with his pants down to his ankles, reading a newspaper.

He had told me he needed an opening line and I wrote about fifty. What a terrific premise, what a field day. Then I chose the best five, wrote them on one page, and gave it to him.

One that he didn't use was, "Gary, get over here and lick me clean."

A few years later, Flink Fla Doogie does eat poop—his own—as a monkey in the "Tarzan and the Land of the Big Titty Women" sketch on the *Butt Bongo Fiesta* video.

The line Howard did use?

First the show announcer bellowed, "*And now!* Live from Newark, New Jersey, the Carjack Capital of the World, it's the Miss Howard Stern New Year's Eve Pageant, starring Howard Stern!"

(Although Newark being the carjack capital of the world was an undisputed fact—that's why we used it—the city fathers are pissed off to this day.)

The toilet rose to stage level, Howard turned to the audience and from behind his newspaper he said, "You people just paid forty-nine ninety-five to watch me take a shit."

1994

THE PATTI DAVIS REAGAN JOKE

In September of 1994, I got a call from my old pal Eric Mittleman, who was a producer at the Playboy Channel. At that point, he was producing a show called *Hot Rocks*, which consisted of rock videos that were too explicit for MTV or VH-1, and hosted by Playboy's up-and-coming star, former Playboy Playmate Jenny McCarthy. He asked me if I would cohost a Playboy party at Webster Hall (a huge, hip dance bar–hangout in Manhattan) with Jenny, and also be a guest on the *Hot Rocks* show they were taping there on location the same night. I said sure. I could tell filthy jokes, Jenny would plug my new Polygram video (*Jackie The Joke Man In Concert*), and I'd plug *Hot Rocks* on *The Howard Stern Show*. We'd all win.

I asked the publicist for Playboy to get me a list of any celebrities who might be at the party so I could write a few "spontaneous" comments about them in advance, so that while Jenny and I were on stage doing whatever was required of us as the hosts, I could point them out and have a witty line or two to say about them.

The guests were the typical lineup for Manhattan events. Grandpa Al Lewis, Gilbert Gottfried, Dr. Judy Kuriansky, and so on . . . but also Patti Davis Reagan, daughter of former president Ronald Reagan, who had posed for a *Playboy* layout that year (you may read this as a way-too-late means of making up to her, but she looked really great).

On my drive back in to the city from Long Island for the Thursday night party, I wrote a few stupid lines about each of the potential celebrity guests. That's when I wrote the joke about Patti and her father. I said to myself, "Jesus, what a funny, well-crafted joke. It's a bit vicious and callous, but what great joke isn't?"

And who knew that since Ronald's disease had struck that Patti had started to rebuild her relationship with the family she had not only estranged, but obviously tried to completely freak out by being the first daughter of an American president—not to mention a living American president—to pose totally nude in an international skin magazine?

The party, like all of these type parties, was frighteningly crowded, because they invite a zillion people to ensure that it's an "event." So when Jenny and I went on stage to host the festivities, there was no way to spot anyone in the crowd. I flirted with her and said a few rude things, she put up with me and was pretty rude back, and in general we were pretty good together. I had never heard of her before, and I have to say I really enjoyed myself on stage with her, because she was not just gorgeous but quick and funny. We gave away whatever awards there were and then ran to the room to tape the *Hot Rocks* video wraparound segments.

It was an austere setup. Eric, a sound guy, a light guy, a cameraman, and me and Jenny sitting at a table, talking. We had a few beers sitting out of the camera shot and were having a great time. She roared at my jokes, laughing louder the filthier I got. The crew was laughing, Eric was laughing, it was so easy and fun. They were taping two shows with me as the guest, which entailed about eight separate segments.

After about the fifth segment, when they weren't rolling, I said, "I wrote some stuff on the way in, and I think I have a great joke, but it's pretty harsh. Want to hear it?"

Of course they did. I told them the Ronald Reagan joke and they screamed.

I said, "Should I tell it on the show?"

They all said, "Fuck, yeah."

So during the next segment, I told the joke to Jenny, and she and the crew screamed all over again.

By the time we were done taping the eight or so segments, which didn't amount to a lot of airtime but took a while to get on tape, I had polished off quite a few beers and they had laughed every time I opened my mouth for the duration, so I was glowing.

The room we were using to tape the *Hot Rocks* show was immediately next door to the Webster Hall VIP bar for the Playboy party. After thanking Eric and the crew and hugging Jenny in appreciation for being such a great cohost and then TV host and then audience to my stupid jokes, I went over to the VIP bar, and . . .

Standing right in front of me when I opened the door was Patti Davis Reagan, who I knew from when she appeared on *The Howard Stern Show* earlier that year to promote her naked *Playboy* layout.

Pumped from my successful Playboy tapings, feeling funny and a little bit buzzed (all of this can be read as "not thinking"), I said, "Hi, Patti. I wrote a joke about you today." And I proceeded to tell it to her.

I wasn't even through with the joke when I realized her face was starting to distort. I had just told her a joke that was funny to every English-speaking person on the planet—except her.

As I said, I had no idea she had recently started trying to mend things with her family. Her posing nude in a magazine was certainly more of an affront to her father than my silly joke.

That said, I'm probably very lucky she didn't have a machete or a pistol. She went ballistic.

And there were reporters and photographers everywhere. The cameras were clicking like hail on a tin roof as I tripped over my words, talking at the speed of stupid trying to apologize.

When it wasn't in the papers on Friday, I figured it was a non-incident.

What had happened was the party had been too late on Thursday for any gossip to make the Friday papers, so it was on Page Six of the *New York Post* on Saturday. When I walked into work on Monday (a Long Island boy, I never looked at the *Post* on weekends), I had no idea I was going to be ambushed at 6:00 a.m.

Robin opened the show with, "He did it again, Howard," read the Page Six piece, about how I had freaked out Patti with an incredibly offensive joke, and Howard immediately started in on how inappropriate I act wherever I go.

This had been going on a while when MuchButt&Gums ran into the studio and said, "Voff, ah hate to interrupt, but the listeners want to hear the joke."

I was, of course, thrilled, because the joke is so fucking funny. I told it, and Howard and Robin and Fred did their best to not laugh and to feign being mortified.

Why was Patti Davis Reagan the first to realize that Ronald Reagan had Alzheimer's?

He started returning her phone calls.

A great joke. Very, very funny, to everybody—everybody, that is, except Patti Davis Reagan.

They rode me for an hour, and then the next day they rode me for another hour, during which Patti called in. After them kissing her ass for a while, I'd had enough of all the hypocritical bullshit, both theirs and hers.

Howard was telling Patti what a great body she had, and I mumbled, "Yeah, that's why I felt her up while I was telling her the joke."

And she freaked out again. And they started yelling at me again. Who gives a shit?

Then a guy called in to add more logs on the Jackie is an insensitive prick fire.

He said, "I saw Jackie and Nancy in Fortunoff's five years ago and he gave me his autograph, and then he asked me why I looked so sad. I told him my grandmother had died the day before. And Jackie said, 'Oh, yeah? Did she have any loot?'"

And Howard commiserated with the guy for about ten minutes about what an obnoxious, unfeeling schmuck I am. Assholes. *Loot?* Who uses that word besides Frank Sinatra? It was total horseshit. But very funny.

I called Eric right away and insisted he edit my Reagan joke from the *Hot Rocks* show. I felt it was the right thing to do. If she felt that strongly about it, what the hell.

Maybe I shouldn't have told Patti that joke at that point in time. Maybe I should never have told her that joke at all.

But it's a funny fucking joke.

By the way, if you're keeping score, Sirianni says the guy's Fortunoff story is true.

1994

THE TALE OF THE JACKIE PUPPET

The "Gary Puppet" is a very unflattering, though somewhat accurate, representation of "Boy Gary" Dell'Abate and his unbelievably pronounced teefs. It's a ventriloquist's dummy that, before it was permanently mounted next to Howard to deliver Gary's input from the microphone in his office during the show, Fred used to often pick up and bring to life, much to our delight and Gary's dismay. It had been sent to the show by a fan in the late eighties and we fell in love with it. Just sitting in various places in the 600 Madison Avenue studio, it added lots of mirth to an already pretty funny room.

One day, when I got home from work, there was a pickup parked in my driveway, so I parked in front of the house and walked over to the driver's side of the truck. It was our friend Billy Bourne with a guy I didn't know sitting shotgun. Sitting up on the seat between them was a small, unmistakable replica of me. It was also a ventriloquist's dummy.

The scary little bastard had receding scraggly blond hair, thus a huge forehead, squinty eyes generously adorned with crow's feet, and a big, dopey smile with a working mouth. He had a joint jammed between his lips, a scaled-down can of Budweiser in his hand, and was wearing a tiny (516) 922-WINE T-shirt (my dirty joke line that's still going strong).

My God, it was *so* unmistakably me.

180

I took the joint from the dummy's mouth (what could he do?) and as we smoked it, I said, "Jesus, this is great. Where'd it come from?"

Billy said, "It's Thai weed I copped in Oyster Bay."

I said, "Not the *pot*, you dweeb. This dummy."

Billy nodded toward the other guy in the cab and said, "This is Tom Andresakes. He made it. He lives on Centre Island [which was down the street from us] and he's a huge fan."

Tom said, "It's nice to finally meet you. One day a few weeks ago, I figured, 'Hey, if there's a Gary Puppet, maybe there should be a Jackie Puppet, too.' So I made one."

He handed it to me and I played with it a few minutes. It was just wild. But as goofy as the thing was, as much as a slap in my face this balding, aging dummy was, I realized immediately that I couldn't bring it to the show because, coming from me, it would just be another Jackie self-aggrandizing self-promotion gimmick.

I said, "Guys, I love it. It's *great*. But if I bring it in, Howard will see it as me trying to get more attention and probably toss it. So Tom, you should come to the studio out of the blue one day and surprise us with it. Have you got a girlfriend?"

Billy said, "Tom's got a beautiful young wife, Amy."

I said, "Great. *Great*. Okay. So here's what you do. Tom, you and your wife just show up at K-Rock one day during the show. You and the puppet should be enough, but the fact that she's real pretty increases our odds that you'll get in.

"Tell Gary how much you love it when they goof on me, and that you made this Jackie dummy so they'd have more ammunition to break my balls."

As big fans of the show they knew I was right and agreed on the battle plan.

A few days later, in the middle of the show, Porcelain Pete came walking through the studio door smiling, that piano in the lower third of his face glistening, and said, "Howidd, there's a gah in the lobby with a Jackie puppet he made hisseff. It's prett-tty funny and he's got a real nice lookin' wahf. Should ah bring 'em in?"

With no hesitation Howard said, "Yeah, let's have a look."

I smiled to myself as I looked up at Howard and Gary, feigning annoyance at what was going down.

Gary ran out and immediately returned with Tom, who was carrying the puppet, and Amy, who looked incredible. I smiled to myself again as Gary introduced Tom and his wife to all of us. I made knowing eye contact with each of them as we pulled off our scam.

Tom explained to Howard that there was already a Gary Puppet and that he thought a Jackie Puppet would be a nice addition to our little family.

The puppet was an instant hit. A star was born. Everybody took turns working the puppet and doing their version of my voice, which at the time was the rage at the station. General Manager Tom Chiusano came running in right away and he alone must have worked the thing for fifteen minutes. It was very funny, as they all had a field day breaking my stones, and I continued my charade of being a bit miffed because I was the butt of the thing yet flattered by the effort Tom had made to create a likeness of me.

But once Billy West picked up Jackie Puppet and took off into the stratosphere with his cackling mercurial Jackie voice it was all over. In his hands, the semi-innocent dummy became a boisterous demon; a rude, insulting, guffawing attack dog. Jackie Puppet bushwhacked Conan O'Brien so viciously when he came on the show to celebrate his one-year TV anniversary that Conan found himself actually arguing with the thing.

The damn puppet was nearly constantly chiding me. Nothing was funnier than Billy's guffawing, chortling, unearthly-sounding "Jackie" voice that could cut through steel. Billy would pop in with it totally at random, and it was damn near always perfect comedy.

The puppet was for all practical purposes a member of the show. For years, he had lipstick on his cheek where he had been kissed by actress Sally Kirkland. The joint never made it out of the truck, the midget Budweiser can has long since disappeared, and at some point, one by one, many of his poor little fingers were broken off. And after I left, supposedly they sat him in a toilet bowl. But when he burned, he burned bright. Man, did he burn bright.

I never told Howard or any of the gang how I finagled Jackie Puppet onto the show. Sure, maybe if I had brought it in myself it would have been accepted and would have achieved the same notoriety. But that's certainly not the way I would have bet.

The funniest thing is that since back when Billy West created that manic Jackie Puppet character, to this day, people say to me, "Jackie, you're a nice guy, but you can't do you. You do a lousy Jackie."

I'm just not in Billy's league when it comes to doing me.

Fuck you, Brad.

1996

THE HANK NOTE AND MUCH MORE

Over the span of my years on the show, I wrote many hundreds of notes for Howard . . . to this day all stacked neatly in my mother's attic . . . but there's only one note I ever hung up over my desk, where it remained for a very long time.

There were some templates I used over and over, one of them being, "If you're just tuning in," or, "If you're just joining the show." I'd give a hopefully humorous update of what Howard was currently up to that would underscore the craziness and also serve to actually update whoever had just come aboard.

During a commercial break during a show presumably around Easter time, I went to the restroom. As I was standing at a urinal, I thought I heard somebody, but when I glanced to my right, there was nobody there.

But when I tilted my head down, standing there was a very small man in a pink bunny outfit. I said hello, and he mumbled something, which made it immediately obvious he was a half a sheet to the wind.

It was a very feisty and funny little guy who was about to make his first appearance on *The Howard Stern Show*. He was very, very bombed, stumbled into the studio and in a wink, was christened Hank the Angry Drunken Dwarf.

Somehow, we had a Breathalyzer kit in the office and Howard had Bababoo Flooey give Hank the test, which I'm sure resulted in a reading that was off the chart.

I was inspired to write this note:

IF YOU'RE JUST TUNING IN,
WE'RE GIVING A BREATHALYZER TEST
TO A DRUNKEN DWARF IN A PINK BUNNY COSTUME

It just strikes me as quintessential *Howard Stern Show*. I think it really tells the tale of what the show's all about as best as can be stated in a single note. So I put it up and have never tired of explaining why it's there.

When *The Howard Stern Show* started morning drive at K-Rock in February 1986, Susan Berkowitz was our traffic reporter, who called in from a helicopter.

Of course, Howard would talk any and all kinds of sex with her. That is, stuff that he could get away with in the mid-eighties, or at least thought he could. He'd make her crazy, she'd get all flustered, and sooner rather than later she was given the affectionate name Susan Berserkowitz.

Susan lost a bet to Howard, so she had to sing an off-color song during one of her traffic reports that Fred and I wrote for her. It wound up being the first thing the show was ever cited for by the FCC. I was actually bursting with pride when I saw the lyrics to our parody of "I Gotta Be Me" blazing across a legal US government document:

WHETHER IT'S RIGHT, OR WHETHER IT'S WRONG,
I PROMISED HOWARD AND ROBIN, FRED, JACKIE AND GARY THIS SONG . . .
I LOVE SODOMY, I LOVE SODOMY,
TO GET ON MY KNEES, AND DO WHAT YOU PLEASE, I LOVE SODOMY . . .

The only other notes that ever adorned my house were from a day when Howard was talking about something that took place in West Hempstead, Long Island, and immediately after I quickly wrote the one word:

ZIMBABWE

And as I put it in the note tray under the E! TV camera, Fred Norris passed me a note that said "Zimbabwe." Both notes were just the one word, spelled properly, and it was wild. That happened lots of times, where Fred and I went to exactly the same place or frighteningly close, but that was the simplest and most fun of them all. I had them both on the door to our basement office for years.

A note that was a very subtle turning point in the show, which nobody noticed, happened just after we went to mornings in 1986. The more time I spent on the show, the more in step I got and the more ways I saw to add stuff, new premises, and new targets.

It happened one day when Howard was going on and on about how bad his life was, how wretched the press was to him (and they were), and in general how crappy it was to be him.

It was fall 1986, we had just started on morning drive at K-Rock, and at the time, he was and had been the wildest guy on radio, ever, for quite a while. He attacked anything and everything. And he often took shots at his own career and family and whatever came into his bubbling brain.

But he had never been self-critical about his looks. He had never gone there.

And in the middle of his rant about his horrible existence, I put up a note. He hesitated . . . and then let it fly. Fred's eyebrows lifted and Robin took pause . . . and after a healthy beat they roared along with me.

The note was:

WALK A MILE IN MY NOSE, ROBIN

It opened an entire new line of potential fun, and goofing on himself made him so much more likeable. When you take it on the chin yourself, it's much easier for people to swallow you smacking everybody else around.

Speaking of targets, over the years countless fans have asked about Gary's breath and teeth, stuff like, "Does Gary's breath really stink?" and other sensitive questions of that nature.

The truth is that after we went to mornings and I had my own chair and microphone Gary would often bend over and speak into my microphone or Fred's. And yes, his breath was frightening. Bad breath squared, very offensive. And my mike would often hold the stink for a while after he left.

Very, very gradually it somehow made it into our conversations during commercial breaks. I'm sure he left Fred's mike stinky, too. And Fred and I tend to notice stuff. Maybe I mentioned Gary's breath to Fred or vice versa, and maybe we laughed about it, and then Howard asked us what was so funny . . . I really can't remember. Hey, maybe they had discussed it before I even came onto the scene on a regular basis, who knows? As I said, it reared its head very gradually.

It finally escalated to where Howard, Robin, Fred, and I decided Gary needed an intervention, that we had to say something to him about it. And we did. And as heartless as it sounds, it was worse. I'll never forget the Listerine commercial from the fifties, "Even your best friends won't tell you . . ."

Booie Dell'Adolly thought we were just breaking balls, but in time we got through to him that his breath was indeed very foul. He went to the dentist and found the root(s) of the problem were the caps on his teeth. And we had long been on him about his tombstone caps. So, he immediately fixed the problem years later by getting all new caps.

One of the funniest things in the history of a very funny show was when Gary Bella Booie unveiled his brand new teeth on the air and the new caps looked *exactly* like the old ones. I thought my heart was going to stop. My God, it was so damn uncomfortable, it was comedy like you write home about.

I know I keep saying Fred Norris is one of the smartest, fastest, and funniest people I've ever encountered, and I've met a lot of talented people. Working with him was sheer joy. He made *me* faster and funnier, like playing tennis against somebody better brings your game up. So I hear. I play Scrabble.

That said, it was great fun to break his balls. He's a very sensitive man, which may sound odd coming from me to any readers who've heard Fred attack me unmercifully on the current *Howard Stern Show*, but breaking balls was my job description. He's also a big and very strong man who could easily tear me limb from limb if he chose. So in the back of my mind, even after all those years, I always harbored the thought, "Yikes, I hope he knows I'm fucking around."

In my opinion, the worst I ever gave it to him was with a running joke that ran way, way too long. A childish, dopey joke that I laughed progressively harder and harder at with each rerun.

One year, the day after Halloween, I put up this note:

FRED, TAKE OFF THE MASK

Howard read it and I screamed . . . Howard chortled . . . and Fred wasn't the least bit amused. So childish and so stupid, but so damn funny. Robin couldn't help but laugh at our idiocy.

I saved the note, and a few days later, I put it up and Howard read it again. And I screamed louder. Fred was much less than amused.

Maybe a week later, I put it up again. And after a length of time, I put it up again. I laughed and laughed harder and harder, and Fred's probably still pissed about it.

Once we heard about Robin's fondness for anal sex, which she unbelievably divulged, I couldn't stay out of there. The day Frank Sinatra died, in 1998, for no apparent reason I sat and rapidly scrawled what has to be the funniest song parody I ever came up with. I parodied "My Way," one of Frank's classic anthems, and the subject matter was Robin's love of back door lovemaking. I sang it to her the next morning on the show and it's one of my fondest memories. Halfway through, Howard turned off my microphone. Fred kept playing the track so I stood up and belted it out to the bitter end.

Maybe my finest hour on *The Howard Stern Show.* Countless fans have told me they'll always remember where they were when they heard it.

None of my former cast mates want me back on *The Howard Stern Show.* And I can't say as I blame them. As I said, breaking balls, including theirs, was my job description, and I'm sure their on-air lives are so, so much sweeter for them without me fueling Howard's fire with comments about Robin's pomposity and her welcome sphincter, how scary Fred can seem, and Gary's big ass (let alone the piano stuck between his gums). The day I left, their holiday started.

As the years passed, Howard and I were truly sharing a brain. He'd often just read what I wrote out loud as he was reading it for the first time. He trusted me. Occasionally that would fuck him up, and that was even funnier.

Sometimes—very rarely, I have to say—but sometimes he'd read my handwriting wrong and what he said was like he just stepped in from Mars.

But amazingly, it never mattered. He'd make it work. He'd sell it and move on.

Unreal? Hell, yes.

Once he told me he saw my handwriting in his dream. I didn't ask him if it was a nightmare.

I loved it when the media quoted Howard and it was word-for-word from a specific note. Since it was always something funny, very often the articles would start with one of those quotes.

In 1995, Howard and his wife Alison and K-Rock announced the Sterns' marriage separation on a Friday afternoon, long after the show was over, so that Monday morning the entire world was listening to hear Howard's comments on his new status.

One of his opening lines, which was quoted in newspapers and periodicals around the globe, he read off my first note of the day:

ALL BROADS PLEASE CALL

It was the Greatest Show On Earth.

1997

PAYING RODNEY WITH JOKES

It's time to finally set the record straight about me supposedly owing Rodney Dangerfield money, a myth that was given birth on one of Rodney's appearances on *The Howard Stern Show*.

In 1978, I blindly sent Rodney six pages of jokes, he picked out four, and sent me a check for two hundred dollars. Fifty dollars a joke was what he paid, to me and to whomever he bought a joke(s) from. As simple an exchange as you can get.

Over the next few years, I sent him many, many pages of jokes, and he only bought, I think, two. But that was normal. Rodney was very, very picky, he knew just what he needed, just what jokes worked really well for him. Then the ones he chose, he tried out on stage over and over to be sure they were surefire no-miss.

That's why he was always so ridiculously funny.

As I told you earlier, Rodney had also taken me on the road with him for two weeks in March 1980 and we had a splendid time.

In late 1980, I was struggling along hand-to-mouth, living and working in my mother's attic, and had run out of copies of my first album. I had sold many of them and I'm sure had mailed out just as many in the name of promotion. I had nothing to lose, so I wrote Rodney and asked if he'd loan me a thousand dollars to get my album reprinted.

He called me as soon as he got my letter and said, "Yeah, no problem, I'll loan you the grand. Come on in and get the check," and I did.

I showed up at his apartment and, as always, he answered the door in his trusty tattered blue bathrobe, wide open, with his former instruments of destruction hanging like saddlebags. You try not to be thrown, but come on . . .

I thanked him to the point of annoyance and left.

Time went by, we had some communication, I kept sending pages and pages of jokes, but he never bought any. Then I saw him do a few jokes on television that I sent him but he had never responded about. And then I listened to his new *Rapping Rodney* album, and there were a few jokes on there that I had sent, but that he had never bought.

I am emphatically *not* accusing Rodney of anything underhanded. He smoked a lot of pot, did lots of cocaine, drank a lot, smoked endless cigarettes, and was always at the clubs trying out new jokes, jokes that were arriving in the mail as well as being handed him by comics on a daily basis. Bookkeeping was not his strong suit, if he bothered with it at all. I was sure the remuneration for the jokes had simply slipped through the cracks.

But I wanted to at least have him acknowledge it had happened. I went to Dangerfield's on a night he was there and went down to his dressing room after the show.

I said, "Boss, some of the jokes I sent that I thought you had passed on turned up on TV and on your album."

He didn't question it even a little.

He said, "Sorry about that. Okay, you owed me a thousand bucks . . . what was it, let's say it was about ten jokes, that's five hundred. So you owe me another ten jokes, and we'll be square."

I said, "Sounds perfect."

And it was. The price was fifty dollars a joke, so the math wasn't exactly calculus.

After that night, I kept sending pages of jokes, but he never "bought" any, never responded to say, "Okay, I'm using three of these, knock off a hundred fifty," never anything like that.

About a year later, I had completed my second album, *Goin' Ape*, and it was ready for pressing. But I was broke—*so* broke. So I wrote to

Rodney again, asking him to loan me two thousand dollars so I could print my second LP.

And he never responded. He ignored the letter, which was certainly his prerogative, and that was that.

I continued to send him jokes, but he never bought any—never acknowledged any. To the best of my knowledge he never used any of them, either.

Over the years, I ran into him a few times here and there.

In Fort Lauderdale, he said, "Asking for the two grand was ballsy," but that he wasn't pissed. "Hey, I could never be pissed at you, you gave me the best fucking joke I ever had . . ."

He always loved the two-bagger. That joke, an old Southern expression that came to me by way of Peru, had sealed me with him forever.

Cut to many years later. Since I had first started on the *Stern Show*, I had told the gang many wonderful Rodney stories, as damn near everything that went down when I was with him was so, so funny. But Rodney and I had no contact at all.

The first time Rodney called in to the *Stern Show*, Howard asked him about me, and he said, "Jackie Martling? Yeah, we were friends for about ten minutes in the eighties."

In all fairness to me, back in those days, I wasn't the first or the last person to move in and out of Rodney's circle of friends. He was mercurial, to say the least.

So now it's 1997, Rodney comes on one morning, and he's of course a riot. By the luck of the draw, journalist David Handelman was writing an article on the show for *TV Guide* and just happened to be sitting in on what wound up being an often-visited part of Stern history.

After Rodney's interview, as he was leaving, Mike Gange, a producer for the Howard Stern E! show, asked Rodney if he remembered me, and Rodney must have mumbled, "Yeah, I know Jackie. I lent him a thousand bucks, and he never paid me back. Then he asked me for another two thousand . . ."

I'll never know if Rodney simply had no recollection of what had actually gone down with me and what I owed him—as I said, he was always so high back in the early eighties, especially in his dressing room after a show—or if he knew exactly what had happened back then, but was stirring the pot for more Stern airtime. I wouldn't have thought it was that calculated on his part, but how could he have not remembered that yet recall I had written to him for more money. Hmmm . . .

Immediately recognizing a golden opportunity for some Jackie bashing, Gange asks Rodney to wait, goes back in, tells Howard that Rodney has a money issue with Jackie, and Howard has Rodney come back in. Rodney sits back down and starts explaining and soon Howard has Jackie ripping Rodney off for three thousand dollars.

The minute I tried to explain what had happened, that I had paid back part of it and was supposed to pay back the balance of the thousand dollars "in jokes," was met with not only instant ridicule, but Rodney himself said, "I don't know anything about anybody paying anything in jokes," which sealed off any chance I had of getting across what had taken place in his dressing room all those years back.

I don't think I even went near "Rodney, I heard you use some jokes on television that I sent you that you never bought from me," or anything the least bit accusatory like that. I just tried to explain that he had initially bought four jokes from me for two hundred dollars, that fifty bucks was what Rodney always paid for a joke, and that "ten jokes for five hundred dollars" was very simple math.

Rodney danced around that, because he certainly wasn't a fan of the world knowing he bought most of his jokes. Comics of course knew it, but the average Joe had no idea. Hell, a good portion of comedy audiences used to think comedians were making it up as they went along. And the truth is, they couldn't care less.

The crux of this story is I loved Rodney way too much to say, "Boss, you were so drunk and stoned and coked up back then, you have no idea what went down." I wasn't about to throw him under the bus—not that anybody would have believed me. He was an icon and I loved him as much if not more than anybody, so I took one for the team.

The best takeaway from this is that the concept of me paying Rodney back in jokes was not only a genuine agreement between us, but that it was *his idea*. Had I thought of it, I doubt I would ever have suggested it.

I got so frustrated with the way everybody in the room ganged up on me, never letting a syllable of truth through, I took a blank check out of my wallet, wrote it out for a thousand dollars, payable to Rodney Dangerfield, and took it over to him.

Rodney wouldn't take it . . . but David Handelman did. I bet David still has it tacked up somewhere.

If you ask someone for two thousand dollars and they never respond to your request, you don't owe them that two thousand . . . do you?

But, of course, as I said, by the time Rodney left, Howard had me owing him three thousand dollars.

And to this day, I get emails, Facebook messages, people coming up to me at shows and in public, everywhere, saying, "Pay Rodney back, man!"

And, most amazingly, Rodney being dead has hardly slowed them up.

The hardest thing to believe is that after the show, Rodney's office called and asked me if I wanted to continue our feud that night at his show at the Beacon. I guess everybody had really enjoyed the skirmish, including Rodney.

But I was shot. They'd turned me inside out, made it look like I had been crappy to my hero.

As much as I know the *Stern Show* is bullshit, I just didn't have any playfulness in me to go continue the feud—and it's still one of my greatest regrets.

1997

THE BATTLE OF THE SUPERHEROES

Spring 1997, the *Stern Show* gang was in Los Angeles for the West Coast premiere of Howard's terrific feature film *Private Parts* at Grauman's Chinese Theatre. The movie was number one in the country and, at least speaking for myself, as small a part as I had, it was about as exciting as anything could ever be. The movie industry was buzzing, mostly with the sweet surprise that the movie was so damn good.

The night before the screening, Fa La Flutie, Stammerzer John, and me, and our wives, were on the second level of the infamous Skybar at the Mondrian Hotel, which you accessed by way of a narrow stairway that led up from the big area around the pool. And we were the shit.

For that brief moment, we were movie stars and the world was our oyster. We were the belles of the ball (belles with balls?).

After a while, somehow, the three of us guys were entrenched in a wonderful conversation with George Clooney, John Stamos, and Dean Cain, all huge fans and—believe it or not—were as thrilled to be talking to us as we were to be talking to them. Yeah, it was a pinch me moment.

I vividly remember George, who I already knew by way of his assistant Amy Cohen, saying, "Guys, soak it all in. Enjoy the fuck out of this, because trust me, it goes away as quickly as it comes."

We were having a great time and laughing our asses off. Eventually, George and Dean had drifted away and were standing at the top of the stairs, greeting and befriending one by one the gorgeous women who were coming up to our level. After meeting them, the women were tending to stay close in an attempt to keep their chatter with the boys alive.

John Stamos, who was still rollicking with us, glanced over at George and Dean and the stunning harem that was accumulating, turned back to us, smiled, shook his head, and said, "Look at those poor girls. They can't make up their minds. Superman or Batman, Superman or Batman . . ."

All I remember is the thought going through my boozy head, "Holy fuck, are we in Hollywood."

1998

DECORUM IN THE WORKPLACE

From the very first day I walked into the radio studio, I was a loose cannon. I'd been a musician and comedian working in bars and nightclubs and, in general, not places that required me—or any of us—to act our ages or even like decent human beings. We were and are a low form of life and prefer to keep it that way. There are exceptions, but for the most part, comedians are under the barrel between the slugs and the maggots. Talk foul, act foul, and walk around wondering why the hot women aren't flocking to us.

Actually, for all the grime, musicians do very well with the babes. Even the bad ones.

The quintessential difference between a musician and a comedian is that when the worst bass player in the worst band in the skankiest bar goes on break, women run to him and hand him their phone numbers, hotel keys, and panties.

When a famous comedian walks off stage in a classy venue, a nice-looking woman will go up to him, point, and say, "My husband thinks you're very funny."

I wrote a joke about it back in 1985:

"Music's great . . . comedy sucks. Look at Billy Joel. Billy Joel's fucking girls that look like Christie Brinkley, and I'm fucking girls that look like Billy Joel."

So I was always having fun running amok in the halls and offices and studios of K-Rock. Occasionally, I'd throw Robin down on a couch and hump her leg, just being a jerk.

Howard would say, "Man, you really dig her, don't you?"

How could I begin to explain that if I actually had designs on someone, even I wouldn't approach her like that?

In the early nineties—and I think we can safely say long before that—women started taking some offense to the freewheeling antics of some of the men they worked with, either with what they were saying or doing or even touching or all of the above. And cases of sexual harassment started popping up in the news when they had previously been very rare. There were no cases in our offices, but that didn't mean it wasn't a bit loose here and there . . . I like to think it was because we were a fun group. Respect is a state of mind that I felt we all shared.

Please don't get me wrong. I'd wither and die on the vine if I couldn't flirt. But, somehow, I felt I never went over the line. Unless I was pulled. Of course, I'm still waiting for that glorious event.

I wonder if Gloria Allred is a talented fellatrix?

At some point, one or a few of the powers-that-be decided that all of the stations in the Infinity Broadcasting group needed to make sure their employees were well versed in what was and wasn't appropriate behavior when they were on the clock. Our general manager, Tom Chiusano, a good friend even though he was the person I battled with at salary time, was given the task of heading up our station's all-employees meeting. He'd deliver the required speech after we each grabbed a copy of the pamphlet that accompanied his soliloquy, *The Official Infinity Broadcasting Guidelines to Political Correctness at a Radio Station*. I couldn't make that up.

We were all assembled in a big room waiting for him. It was an incredibly pregnant situation, screaming for Jackie and Fred Norris, the bad boys representing K-Rock's wild morning show, to break balls.

There was a television set at the front of the room. I quickly grabbed a piece of paper, drew a huge, very simple stick figure sketch of an immense hairy cock and balls, and taped it to the television screen.

Tom walked in, everybody faced him, and he started the meeting— standing directly in front of the TV set with my artwork hanging not a foot behind him. Everybody held it together just long enough so that when he finally realized something was very amiss and turned around and saw it, he got really pissed off. He tore it up and then attempted to finish what he set out to do, with the pecker image firmly emblazoned in everybody's mind and the snickering never quite stopping.

He was very upset with me, and all of us, for not realizing the importance of his talk. He was even more upset when Howard got wind of what had gone down and we all laughed about it on the air for the next few years.

That, dear reader, is what we call hijinks. Wonderful, harmless hijinks.

The amazing and very disappointing postscript to this chapter is that there was no sexual frolicking whatsoever in our studios or offices or halls.

I never did anything with anyone, never saw anybody else do anything with anyone, and never even heard a story or even a rumor that somebody blew somebody in a back office or somebody banged somebody in the bathroom. Not once in all those years.

That, of course, doesn't mean it never happened. Just, if it did, neither me or any of my cast mates knew about it. All those people and all those cubbyholes and all those years . . . I really hope *somebody* was getting laid or sucked or whatever.

Of course, if you were trying to keep anything hush-hush, we certainly weren't the show to trust with your secret(s).

1998

I'LL GIVE IT A TEN

The years I was there and before and since, Howard's had all kinds of people on the show. And that has to go down as one of the world's great understatements. Rock stars, politicians, homeless people, movie stars, morons, athletes, television stars, virgins, writers, broadcasters, comedians, little people (to me that term sounds way more insulting than midgets), porn stars, fans and super fans . . . the list could fill this book (it almost just did). Many famous and infamous people and others who came on and loved it became regulars or semi-regulars, stopping in every once in a while over the years.

One of the great gentle creatures I always enjoyed, as did my fellow *Stern Show* writer and Master of the Sound Bites Fred Norris, was Gary the Retard. Fred's and my taste ran remarkably parallel, getting perhaps our ultimate minute-by-minute enjoyment from the earlier on-show antics of "world's angriest comedian" Pat Cooper.

Gary's mentally challenged. Not completely debilitated, but most definitely more than a few cards short of fifty-two. When the show came across him, or vice versa, he lived in the Pacific Northwest, was a huge fan, and somehow wound up in the studio many times. I was never privy as to whether we were getting him there or he was getting himself there. I think it was a bit of each. Nonetheless, it was always great fun.

Howard treated Gary with the utmost respect. The fun was inserting him in somewhat normal situations and watching the fur fly. We sent him on dates, took him to the strip club Scores, used him in prerecorded bits. He loved it (I hope) and we all loved it.

This particular show, Gary was one of three judges for a bit much like television's *America's Got Talent* (!). They were given the task of rating each of the contestants' performances with a score from one to ten.

The first contestant performed, the judges gave them a score, and then one by one Howard asked the judges for the score they'd given. When he got to Gary, Gary of course had to be reprogrammed what he had to do.

So when he got to Gary, Howard said, "Okay, Gary the Retard, what score would you like to give, from one to ten?"

There was a really long pause, and then Gary said, "I'll give it a ten."

Very generous.

The next contestant performed, and the judges gave them a score.

When Howard got to Gary, he said, "Okay, Gary, what score did *you* give, from one to ten?"

This time there was a much longer pause, and then Gary said, "I think I'll give it a ten."

The pause had been so long that the comedy was beyond exquisite. Fred and I, as well as everybody else, howled.

Then the next contestant performed, the judges gave them a score, and when it got to Gary, Howard said, "Okay, Gary, what score did *you* give, from one to ten?"

Now there was a really, really, really long pause. I can still remember it, as well as where I was when JFK got shot. It feels like it's still taking place. It was interminable, but Howard's instinctive genius let it just tick by. We were about to explode. I think we all knew fucking well what he was going to say . . .

. . . and then Gary said, "Ten."

It was like a bomb went off. So much suspense, everybody on eggshells, for no apparent reason. The beauty is that no comedian or actor in a million years would *ever* have the balls to leave that huge a span of dead air. It played like sheer comedic genius.

I thought, as I think most everybody else did, that Gary was giving everybody a perfect score because he didn't want to be mean. But in retrospect, that was way too cerebral a place to take the explanation.

Later, Fred said to me, "I figured out why Gary gave everybody a ten. It was the last thing he heard. Each time, Howard said, 'Gary, what score would you like to give between one and ten?' And so 'ten' was the last thing Gary heard, so he simply repeated back 'ten' each time."

Fred's a genius.

That was easily the hardest I ever laughed on *The Howard Stern Show*, and I laughed a lot. But my *God*, that was one for the books (obviously).

2000

JACKIE TELLS JIMMY FALLON TO BAG IT

Once I started to get somewhat known, in the mid-eighties, after about the zillionth person came up to me and said, "I want to be a comedian, what should I do?" I came up with a stock response.

I'd say, "Give up. You haven't got a chance. Forget it."

Which is not intended to be at all mean, but because if me saying "don't do it" is enough to stop you, or even give you *pause*, you *shouldn't* go for it. Because you're going to face *so*, so many hurdles on your way to becoming a comedian that me telling you to give up is relatively no hurdle at all. It's meant to be kind of a first test . . . do you really want to do it?

Around 2007, in her daily column in the *New York Post*, Cindy Adams quoted Matt Damon as having said, "People are always telling me they want to be an actor. I tell them it's too hard, don't bother. Hey, if that stops them in their tracks, they're not cut out for it."

Fall 2013, in a Q&A at the Gold Coast Film Festival, Sean Young was asked the same question and responded the same way, with the same explanation.

Great minds.

After Jimmy Fallon became a *Saturday Night Live* cast member in 1998, he was soon cast in the film *Almost Famous*, and when it was about to be released, he called in to *The Howard Stern Show* to promote it. He had never been on Howard's show, so both he and Howard were excited to talk.

Jimmy said, "I met you guys years ago, Howard. I'm from upstate, outside of Albany. You guys took a road trip up to the capital when you were thinking of running for governor, and I went to the bar of the hotel where I heard you guys were staying, hoping to meet you. Of course, Jackie was in the bar. I went up to him and told him I wanted to be a comedian, and he told me to quit."

That's all Howard needed to hear. Forget about me getting in one syllable of my reasoning for saying it. I never heard the end of how I tried to stifle a great talent and what a loser I was for doing it.

Jimmy and I have laughed about it for years. I last saw him in Christopher Cross's dressing room years ago when Chris was booked to perform his hit song "Sailing" on one of Jimmy's yachting-themed shows.

Jimmy said, "Jackie, I love to tell that story. My buddies all love it, too. You gotta come on the show and tell it."

Needless to say, I've called repeatedly. I guess *The Tonight Show* bookers didn't get the memo.

2000

LES PAUL . . .
OH, AND KEITH RICHARDS

For years, Adam Sands, a good friend of *Stern Show* fixture Steve Grillo and a very popular New York promoter and publicist, had been trying to get Fred Norris and me to go see the Les Paul Trio, guitar legend Les Paul's show at Iridium in New York City. He had a gut feeling Les and I would really hit it off.

In 1998, I rented an apartment on Fifty-Sixth Street and Broadway, a stone's throw from the club, but somehow I still never managed to get there.

One fateful night in June 2000, Cari Ash, ex-wife of the grandson and namesake of the legendary music store mogul Sam Ash, called and said, "Martling, tonight's Les Paul's eighty-fifth birthday, and you and Nancy are going with me. He's terrific, plus you never know who'll show up. Some of the Rolling Stones are supposed to be there, everybody loves Les, and I know you guys'll love him. The limo will be there at nine and you guys are getting in or I'm going to come up and drag you down."

She'd made it too easy and too irresistible. At nine, we jumped into the limo with Cari and her gang and drove up Eighth Avenue the seven short blocks to where Iridium used to be (it's now at Broadway and Fifty-First, under Ellen's Stardust Diner). We descended the stairs that led to a room packed to the hilt with celebrities and music greats. When we walked in, the maître d' rushed to Cari and proceeded to lead us through the packed club to some of the best seats in the house, against the right wall of the very small showroom. Adam was of course thrilled to see I'd finally made it there.

We'd barely begun drinking (it was 2000, I wasn't sober yet) and carrying on when Cari said, "Look over there."

Keith Richards and an older couple were just sitting down, right across the aisle from us. He was in all of his rock and roll eminence . . . silk shirt, bright-colored scarf, hair braided in cornrows with beads in them, puffing away at his cigarette, smiling broadly, obviously glad to be there.

Soon Les came walking down the aisle on his way to the stage. Adam was walking with him, and they passed right by our table.

As they were passing, I heard Les say to Adam, "So Jackie The Joke Man is here tonight?"

I was sure I had heard him wrong. But I soon learned that a good many old folks don't sleep through the night and that Les would often be awake during the hellish hours we were on the air. It turned out he listened almost every morning, was a huge fan of the *Stern Show*, and was intrigued by what Adam had explained my role was.

After the opening few songs, right out of the blue, Les said, "There's a guy here tonight I've always wanted to meet. Jackie The Joke Man, come on up here."

He, of course, caught me totally off guard. I got up and was a bit flabbergasted as I made my way to the bandstand.

And suddenly there I was, on stage with a living legend—the man who invented the electric guitar and multitrack recording and more—and he was the spitting image of my father, who had passed away seven years earlier.

Like my father in so many ways, Les was a slight man, once a redhead and now with a very receding hairline, thick glasses, a bit of arthritis in his hands and fingers, the same quick smile, and that devilish twinkle in his eye. It was spooky and wonderful. I mean, I actually felt like I was standing there with Pop. For the most part I'm pretty at ease on stage, but I was instantly *very* comfortable up there with him.

He said, "So you tell jokes? Go ahead, Jackie The Joke Man, give us a sample."

I said, "Well, Les, there's a pretty good chance they'll be a bit off-color," and he said, "Whatever, go ahead, we can handle anything you've got."

Now, as I was to quickly learn, Les Paul had a very, *very* varied audience. He was Bing Crosby's bandleader in the forties, and he and his wife and partner Mary Ford sold millions of records in the early fifties, the days of *Your Hit Parade*. But then he created Gibson's Les Paul electric guitar(s) and he was an instant hero to millions of young rock and rollers from the late fifties right up to present day. So you never knew who was going to be in his audiences. But for the most part, they're older, gentle, music-lover types.

So the great Les Paul had teed me up to this electric crowd. The *Stern Show* was at its very height, I was still drinking and feeling very much up to the opportunity he was handing me, and I was off to the races. I rattled off five or six of my best very funny but very foul jokes.

I was watching Les as well as the crowd. The harder he laughed, the dirtier I got, and vice versa. In no time at all, the place was erupting with every punch line and I figured I'd get off on a high note. I told one last very obscene joke, thanked Les, jumped off the stage, and made my way back to my seat to pretty amazing applause.

Les was shaking his head in disbelief. I think I may have been dirtier, and funnier, than he'd anticipated. But he'd loved it, a lot, and he was still laughing, mumbling to himself, "So that's Jackie The Joke Man?"

Then Les announces, "My old friend Keith Richards is here tonight. Come on up, Keith, let's see what you remember," and the audience, who mostly had no idea Keith was in the house, went berserk.

Keith took the stage, and as he was strapping on a guitar, he said, "It'll be a bit tough following that bloke."

I couldn't believe my ears. I was still pretty dazed by the proceedings, but I'm sure that had me beaming like a Cheshire cat.

Right here I need to mention that the older couple with Keith were his mother and stepfather.

Les said, "Keith, that's your mother out there, I know Doris. Folks, Keith's mom is a great blues singer. Doris, come on up and do something for us."

But he couldn't coax her up on stage. After Keith played a few blues songs, he went back to his seat, and as Les and the trio were about to play a song, Les was still shaking his head, like he was still trying to digest me and my dirty jokes.

He said, "That was Jackie The Joke Man, huh? Jackie, come on back up here."

(A quick note: From that night until Les's passing in 2009, I went to Les's show about sixty times, and I never saw him ask anyone back on stage a second time. Ever.)

I couldn't believe it. Back up I went.

When I got up there, I turned to the jammed house—Les's birthday was always a very hot ticket, and they were literally packed in like sardines—and I said, "Keith, I'm so sorry. If I'd known your mother was in the audience, I would never have told those off-color jokes."

Which I said totally tongue in cheek, because as a blues singer as well as the mother of a rock and roller, she'd certainly heard every foul thing that was ever uttered and then some. It was funny, Keith looked older than her.

Keith stood up at his table, and yelled, "Oh, *yeah?* Well, I'll tell you something about *your* mum . . ."

I said to the crowd, "I'm getting heckled by a Rolling Stone. *That* doesn't suck, does it?"

And they went wild. I mean, they went *wild*.

Then I turned to Les and he started asking me about the radio show, typical questions about what my function was in the studio, stuff that lots of people asked (and still do).

"So you're sitting there every day in the studio with Howard? Tell me about how his radio show works. Adam tells me you write jokes as the show's in progress?"

Again, I was so damn comfortable on stage with Les it's hard to express. Though it was only my second time on stage with this wonderful man, though we had only known each other for a few precious minutes, I could sense his total trust in me, in wherever I chose to go—which is huge on stage. There are lots of bands and television shows where the characters still don't have that mutual feeling.

I said, "Les, I can't begin to tell you how blown away I am, how flattered I am that you know who I am and that you're interested in the whole Stern thing. And probably there's a few *Stern Show* fans in the crowd who're interested, too. But it's your birthday and these people are here to see you and hear you play your music and to celebrate your birthday with you.

"So do your show, and when you're done, we'll go to the bar, have a few drinks, and we can talk about the *Stern Show*. And maybe Keith'll join us. And who knows? Maybe Keith'll even buy. And if he doesn't have any money on him, maybe he can pay with those fucking beads he's got in his hair."

I watched Les crack up, and as he doubled over, the crowd exploded with laughter.

I turned to the crowd and said, "Now *I'm* fucking with *a Rolling Stone*. That doesn't suck, does it?"

And man, did they howl and cheer. Louder and longer than the first time. When I got to my seat, they were just calming down. It was just fucking rarefied in there. A pinch me moment if ever there was a pinch me moment.

After the show, Les and Keith and I sat in Les's dressing room for quite a while, and it was just too incredible. We joked and laughed and told stories as though we shared a brain. One of the finest nights ever, in a long line of fine nights.

I left totally intrigued by my new friend. Adam told me Les rehearsed the band every Monday afternoon before their two shows that night.

The next week, I was eating lunch at Fiorello's on Broadway with my pal Lisa France when it hit me that it was Monday and that Marlow's, with Iridium down below, was just a few feet away.

I said to Lisa, "After we eat, I'm going to introduce you to a new pal of mine."

We finished up, walked down to Sixty-Third Street, went in, walked downstairs, and sure enough, there was Les and the band on stage.

It was very dark in the showroom.

I made my way up close and said, "Les, it's Jackie. I want to introduce you to a pretty girl."

Actually tickled to see me, or more likely the pretty girl, he quickly excused himself to come down and say hello, and when he got a look at Lisa, who's a knockout, eighty-five suddenly became thirty-five.

I said, "Les, this is Lisa France. She's a film director and a big fan. I have to tell you, I'm still sailing from joining you on stage last week. I don't want to interrupt your band practice, but I want to give you a joke for your show that I think you'll love."

Les loved to tell stories and joke around on stage. I could tell he enjoyed that as much as playing the guitar.

One of my favorites was when he'd tell the crowd, "A long time ago I was in a band with Frankie Hebert, who was a mortician. One time, I went to pick him up and he said he'd be just a few minutes, he had to dress a body first, and hey, could I come help him.

"I said sure. We went down into his laboratory or whatever you call the place where they drain the blood from the bodies, and there was a stiff lying there. He picked up a suit jacket and a pair of scissors and started cutting up the middle of the back, cutting the jacket in half.

"I said, 'What're you doing?'

"He said, 'You didn't think we were going to do it the *hard* way, did you?'"

"Frankie was a musician and a mortician, and to this day, I don't know which one was his hobby."

Priceless.

Les was humble, so often I'd take the stage and after a few jokes I'd tell my favorite Les story, one he rarely told, because I knew the crowd would love it.

In the fifties there were two kids in a band who went to audition for a job. The guy liked them, but he didn't like their repertoire.

He told them, "Go home and learn some Les Paul and Mary Ford songs."

They did, they came back and auditioned again, and they got the gig.

It was John Lennon and Paul McCartney.

When Paul first told that story to Les, he was standing in the precise place I was standing each time I recounted it.

And when I had finished the story, Les would counter with, "When Paul told me the story, he was with Heather. I should've knocked on her wooden leg three times to wish them good luck."

The joke I gave him when I went to see him that day with Lisa he wound up using in every show from then on. He'd always work it in.

It worked best on the many nights beautiful blonde Australian stand-up bassist Nicki Parrott was playing in the trio. Nicki would come up front and perform an incredibly slow, sexy song she'd written for and about Les, all the while cooing and unashamedly flirting with him.

When she'd finish, Les would turn to the crowd and say, "I feel like a condemned building with a new flagpole."

Until a few weeks before he passed, just shy of ninety-four years old, Les and the Les Paul Trio were still doing two shows at Iridium every Monday night. And not to pay the rent—his estate made more money while I was typing this sentence than most of us will ever see. It was the love of the game.

The club being so close to my apartment, I went to Les's late show fairly often and he'd always invite me up. I'd jump on stage and fire off a few insults at Lou Pallo, Les's guitar player of three decades and a wonderful man, banter with Les a bit, maybe tell the audience a Les story he hadn't told as yet, and then shoot off a healthy dose of foul jokes.

What I do, of course, had absolutely no place in Les Paul's gentle, jazzy show, which at different times was frequented by the likes of Paul McCartney, Slash, Merle Haggard, Steve Miller, Richie Sambora, Al DiMeola, Bucky Pizzarelli, Richie Cannata . . . just about anyone of note in the music industry. But Les loved me, insisting I join him on stage whenever I was in the house, and laughed at my jokes damn near as heartily as me.

I've got dozens of photos of the two of us on stage, caught in the act of yukking like five-year-olds at my pee-pee and ca-ca jokes.

Like so many millions of others, I admired Les and treasured him— but I also, very fortunately, counted him as a dear friend.

Again, we lost Les years back. The heft of what he gave us, what he left in his wake, can't be overstated.

I miss making him laugh. We were soul mates.

Thanks, Adam.

Every time I joined Les on stage, he'd insist I finish my set with this, his favorite of my jokes:

A guy from France, a guy from California, and a guy from New York get caught by cannibals.

They say to the guy from France, "We're going to boil you and eat you."

He says, "Sacré bleu! Zis is terrible! You cannot boil me and eat me! Sacré bleu!"

They say to the guy from California, "We're going to cut you up and use your bones to make weapons."

The guy from California says, "Sacré bleu! Zis is ..."

No ...

He says, "Oh, wow, man. You can't do that, man. You can't cut me up and use my bones, man ... that's bogus, dudes ..."

They say to the New Yorker, "And you ... we're going to peel off all of your skin and use your skin to make a canoe."

The New Yorker grabs a fork from one of the cannibals, starts stabbing himself in the chest again and again, and says, "Yeah? Well, here's your fucking canoe, you asshole. I got your fucking canoe right here. Here's your fucking canoe, Jack. Your mother should ride in this canoe, you fucking cock- sucker, you scumbag bastard ..."

2000

THE TOAST

In the summer of 2000, the very large, very bubbly, voraciously media-hungry as well as food-hungry and at the time very rich attorney Dominic Barbara, a good friend of and frequent caller to *The Howard Stern Show*, invited a bunch of the cast and crew to his beautiful spread on Shelter Island for a three-day weekend. My wife's band had a gig so I drove out alone on Saturday morning. When I got there, Howard and his new girlfriend Beth Ostrosky, Stuttering Johnson Melonhead and his wife Suzanna, our E! television producer Scott Einziger and his girlfriend Maya, Richie Notar from Nobu, and Dominic and his wife Irma were already immersed in Dominic's over-the-top hospitality.

Getting there was a bit of an ordeal, as the long ride out had culminated with taking a ferry to the island, but I remember it was a perfect day for a cruise and when I finally got there they were all so glad to see me that the hassle of the trip immediately melted away.

My God, it was a pleasure palace. Like the rest of us, Dominic is an arrested adolescent (*hmm* . . . speaking of which, I may be the only one of us who was ever actually arrested, but enough times to cover all of them). A huge house and grounds, an oversize outdoor pool, an indoor pool, pinball games, a pool table, a poker table, huge televisions, stacks of videos, many bedrooms, and a kitchen and bar packed with anything you could want. The surreal icing on the cake was every board game I'd ever played ... Monopoly, Risk, Clue, Parcheesi, even Candyland. Always wanting Howard's time with him to be exquisite, Dominic had more than prepared for this invasion. In retrospect, I'm sure Dominic had Howard's gal Friday Laura tend to it.

We floated in the pool and drank for most of that afternoon and it was really relaxing and fun.

I remember floating over next to Howard and saying, half (only half) kidding, "If we had a four-day workweek, this could be us every weekend."

He said, "I've tried, but Mel [Karmazin] won't go for it. I'd love to have a four-day week."

As I type, Howard's down to a three-day week. By the time this book is published he may very well have a three-*hour* workweek.

Howard looked and sounded very happy and I believed him. Many times I didn't take him at face value, but it seemed he had been changing a bit. I wondered if he had honestly been attempting to make a dent at repressing the severe workaholism that haunts so many of us.

Of course, I'd been screaming four-day week for years. I'd bark it whenever we were discussing ways we could make doing the show easier. Those very informal discussions happened more frequently as the years wore on and the early morning hours continued to beat us up more and more. I know by the end of my tenure, never being caught up on sleep had really taken a toll on me. After all these years off the show— sixteen if you're keeping score—the joy of the freedom hasn't worn off at all. I'm still ecstatic about not having to set my alarm for 4:20 a.m.

Saturday night, we had reservations at Sunset Beach, a popular restaurant in town. Shelter Island is a very exclusive area and the restaurant was jammed with the wealthy locals and a few celebrities. The place was naturally thrilled to welcome Howard Stern and his entourage and the hostess led us to one of the long banquet tables on the tented rooftop. The left side of the table was Dominic, then Howard, then me, then John, then Scott, with Richie and the girls across the table from us. We had been partying all day and were very merry.

There was another long banquet table parallel to us, and then another long banquet table that continued lengthwise down from that one after the break of an aisle, so that there was a table diagonally away from us. It was tight quarters, so the people at that table were pretty close to us. Actually, everybody on the small rooftop was part of a pretty intimate setting.

At the table diagonally away from us was Michael Gelman, his wife, and their party of about ten people. At the time Gelman was the producer of *Live with Regis and Kathie Lee*, which Howard spent endless hours berating, mainly attacking Kathie Lee and her philandering husband Frank Gifford (what a gift to our show his dalliances had been).

Gelman was rarely, if ever, the focal point of Howard's attacks, but he definitely represented what could gently be termed, in what I'd refer to in a friendly way, as "the enemy." The buzz that he was a few arm's lengths away got to us almost immediately and it put a small amount of tension in the already rarefied air.

I say rarefied because whenever I was with Howard and whoever he had in tow, no matter where it was, the incredible degree of his celebrity always made it very, very different than being with regular people. It even made it very different than being with a normal celebrity. It's not due to anything he tries to cause, it's just a fact of American life. His fame and stature, his superstardom, makes his presence an event anywhere he goes, which is at once wonderful and frightening, a blessing and a curse.

Gelman was sitting at the far end on what was the opposite side to where Howard was sitting, so he was as far away from Howard as he could be and still be at that table. Meanwhile, the many beers had started to back up and it was time to break the seal. John, Scott, and I excused ourselves and left for the men's room.

As we were tucking ourselves back in, I said, "Gelman's here. This is such a pregnant setup, we have to fuck around."

John and Scott looked at me and said, almost in unison, "Not me," and scattered like cockroaches suddenly exposed to daylight.

As they bolted, I yelled to them, "Hey, I'll take the heat for whatever we do," but it was already too late, they were gone. They had zoomed back upstairs.

I love to break Howard's chops, always innocently, and, in fact, from the very beginning I think I somehow always felt it was almost expected of me. I'm pretty sure that's part of the reason I was thrown into the mix in the first place, or at least something I had grown into. If not, hey, it's a great rationalization.

But the other schmendricks, they were somewhat afraid to pull anything on the boss.

I found our waitress by the bar, handed her twenty dollars, and asked her to please bring Howard a drink and tell him it's from Mr. Gelman, who's seated at the other table. I smiled, told her it was a little joke I was pulling, and she smiled back and said okay.

I returned to my seat and a few minutes later the waitress came over with a drink, handed it to Howard, and said in his ear (I imagine), "This is from Mr. Gelman, who's sitting at the table over there," and she motioned to Kathie Lee-Ville.

As she turned and walked toward me, I looked up and smiled, and she smiled back.

Howard looked at the drink for just a second, and then stood up, all six foot five of him, raised his glass way high in the direction of Gelman, and said loudly, with a toasting gesture, "Gelman! To you!"

Gelman, of course, had absolutely no idea what the hell was going on or what Howard was talking about, and the combination of his clueless blank stare and the incredulously puzzled looks on the people he was with made that immediately apparent.

For the next few seconds, but what I'm sure seemed like forever to him, Howard was trying to figure out exactly what had just taken place as he slowly sat back down, folding all six foot five of himself back into his chair.

As his ass hit his chair, totally confused and embarrassed, he leaned over and softly said to me, "The waitress told me this drink was from Gelman."

Grinning like the Cheshire cat I said, "I know. That's what I told her to tell you."

I roared. I laughed so hard, I don't even remember if Einziger and the Stammerer were enjoying it. As the rest of the table was gradually brought in on the joke, everybody who dared to laugh laughed, and to me it of course just got funnier and funnier.

Being the butt of a joke is nobody's favorite, and Howard is certainly no exception. I think he was a bit pissed the rest of the weekend. But it was the perfect practical joke. The situation had been way too ripe not to harvest.

When I walked into the studio on Tuesday (it was a three-day weekend, remember?), I had no idea how my stunt was going to play out on the radio. You never knew, which was consistently a major part of what made being on the show so much fun—and so scary. Goofing and breaking balls were the whole show, but it was different when Howard was the breakee. To tell the truth, it was such a perfect hit that I wasn't even sure if it would make it to the air.

But Howard was sheepishly smiling. As he related the story to Robin, and she cackled, being careful not to give me too much credit, it was obvious it had been a hoot. And then the *pièce de résistance*.

He turned to me and said, "When I told my daughters what you pulled, they laughed their asses off," and then he shook his head and cracked up.

That's one of my favorite stories. Probably because it happened at the point where I felt the closest I had ever or would ever feel to Howard, as well as most of the people there that weekend.

This was the same summer Howard showed up unannounced at my beach, in the afternoon, twice. I had known him since 1983, and he had never come over during the day before. But here he was, once with his daughter Emily, the three of us actually swimming in Long Island Sound, and once with his dog Jolly.

When he showed up with Jolly, I asked him if he'd ever taken her swimming. He said no, so we took her down to the water and I taught her how to swim. Well, I coaxed her into the water, and she swam, since all dogs are natural swimmers, and it was very apparent that she loved it. Howard was more thrilled with me than if we had just completed a killer Sternak.

I distinctly remember thinking to myself, "My God, that's so refreshingly normal of him." But I didn't want to spoil the moment by noting that.

At that point, it really seemed like he might have been reaching out, that he might want to be closer friends with me or just wanted more normalcy or both. But you never knew. We hung out at a few concerts with our ladies, but never did anything or went anywhere as a twosome.

When I first met the gang in 1983, I was surprised to learn that they didn't go out to dinner together or hang out on weekends. But almost immediately I saw and understood that the distances between everyone in the cast was healthy and totally necessary for the show. But after the many, many years together, I really thought those ranks could have been closed a bit, that as weathered professionals we could have more than very occasionally broken bread and yet kept our all-important in-battles vitally alive.

But it was Howard's call and it just didn't happen much.

As I look back, I realize I never reached out much, either, except for the few dinner parties Sirianni and I threw for the gang, and our classic Fourth of July and other beach parties. But due to my position on the show, I had never felt it was my place to approach him about the two of us traipsing around socially. Not to mention that before his split with Alison, to my knowledge, he went out very little at all. All these are of course very stupid and very poor excuses. The worst a person can do if you call and ask them if they want to hang out is say, "No."

Hmm . . . And then go on the air to twelve million listeners and bitch, "Robin, Jackie actually thought I'd go out with him Friday night."

But letting people have it on the radio was his job. So it remains a poor excuse and I'm honestly sorry I didn't at least try to befriend him more.

So during my final year on the show and before the start of my last negotiation, which ended up with me off the show for good, we had actually begun to do more stuff. After Howard had gotten divorced, he'd started to relate to me some of what he was up to, about his dates and his occasional drinking and whatever.

Maybe had I stayed with the show, especially since I became single, too, we'd have hung out a bit. Although he got very close to his girlfriend Beth very quickly, so I guess he couldn't really have been termed "single" anymore.

That's so funny. One of the only things Robin and I ever agreed on— that is, that springs to mind here—was on the air, years ago, whenever

Howard was talking about divorce in general and what he'd be like if he ever split up with Alison.

He'd say, "If I was ever single, I'd never get involved again. I'd be out with a million babes, free forever."

Robin would always laugh and say, "That's not you. If you ever got divorced, you'd be coupled up again within a year."

And I remember saying, "As much as I hate to agree with her about anything, she's on the money here."

And she was.

2001

THE END

So, at some point, near the end of the nineties, I knew I had to get off *The Howard Stern Show*. There were a lot of contributing factors, big and small, that seemed to multiply with each year, and then each month, that were all muddled together, so the actual trigger or triggers aren't precisely clear. I think it was more of a general gut instinct, which included a nagging "I really should get out of here and create something of my own before I die" feeling. Looking back, maybe I was stockpiling the reasons as an aid to help me stand my ground for the (whopping?) pay increase I was going to request. I'm not sure . . . it was all bubbling in my head like a stew.

Of course, the main reason was exhaustion. I simply couldn't ever, ever get in my damn bed and go to sleep at eight or nine o'clock. For fifteen years, I'd had to get up at 4:20 schmendricks a.m., five days a week, yet I went to bed sometimes at ten, but most often between eleven and twelve, *every night*. Except, of course, on Fridays, when even if I felt like I was going to drop dead from being up since before the crack of dawn, I went out and did something socially, because "it was the weekend." I'd bet that in the course of the fifteen years I climbed into bed at nine o'clock or earlier three times tops.

And I'd damn near never, ever take a nap. That's most likely all I would have had to do to right myself a bit, but I just couldn't do naps. It's so funny. I'm sixty-nine now, and all I want to do is take a nap. I wake up in the morning and wonder, "*Hmm*... when will I get to lie down again?" The thought of still having that job, where the smartest thing I could do for myself and all around me is take a nap every day, makes my head spin. Could I teach myself to nap *now*? Ho boy.

Some weekends I'd get recharged, sleeping in would get me somewhat back in the ball game, but by Wednesday, things would be bleak again. I'd get back from Manhattan to my Bayville office on the North Shore of Long Island, be sitting at my computer bleary-eyed and complaining, and Nancy would say, "For God's sakes, go home and take a nap." But for whatever reasons, I just couldn't or wouldn't do it.

This was compounded with often racing to the airport on a Friday to zoom off to do stand-up gigs that were too hard (no, *impossible*) to refuse after the years of telling those same jokes for a tiny fraction of the money that was being offered. The proverbial Golden Handcuffs.

Believe me, I know you comics and show business people are reading this, gritting your teeth, and snorting, "That lucky cocksucker. He had it sacked. Big money and he gets to sleep in his own bed almost every night. Let *me* at that job. What the fuck was he thinking to give that up?"

But you had to live it to understand. It wasn't a film that would wrap in seven weeks. It was in no way finite. It was end over end, work-vacation-work, month in month-out, for fifteen years. I was cooked, fried, and fricasseed.

The last few years on the show, I was relatively rich and unquestionably miserable. *Nothing* compensates your feel-good quotient when you're totally run down. On Sundays, after two days of sleep, I'd actually say to myself and whoever was listening, "Is this what the world looks like to everybody else? It's in *color*. It ain't so bad."

I'm very aware—I always have been, but now more than ever—that I have lots of problems. Deep, extensive problems, I think. Let's go with yes, I do. Hopefully, I manipulated whatever they brew inside me into an offbeat career that often makes others laugh and in turn makes me feel a bit better. But being exhausted really magnified and worsened my psyche. I was very sleep deprived and very unhappy a lot of the time.

Of course, I was very rarely, if ever, unhappy when I was sitting in my seat on the show, pumped full of coffee, laughing and goofing on the world and having the world goof on me. That was *spectacular*. It was merely the rest of my existence that sucked. And call me crazy, but that mattered—matters—to me.

I know going to bed a bit early seems like a simple compromise for success, fame, and riches. And it is. And I know it sounds absurd that I couldn't do it. But after fifteen years, I finally realized I just couldn't, and wouldn't, and was never going to be able to do it. You know, the definition of insanity . . .

So when I had really had it and was seriously thinking about bailing from the show, a good friend said, "Before you jump ship, why not try getting an apartment in New York? You could get up an hour later and not have to commute both ways every day. That could help solve the problem."

It was a great idea. Believe it or not, I hadn't actually considered it before. I didn't want to buy a place in the city, nor did I have the energy or was I informed enough to go about it. And renting is burning money. But when the choices were viewed as "an apartment in New York or no *Stern Show*," it was a no-brainer. Nancy and I knew how to be apart (all too well), so that wasn't a problem.

My friend knew of a vacancy in a building near the station, I went and looked at it, went home, looked my therapist of two weeks in the eye, and said, "I'm going to do something major for myself. I'm going to rent an apartment in New York City. Even if it doesn't fix my life, it certainly can't hurt." And he agreed wholeheartedly.

I went in, signed the lease, went back and told the therapist I had made the move, and never saw him again.

Of course, as I way too often don't, I didn't think the idea through. Sure, now I could get up at 5:30 a.m. instead of 4:30 a.m. But out in sleepy Bayville, at least they roll back the streets at 7:00 p.m., and the only distraction is TV or Scrabble. Now I was in Manhattan—endless neon, screaming, "Come play." Fix schmix. One night I was sitting in Whiskey Blue next to Rachel Hunter and we all headed downtown at 2:00 a.m. Would *you* have gone home? Too many nights of rolling in at 4:00, and then jumping up out of bed nearly as soon as my head hit the pillow.

And then sitting in my seat at work at 11:00 a.m., the broadcast over, staring at the pile of lines I had written for the show that day and wondering where they came from. Who wrote *those?* Yeah, I had solved that problem.

And I knew there was no way I was going to stop drinking in this madness, as much as I knew I had to. As wrong as I now realize it was, there had to be some reward beckoning me to keep going. I needed to have Budweiser-soaked carrots hanging in front of me to spur me on. Foolhardily, I could only see the whole thing as a whole thing—an all-or-none proposition.

Another factor, which seemed to escape everyone, is that they had sat Benjy (Benjamin Bronk, an intern at the time) right next to me. In my little space, which was already tight. Elbow to elbow, doing the same thing as me, writing lines on the fly for Howard. For me to read, in addition to often reading Fred's lines, and then in addition to what I had written, having to decide which of the three pages to toss in front of Howard. Fred and I already had it covered—the show was a well-oiled engine and a juggernaut. It simply wasn't necessary. It was as if to say, "Should you decide to go anywhere, this guy can simply move over."

I'm not blaming Benjy. We all want to work, we all want to get ahead, we all want to be funny and want the world to know it. Everyone wanted to write lines for Howard. Stuttering John used to put lines on the computer screen in front of Howard above his descriptions of the phone calls he was putting through. I still don't know how Benjy finagled his way to that seat, but as an old finagler myself, I can only respect it.

To this day, I don't know for sure whose idea it was to put him there, but I'd bet my radio residuals it was Howard's agent—and Benjy's agent—Don Buchwald. I was never asked about it. Just one day, Gary Flooie told me that Benjy was going to sit in for the news. First during the news, at the tail end of the show, and then earlier and earlier. It wasn't only professionally insulting—I mean, as I said, I thought Fred and I had it pretty well covered for all those years—but Benjy was physically in my way. My workspace was small enough without him there.

Over the years on the show, I had become a caffeine addict. Howard's infamous "We'll be right back after these words" was usually followed by endless double-length commercial breaks, and in later years I usually didn't even come back to my seat for the "live" spot in the middle of the double sets of commercials unless it was a Heineken spot, so more often than not, I had as long as ten minutes to myself. During almost every commercial break, I was up to pee, or to get more coffee, or most often both. And every time, I had to climb around Benjy to get out and back in, like I was at a crowded movie and had to take a leak. And every single time, I got that crappy feeling in the pit of my stomach, the feeling that the situation sucked, that it was not only insulting, but worse, that it had absolutely been created to do just that. And I'll debate that with anyone.

It was such a blatant slap in the face, and I didn't know who to say what to. I didn't gripe about it. I wasn't going to take the bait and complain about my work situation and have Howard berate me on the air as a prima donna, as me denying Benjy a chance, or whatever. But it really felt like a big, hairy "fuck you" to me. I just let it fester in the back of my head to bolster my position when I decided to stand my ground for what I planned on asking for.

Also, from the minute I had returned from my previous contract holdout three years before, Howard had made a point of very often riding me with, "You better not ever pull that crap again. You walk again, you're out." And every time he did that, it cemented in my mind that at contract time, I most certainly would stand fast for what I wanted, using whatever means I had to. I guess we both stuck to our guns.

And, of course, there was me and Nancy. We knew for a long time, for years, that we were going to split up. We were very slow to get to it because there was just never any time. Even if I was going to be magnanimous enough to let her stay in our home, the little free time I had I certainly didn't want to spend apartment/house hunting and then moving into bachelor quarters.

But mainly, as far as my relationship was concerned, I was acutely aware that our marriage breaking up would certainly be plenty painful enough and the thought of it unspooling in front of the Stern listeners was chilling. I didn't even want to imagine the insensitive phone calls . . . Yow. So I knew that if I were no longer on the show, one small fringe benefit would be that Nancy and I could go our separate ways at least somewhat privately.

In discussing the negotiations, I'm going to use "we," meaning my lawyer and me. It sounds more professional, and "we" asking for more money reads much nicer than "I." By the way, the *Stern Show* screamed at me for years for not having representation, and then when I got great representation, they continuously got bent out of shape, railing on and on about "Jackie and his lawyer."

When we started negotiating, I was fifty-two, close to fifty-three. I knew that if I signed for another five years, at the end of the new contract, if I wasn't dead, besides being thoroughly spent, I'd be fifty-eight, very well-off, probably still drinking like a fish, still be in my marriage because I'd have been too exhausted to do anything about it, and most likely too beat to start anything of my own. Not to mention I'd certainly be faced with the same situation, because Howard is never going to stop doing *The Howard Stern Show*. It's as much a part of him as breathing. The day Howard dies, he'll have been on the radio that morning.

When I say, "When we started negotiating," it makes me smile. Everyone conveniently forgets that we couldn't begin discussing my deal until two weeks before the contract was due to be up on December 31, 2000, because until mid-December, Howard was still saying that *he* was done, that *he* wasn't re-signing, so it made no sense for anyone else to work out their deals. Meanwhile, the "anyone else" was only me. Howard Stern and Robin Quivers and Fred Norris were a package.

When Don Buchwald signed a deal, it was for all three of them, and everyone else, all the people under me, were station employees who would be automatically back on the bandwagon if and when that happened.

Everyone knew—or, at the very least, *I* knew—that Howard would re-sign, but it didn't happen until one of our last days before we all left for Christmas vacation. He had held out for what he wanted. And then he signed. Only then was it my turn. And so typically hypocritical, in the ensuing months, he rode me like a bastard for daring to hold out and trying to get what I wanted. For doing precisely what he had been doing only weeks earlier.

Of course, like nearly everybody, I have my price. So I decided to draw a line in the sand, and if I got what I asked for, or close, I'd stay. That was my deal with myself.

For a bunch of years, I'd been making good money. *Lots* of money. More money than someone on the radio should ever make, especially a side person. After years of gut-wrenching holdouts and standing as firm as I could whenever I could, I had at least gotten my salary up into a decent ballpark. We had gone down slightly in the ratings, so I wasn't hitting bonuses like I had a few times the first year of that last contract, which had sweetened the pot nicely a few times, but I had never really expected to hit my bonus—it had just been a way to break the vapor lock of the previous negotiation.

My final year on the show my base was just shy of $578,000. A fantastic salary. But we weren't just another show and we weren't just another *great* show; we were the Beatles of radio. (Yeah, they always broke my balls about using that analogy, but fuck, we *were*.) Howard was making gazillions, K-Rock and our affiliates were *printing* money, and I felt, as someone who had been there since almost the very beginning, who helped create this monster, to whatever degree (I know how debatable that is), I wanted in on the rewards.

And it made me crazy that adding or losing stations didn't affect my wages. I had been there fifteen years. I wanted to be *involved*, to be a partner, however minimally. You work at a law firm, after a certain amount of time, you're a junior partner. Even if you're way down on the masthead, you're a junior partner. Or you leave to find yourself a firm that respects your contributions.

If Gary came in and said, "Hey, Voff, today we add Toronto and Montreal as new affiliates," I wanted it to affect me, to affect my compensation. Our successes should have put a few more shekels in my pay envelope. It certainly didn't have to be a lot, just so the rise and fall of our show affected me. If he came in and said, "We just lost Dallas and Indianapolis," I wanted that to affect me, too—a few *less* shekels in the envelope. It was like I was playing a game and they were saying, "Give it everything you've got, but pay no attention to the scoreboard."

Of course, they wouldn't do that, because then I'd have known what kind of revenue the show was bringing in and that secret was buried under Jimmy Hoffa. So the only time there would be any pay increases would be at contract time.

Like I said, my last salary was $578,000. It had been $500,000 in 1998, then a 7.5 percent raise to $537,000 in 1999, and then another 7.5 percent raise to $578,000 in 2000. To celebrate and compensate my fifteen years as head writer, on-air personality, an important driving force, and a charter member of the uncontested champs of American drive-time radio, and maybe the Greatest Show On Earth, for my new contract, K-Rock general manager Tom Chiusano offered me a 6 percent raise, to $611,000.

I had decided my line in the sand would be an average of one million dollars a year over the next five years: $800,000, $900,000, $1,000,000, $1,100,000, and $1,200,000. A lot of money, yes, but certainly not unfair figures. My lawyer suggested we take a long shot and ask to start the five years at a million, with $100,000 bumps each year, figuring that after the expected back-and-forth squabbling, we'd hopefully be able to settle for what I needed to make.

Maybe it sounds crazy to some, not so much to others, but that's what I wanted. Hey, I was *done*. But I guess for *that* amount of money, I was willing to die. Howard always rants about how cheap I am. Isn't the ultimate act of a cheapskate to die for a few bucks? So there's your proof.

So my lawyer asked for $1,000,000. After a while Tom recovered.

It was immediately very clear, at least to me, that this was going to take a lot of effort and patience, if it was going to happen at all. I knew, or was at least determined at the time, that we were going to get what I wanted, or reasonably close, or I was through. I had long since shored myself up for it.

It was Christmas vacation and Tom was going to France for the holidays. His health had very recently been through the mill and I wanted him to go enjoy himself without the hassles of my contract. The bottom line is I love the guy, and his wife, and who knows if he'd be getting another shot at Paris. That may sound like I'm trying to position myself as having been a good guy, but it's the truth, and this book, if nothing else, is all about the truth and nothing but.

So I said, "Tom, go have your vacation, and when we get back, I'll continue to work under my old contract, and hopefully we'll eventually agree on a deal."

We came back from Christmas vacation and I worked under my old contract, with the understanding that if and when we came to an agreement, my new salary would be retroactive to the first of the year.

Tom came up to $625,000. We didn't budge. Tom came up to $650,000 and said that was it, as much as he had to offer me. We came down to $900,000. That was the first week in January.

Then, nothing from him for almost two months. Nothing. Nada. Zero. No counteroffer, no phone calls, no emails, no communication whatsoever. Like I said, I was willing to settle at $800,000, with $100,000 bumps. But their side was totally silent.

In the beginning of March, we asked to meet with Tom. On Wednesday afternoon, February 28, at my lawyer's office, Tom reiterated that $650,000 was all they had. It was a five-year deal, with very decent increases: $650,000, $715,000, $765,000, $825,000, and $900,000. ($900,000! *Fuck!*)

He also said that if I didn't sign by that Friday, the offer, which included the retroactive difference in salary, which at this point was a decent hunk of change, would be off the table.

(Tom also made a joke about how he'd love to save my salary and it was totally harmless in the context of the discussion that day. I mentioned it to Howard when I spoke to him that following Monday night and not in the lighthearted vein in which it was delivered. I have since, and here again, apologize to Tom for my being a dick.)

My lawyer said, "Okay. I'm advising Jackie to stay home on Monday until we get this settled."

Tom said, "Okay. But I think you're making a mistake."

We said, "And we think *you're* making a mistake."

I said, "And Tom, Howard of course knows every detail of our negotiations, and you'll be sure to tell him I won't be in Monday, right?"

And Tom assured me, "Of course."

I also emailed Howard that Sunday night to tell him I wouldn't be coming in the next day, or maybe never, if we couldn't come to a deal.

And, of course, the next day, Monday, March 5, Howard, with all of his theatrics, moaned, "Where's Jackie?"

And of course Robin immediately took up the charge, ranting, "He left you high and dry *again*, with no warning?" And from what I was told, she remained on the warpath for a long, long time.

Hell, Howard knew before my *last* walkout, in 1998, that I wasn't coming in on that Monday, and they had played the exact same scene. And—seriously—Robin was just calming down from *that* "unannounced abandonment" when *this* one occurred.

I didn't call Howard that Sunday night—I almost didn't even email him—to tell him that I wasn't coming in that Monday, because I knew he had been made fully aware, and I had always played along with his charade of "keeping him out of the negotiations," even though he was always right there, only the slightest bit removed. But Robin and the listeners wanted my head, all of them so sure that I had tried to screw the show by not telling anyone I wasn't going to be there that day.

After speaking to a lot of people, I took their collective advice and called Howard that Monday night. Continuing the charade, I told him that we wanted to negotiate, but we were hitting a brick wall with Tom, that there had been no communication in months. I assured him that other than that, there was no problem, that it was nothing more than a case of dollars and cents and that we didn't think we were being at all unreasonable.

I could tell as I spoke to him that his relatively new girlfriend was sitting there, because he was acting somewhat "on," and posing a bit. It wasn't the one-to-one Howard I knew and had grown somewhat close to after eighteen years together. So the conversation basically went nowhere. We weren't on the same wavelength. Maybe we wouldn't have been, anyway. I'll never know.

We hung up nicely enough, neither of us knowing how it would play out. Of course, he had 100 percent control of how it would play out—whether or not he'd already decided that the door was going to be shut to me for good by then, again, I'll never know.

Initially, being off the show was much, much harder than I had imagined it would be. I had thought so long and hard about all the nuts and bolts of the situation, but hadn't realized what should have been the most obvious. Forget the money, the fame, the daily routine that structures your life, the sense of belonging, the perks. What I really missed was the actual show, our antics, and the incredibly stimulating workout my coffee-drenched mind got every morning sitting in that seat with my trusty Sharpie pen and my stack of paper, churning out lines like a factory worker, giggling and howling and basking in the wonder that was that room.

It may seem ludicrous now, but I hadn't realized how much of my psyche, my daily juices, my very essence, were derived from laughing like a hyena four or five hours a day, five days a week. Maybe I figured they'd kick in wherever I was. As obvious as it should have been, I never really thought to myself, "You know, you won't be laughing and using your mind like that five hours a day anymore after you leave. Not anywhere else on the planet. It's not a normal situation."

That was a wild wake-up call. But it was just something I had to deal with.

I did feel so, so bad about breaking up the core team. But again, I wasn't *trying* to. Doing the show is really rough, it's a full-time commitment, a life-draining undertaking (there's a weird word choice), and I wanted to be paid handsomely for it. I wanted them to share our incredible, unmatched success with me. What I was asking for wasn't ridiculous. I had been there since the onset of the morning show's rise, I was a founding father, and I wanted my salary to acknowledge it.

But it killed me. For so long, every interview I'd done, I'd always said with great pride, "This morning I worked with the same people that were there when I walked into the WNBC studios for the first time in February of 1983: Howard Stern, Robin Quivers, and Fred Norris. How many people can say that?"

That had been eighteen years ago. Almost nothing lasts that long—rock bands, marriages, TV shows, damn near nothing. And now, I had done it. I had broken up the *Beatles.* I was Joke Yoko.

There was no communication of any kind for almost two months after I had stopped coming to work. The first week of May 2001, I called my lawyer and said, "I've thrown out all my resolve, all my logic, and all my reasoning. Sleep or no sleep, it's too weird. I miss it so much. I'm sure we've let it go too long, but just in case we haven't, please call Tom and tell him we'll take their last offer if it's still on the table."

He called Tom and then called me back and said that he had left a message for Tom to call him.

When Tom called back, he told my lawyer, "After I got the message you called, I saw Howard in the hall. I told him that Jackie's lawyer had called, and that he might be calling to take the offer. And Howard said to me, 'Do we want Jackie back?'"

My lawyer told Tom that was indeed why he'd called and that if the offer was still available, we'd take it. Tom said he'd relate that to Howard and get back to him with Howard's answer either way.

I called Howard, left a message, and he called me back.

After we fucked around playfully for a few minutes like we usually do, I said, "I just wanted to make sure you know that my lawyer just spoke to Tom and told him that if the last offer's still on the table we'll take it."

Howard said, "Okay. Thanks for calling. I haven't hired anyone else yet. We'll let you know."

We never got a call back—not even an email—from Tom, or Howard, or anyone. Not to this day.

I was all over the place. On one hand, it felt great to have stood up for myself and to again be the untied free spirit I'd always been. Most of the time I had no regrets; I knew I had done what I had to do.

Yet at some point, I inexplicably wrote a heartfelt email to Howard telling him I'd made a blunder and really wanted to rejoin the gang. I never got any response to that, either.

I've been told secondhand of lots of things that were said on the air about how I had supposedly said I'd never come back to the show, that I didn't ever want to be there again, that they had kept the seat open for as long as they could, whatever. But again, for the record, we asked for my job back in the beginning of May and Artie Lange, my replacement, wasn't hired until that October.

In fact, fairly soon after 9/11, when everybody in New York was so disheartened and depressed, I wrote Howard another very sincere email, saying I really wanted to return to the show and that I thought the horrible tragedy was a perfect window for me to return, for us to reunite. That New York badly needed *anything* that would symbolize any kind of "return to normalcy," especially anything that would lighten things up at all, and judging from the hundreds and hundreds of emails and the people I ran into everywhere I went (even to this day), so many of the listeners were rooting for my return that it seemed like an ideal time to bury the hatchet, let bygones be bygones, or simply tear down whatever walls that were (are) in the way, and make the show whole again. Just because it would have been a nice thing, a positive thing, for the TriState area. Though very well known to be greatly at odds at the time, Bill Clinton and Al Gore had sat next to each other at a memorial mass, so I wrote in the email: "Even Clinton and Gore are sitting side by side, putting their differences behind them. Surely we should." Yeah, it reads pretty pompous now, but as self-serving as it may read, it seemed like a great idea back then, in the midst of those horrifying weeks and months. It was straight from my heart. I suggested that perhaps we should get together and discuss it.

He wrote back to the effect of, "We're not politicians, we're comedians," and that was that, never addressing getting together. That had been my third attempt at getting together with him, the third time I had asked him point-blank, "Let's get together," and each time when he responded, he failed to address getting together. So as sad as it made me, at the time, I abandoned the idea.

2003

MY OLD PAL DAN

Since forever, I've always responded to every letter and every email (try me, jokeland@aol.com). Over the years, that policy's wound up connecting me with many incredibly interesting people and lots of old (now really old) friends, spanning my entire life since back before there was electricity.

Years ago, I was working in south Florida. On Friday afternoon, I got an email from a guy that read, in essence, could he get two free tickets to my Saturday show the next night at New York Comedy Club in Boca Raton. He signed off "your old pal Dan Fremont" and there was a phone number. (I made up "Fremont," I don't remember his last name.) (He'd probably appreciate its absence, anyway.)

I have a great memory, but as I scanned my mind and my electronic Rolodex, no "Dan Fremont" popped up. My curiosity was, of course, killing me, so I called.

Many years ago, a guy came on *The Howard Stern Show*, the premise being he was going to fart a tune. That, or maybe his goal was to do an incredibly long fart . . . But that's not important.

What's important is that Howard introduced Dan the Farter, he came into the studio and laid plastic on the floor a few short feet in front of Howard and me and Fred (Robin was as always safely tucked behind the

233

Robin Quivers Memorial Glass Window), pulled down his pants and his underpants, bent over, strained, and proceeded to poop onto the plastic.

By the early nineties, we'd been at it on the *Stern Show* for quite a few years. We'd had in a lot of weirdos and seen more than anybody can imagine—but this was an entirely new dimension, in a class (?) by itself.

I'm sure we quickly made with all the classic, "Hey, the guy had to clear his throat" and all that malarkey, and I know we roared as loudly as we ever had, but what I best remember is how violently I gagged. Merely the talk of that kind of activity is enough to set me off—watching me gag or almost gag was probably my SiriusXM cohost Ian McKean Karr's favorite perk working with me every Tuesday night on *Jackie's Joke Hunt*—and here this guy actually made a doo-doo right there.

It steamed and reeked as we went into panic mode, with Howard screaming for somebody to pick it up and get it the hell out of there and everybody else trying to figure out whose job it was to do that. Between laughing and gagging, my head was spinning like a top. I was on Pluto. You may not believe me, but I'm gagging a bit right now as I type.

Needless to say, Dan the Farter was quickly escorted out.

Confounding everybody, and me, to this day, Howard decided to give the guy a second chance.

A few weeks later, Howard introduces Dan the Farter's encore, Dan walks in, lays down plastic in the same place, pulls down his pants and his underpants, bends over, strains a bit, and then to our indescribable amazement and bewilderment he craps again.

Dèjá stool. Same scene. I gagged, we all howled, the show went into panic mode, and again, as quickly as it could happen, somebody dragged the excrement and the excrementer out of the studio.

I'm still trying to wrap my brain around the fact that it happened *once*, and it happened *twice*.

When we were in a second-floor television studio about to shoot the 3D Tarzan sketch for the *Stern Show* video *Butt Bongo Fiesta*, I understood the poor elephant letting go of his bowels in the TV studio after being scared by a journey up the freight elevator. *Ooo-eee* . . . That, my friend, was a gag fest for the ages. (That delightfully scatological footage can be seen next to the credit roll on the video.)

But this was a grown man in a somewhat normal room. And he did it twice.

And now here I was more than a decade later on the phone with "my old pal Dan."

Once upon a radio show, he had defecated in front of me. Twice. "Old pal" was quite a stretch.

I gave him the tickets, of course. Luckily, I had quit drinking by then . . . or I might have had him open the show.

P.S. Dan's a good guy. We hung out after my show and, needless to say, we had some pretty hearty laughs.

But, no, I didn't go eat with the guy.

2017

IS THERE LIFE AFTER STERN?

That's not a million-dollar question. That's a goodbye-millions-of-dollars question.

Actually, it's a ridiculous question. Of course life goes on. It goes on after anything short of death. And even after that if you're one of those.

Since I left the show, has it been a total joyride? No. Do I regret leaving? Sometimes. Did I love every minute of it while it lasted? Just about.

Am I financially set?

To quote Jackie Mason, as I have a zillion times since March 2001, "I never have to work again. Unless I want to *buy* something, that's another story . . ."

Since I left *The Howard Stern Show*, I've laid pretty low. I quit drinking, which I always knew I had to do at some point. Nancy and I divorced and I moved into a home on the beach by myself. The only thing in my life that hasn't changed recently has been the frequency of my masturbation, and that information I choose to keep to myself.

Like I said, I was simply holding out for the money I thought I deserved, or closer to it. Nothing more, nothing less. With very varying degrees of intensity I was of course hoping they'd come back to the table with another counteroffer, which they never did. I knew there was a decent chance, with each passing day after I walked out, that my door to the show may have been slowly closing for good, but I went with it, even knowing full well that leaving the show would be a huge life jolt. Because I knew the jolt would be both positive and negative.

Was I mentally prepared to be off the show for good? As much as I could be, I guess. I weighed the pros and cons countless times and always came to the same decision. The truth is, the money we were talking about wasn't a mind-boggling amount considering the immense success of the show. It's an incredible cash cow. So my lawyer and I were both fairly surprised when they wouldn't continue to negotiate at all. I still don't know whose decision it was to completely halt negotiations, whether it was Howard, CEO Mel Karmazin, Tom Chiusano, or Don Buchwald. I'm sure they always acted in concert, I just wonder who spearheaded the slamming of the door.

People ask if I felt any sense of betrayal by my fellow cast members. And the answer is: no, I didn't. Maybe that's a bit naive, who knows? It's how I choose to feel. We were all very close—or at least went through a lot together—for a long, long time.

I've honestly never listened to the show, so I have no idea what Robin or anyone has said about me, except what's been relayed to me by countless people, all of which seems incredibly varied and inconsistent. I don't think I'll ever know what's been actually said. Hey, do we ever? What is life if not a never-ending game of "Telephone"?

People ask if Howard did all he could do to keep me on the show. Well, after I told him I was willing to take the last deal on the table, he never called. And he certainly got and still gets whatever he wants. So all he had to do was call and say, "The deal's still good, come in Monday." So, did Howard do all he could to keep me? The answer is no.

If anything about the end rubbed me wrong—and just about none of it did, because I made my bed and was fully prepared to lie in it—it was Tom never calling back to say, "No thanks, it's too late."

I went to lunch with Tom and John and Gary in the spring of 2004 to get Tom to admit in person to the guys the true story of my not returning to the show, that no matter what had been bandied about on the air, that two months after I walked, my lawyer and I had called and said I wanted to come back. After at first saying he didn't remember—which was a tough one to swallow—Tom finally copped to it.

People ask me when I first realized I wasn't ever going to be back on the show, was I depressed, relieved, scared, excited . . . what? All I can say is it cured my constipation.

As far as me and Nancy, we had been on the verge of splitting up for years, but no one knew it. I think a lot of people think my leaving the show caused us to break up, but all it did was logistically give us the time and space to go our own ways. It was totally amicable and our decades-long friendship remained and remains intact.

I think it's a little weird, but very few other radio shows have come knocking. I think maybe Howard actually convinced the world that I was very hard to work with, a pain in the ass and a nonstop complainer. *Hmmm . . .*

I'm a very nostalgic guy, so I have a doorbell that plays my theme from the show, a calliope version of the circus music "Entrance of the Gladiators." And it always confuses me, because it makes me think Fred is in my kitchen. And there's nothing scarier than thinking Fred is in your kitchen, except for maybe Fred actually being in your kitchen.

2006

THE JACKIE PUPPET'S MISSING

I left *The Howard Stern Show* in March 2001. The gang remained at K-Rock 92.3FM until Howard's contract expired in December 2005, when they pulled up stakes and moved to Sirius Satellite Radio.

Much of the following is me speculating what happened, filling in the blanks from what I know for sure, to accomplish getting this story across:

At some point after they got to Sirius, I guess someone asked, "Where's the Jackie Puppet?" It wasn't anywhere in or around the new radio studio or the Stern offices at Sirius. Nobody could answer the question, or could even remember seeing it or moving it since they had left K-Rock.

It was suggested that maybe it had been left behind in a closet or somewhere at K-Rock, as no one could remember bringing it to the new location.

Then somebody said, "Jackie came in to K-Rock a few times to do some shows."

I had. I did a test talk show and two interviews on Penn Jillette's show when K-Rock 92.3FM had become Free-FM for five minutes.

They then took a shot in the dark: "Maybe Jackie found it and stole it."

It seems pretty quickly they settled on, "Yes, that would answer it, Jackie has it." And of course, the word got to me.

Never one to not play along with the absurdity of the *Stern Show* and how remarkably off course it can and usually does get when it comes to everything Jackie, I hatched an idea.

I blew up a picture of the Jackie Puppet's head and torso, mounted it on cardboard, held it the proper distance away so the size would be right, and had a pal take a picture of me holding the dummy while also holding up a copy of the front page of that day's *New York Post*, like it was a kidnapping. The picture was perfect.

I emailed the picture to Steve Langford and Lisa G at Howard 100 News and said, "Yeah, I got the puppet, come on out and fetch it."

They were all ready to hop in their news van and come to Long Island when I emailed a side-view picture of me with the very thin cardboard puppet.

Then I called and said, "You morons, of *course* I don't have the puppet."

Then I got a brainstorm.

I called Langford and said, "I know exactly what to do. You guys think I have the puppet or something to do with its disappearance? Get the lie detector guy the show always uses and line up anybody who might have anything to do with this case. I'll go first. You can ask me anything, you'll see right away I had nothing to do with it and you'll also find the culprit."

Langford said, "What a great idea, Jackie. You're a genius. I'll tell Howard and we'll do the lie detector tests as soon as we can."

Steve called Howard and told him my idea,

The next morning, Howard showed up with the Jackie Puppet, which had been at his house the entire time, and it was never addressed again.

2015

YEAH YEAH YEAH

For decades, I argued with Howard about Paul McCartney. One of my regrets about leaving the show was that Paul was finally a guest two months after my much-maligned departure and has made fairly regular appearances since.

The late Noel Redding, bassist in the Jimi Hendrix Experience and a Stern guest multiple times, loved my joke tapes and would often tell me he and Paul and their wives had spent hours telling jokes at dinner the night before. I'd heard from other sources, too, that Paul loves jokes, dirty jokes of course, telling them and hearing them. And joke tellers love to hang with me, which has nothing to do with anything other than if they don't already know, aside from me being a terrific audience and a good laugher, they very quickly realize they're going to walk away with a few new ones, and more than likely great ones at that.

So I've always maintained that if I got to spend five or ten minutes with McCartney he'd both enjoy me and want to connect with me simply because he'd realize I'm a terrific source for jokes.

I don't think that, I *know* that. Joke tellers, the folks who are really into it, have a connection. It's a bond that crosses all barriers, much like people who like to play hockey or who follow the Jets. It's a very strong common denominator.

Thanks to my pal Tom Bernard, copresident of Sony Pictures Classics, I'm on the event invitation list of eminent PR guru Peggy Siegal and on November 20, 2015 (an important date for me, as I crossed something off my bucket list), the lovely Barbara Klein and I were at the Museum of Modern Art for a screening of the incredible film *The Big Short*.

The revelers at the cocktail hour before the screening were an eclectic group—the film's producers Lorne Michaels and Tina Fey, the film's director Adam McCay, actress Candice Bergen—and a host of many folks I'm sure I should have recognized but didn't.

No sooner had Barbara said to me, "I want to do something fun in here . . ." (she's so great), down the stairs came Paul McCartney and his wife Nancy Shevell.

I said to Barbara, "You realize for many moons I've wanted to tell jokes with him, right?"

She said, "Well, then, you've got to go do it."

I said, "Man, I'd love to. But I'm sure there's not a person in this room who doesn't think they've got a perfectly legitimate reason to approach Sir Paul and strike up a conversation about their favorite Beatles song or where they were in 1964. And that'd be crummy. He and his lady should be able to meander about the party unencumbered, that's what New York City is all about."

Of course, she knew that. And of course, as I said it, my mind was racing, thinking about all the near misses I've had trying to get in his presence to fire off a few.

As if we willed it, almost right away here come Paul and Nancy, who had cruised the edge of the gathering and were now walking directly toward us, smiling and nodding and saying polite "hello's" as they approached.

The devil got me.

As they were about to stroll past us, I very gently stopped the cute Beatle and out of Nancy's earshot said, "Can I tell you a joke?"

Only slightly taken aback, he said, "Sure."

So I did . . .

A guy's at a job interview.
The interviewer says, "What do you think is your biggest fault?"

The guy says, "I think my biggest fault is my honesty."
The interviewer says, "I don't think honesty is a fault."
The guy says, "I don't give a fuck what you think."

Paul threw his head back a bit as he laughed out loud, said, "I like that one," and they continued on, making their way to Lorne and Tina.

The most absurd thing about that joke is, years before, my good pal Ed Hamell, a spectacular singer-songwriter and all-around magnificent artist, had been a guest on my SiriusXM radio show, *Jackie's Joke Hunt*, and when he walked in, the first thing he said to me was, "I love your joke emails. The best one in the last batch was . . ."

And he told me that joke. And I howled.

Meanwhile, the joke not only hadn't been in my last emailing, I'd never heard it before.

And when I told him that, Ed actually *argued* with me that it had been in the mailing.

I said, "Hamell, you nincompoop, if my memory's good enough to know damn near every joke in the world, I think it's good enough to know when I hear one I *don't* know."

I've used that joke in every show since. And every show I smile when I get to it, because I think about Ed and I of course think about how funny the joke is and how hard the crowd's going to laugh when they hear it.

The postscript to this tale is that it certainly seemed like Sir Paul hadn't heard that joke before. In which case, I'm almost sure as he walked away, he ran it through his head, to cement it, so it'd enter his repertoire, so *he* could tell it, because it's a downright wonderful joke.

And I'd give odds that in the days after I told it to him, he told the joke three, maybe five or seven times. Or more. Because it was his new baby.

That's what us joke tellers do.

2017

HOW DRY I AM

I've been my definition of sober since Cinco de Mayo (May 5) 2001. The fact it happened to be Cinco de Mayo was not in any way by design, so it has no bearing other than it's odd inasmuch as it's a day of wild celebration for many, many people. I haven't had a drink, but I've smoked pot on and off, more on than off, the entire time. No cocaine or hallucinogens or any designer drugs, just pot and occasionally hash or whatever other incarnations of good old weed.

Folks in AA, as well as many people, claim I'm not sober, because I still get stoned, and that I'm still a drunk, a "dry drunk," not having gone through the steps of sobriety. Fuck them ... I'm sober. And I'm doing just fine at that. I may be a mess by many a yardstick, but I haven't had a drink in well over fifteen years and I've never slipped, other than taking the occasional glug out of a friend's rum and Coke thinking it was my Diet Coke.

And hey, now I'm off Diet Coke.

Perhaps this is a *non sequitur*, but I think it plays in a bit, because I also think everything in life weighs in when it comes to your habits and addictions, good or bad.

The question "Did you have a happy childhood?" pops up often, from therapists or friends or whoever.

I'd tell my first therapist, who was also an alcohol counselor, I had a happy childhood.

And she'd tell me I'd merely convinced myself of it.

Help me here . . . What's the difference?

My kindergarten report card reads, "Jackie has a very sunny disposition and is a pleasure to have in my class."

What'd, I *forge* that?

And as I paraded through my early years, life in school and at home and with friends—with the normal ups and downs—was a total joy. That's my story and I'm sticking to it.

Truth is, I think "Did you have a happy childhood?" is a ridiculous question, because there's no control to the experiment, and happiness is a relative term.

You can't compare your childhood to kids who live in completely different places and situations, because you weren't there. You can't compare your childhood to your friends who were the same age, because you have no idea what was going on behind their closed doors. So the only people you can compare your childhood to are your brothers and sisters, but being different ages, they experienced your family at different stages of its development and well-being, and thus were interacting with an entirely different set of people.

So I tell people the only person I can compare my childhood to is me, and I'd have to say compared to me it was about the same.

That said . . .

I've never figured out what makes us drink or not drink. I had a few childhood experiences that absolutely should have chased me from the demon alcohol, but no. I'll share a few.

My brother Bobby often related that one time when he was just a little kid he was sitting between my father, who was driving, and Pop's older brother Chester, on the way home from a typical well-lubricated Sunday visit with Uncle Clem and Aunt Edith in Bayville, probably to watch the Yankees game, or Great-Uncle Len Hall on *Meet the Press*, or both.

Uncle Chet had been struck between the eyes with a baseball that was hit back to the box while he was pitching a sandlot game in his late twenties and had gradually lost his sight until he was totally blind. He and Aunt Tess and their two sons lived a few doors down from us, so he spent a lot of time at our house drinking with my father. He'd have his son Peter—the same cousin Pete whose dirty poem inspired my life of punch lines—walk him to our house, sit him at the kitchen table with my father, and they were off. He was always singing and carrying on, often with one of us on his lap, occasionally drifting off-color, and us kids were just crazy about him.

The first few miles of the drive from Bayville to East Norwich are spectacular. Very winding and narrow, two-lane West Shore Road runs along Oyster Bay, the actual body of water.

A lifetime of cruising it has not diminished its charm a bit.

A bit tipsy, my father was swerving enough that Bobby was scared and saying stuff like, "Pop! Be careful!"

After Bobby had voiced his concern a few times, Uncle Chet said, with a big smile, "Bob, don't worry about your old man. Believe me, your old man can take a drink. The only time you gotta worry about your old man is when his lower lip starts to sag."

Bobby looked over and Pop's bottom lip was hanging down like a Ubangi.

For countless years, we've laughed and laughed at that story, never stopping long enough to think about just how scary it is.

To us, that seemed perfectly . . . normal. Yow.

One night in the fifties—I have no idea how old I was, but I'm guessing eight, give or take . . . the clues are I know I was pretty young, my father's drinking had kicked in pretty well, the East Norwich Firehouse is now across the street, but it obviously wasn't as yet, and our milkman was involved . . . I woke up to the smell of smoke. I ran downstairs and it got harder to see as the smoke got thicker on my way down.

My father was passed out on the couch in the living room at the bottom of the stairs.

I shook him awake and said, "*Pop!* There's a *fire!*"

He jumped up, and upon inspection, we realized my father had passed out and his lit cigarette was smoldering in the couch. We opened the front door and carried the smoking couch out and down the porch stairs. No sooner had we gotten it out onto the front walk when, thanks to the now-available oxygen, it burst into flames.

I have no recollection if the rest of the family was awake at this point, and I have no idea why we never called in the fire. I'm thinking we were too busy dealing with the situation.

Our house is right on Route 106, but in the mid-fifties East Norwich was a small village, the area was still very rural, and I'm pretty sure not one car passed by while all this was going down.

My father and I carried out endless buckets of water and poured it on until not only was the fire out, but the couch had stopped smoking, at which point we poured on a lot more. Then we opened all the windows so the smoke would clear out and went back to bed.

However much later, I was awakened again, this time by pounding on the front door. I went and shook Pop awake and we ran downstairs. We opened the door and there was the milkman, pointing to the couch on the front walk. It was engulfed in flames . . . it looked like a bonfire. It had slowly smoldered until it was ready to let the oxygen perform its encore.

Once again, we schlepped endless buckets of water and poured it on the couch until we were sure it was out, really out, *reeaalllyyy* out. I don't remember if we broke it up or pulled off the cover material or both, or what we did to ensure it was out for good. It's a blur.

All I'm certain is alcohol was the culprit.

How long would it have been before it ignited in the house? I've had nightmares about it ever since. We never had a fire alarm or fire extinguishers or anything like that in the house, ever. It was all wood, having been most likely built from a kit in 1900. It would have been leveled in a heartbeat.

Family Christmas has always been wonderful, no matter what, but my holiday memories of the fifties are storybook.

When Bobby, Kathy, and I were young kids, each December, if not earlier, we'd make out our Christmas lists. There'd always be a present or two on each of our lists that we really wanted, more than anything else, and Pop was really good at accomplishing that. He'd chase down what we had our hearts set on and more than very often we'd get whatever they were, which with three children so vastly different had to have been a formidable task.

Logically, each Christmas, Pop's drinking would have escalated another twelve months' worth, but thus far it hadn't taken a toll on his role as Santa.

One Christmas morning, we were, as always, up scary early and under the tree tearing into our presents when we slowly started to realize something was wrong. As we finished opening everything, our main gifts hadn't materialized. But as always, our parents had been more than generous.

Much later, when my father appeared, moving very slowly as it had been a very rough night—lots of drinking, lots of wrapping—one by one, we made comments to the effect of, "Hey, Pop, this is all so great. I didn't really need a discus and a shot put . . ." "I love my stuff, I didn't really need that science kit . . ." "Daddy, I don't mind that I didn't get the high-chair doll . . ."

Slowly it started to register with Pop and he said, "Wait . . . *wait!* I *got* all those things."

We all followed him up into the attic, which in addition to being storage for everything the family had accumulated since 1900, was his on-deck circle for each year's gifts.

And there, way back in a corner, was the discus, the shot put, the science kit, and the high-chair doll, as well as a few other glorious items. They were our most important requests and to make sure it was a great Christmas, he had bought them first, so they were the first things to be put up there to await the big day. A bit bombed, he had missed them when he brought everything else downstairs to wrap and then put under the tree.

To put it mildly, we were ecstatic. A good Christmas became a Christmas for the Ages. There hasn't been a holiday season since where we haven't rejoiced in the telling of our Instant Replay Christmas.

Happy ending or not, the story is a direct result of alcohol.

So, so long ago—I hope it was in college, but it very well may have been high school—I picked up a *Reader's Digest* that had an article to the tune of "Thirteen Surefire Signs You're An Alcoholic."

If memory serves me, like so many bartenders did, I went through those thirteen bullet points more than once trying to find a few that didn't apply to me.

But fuck them.

"If you work all week for the reward of a drink on Friday, you're an alcoholic."

Well, yes, I do. Don't know many people who don't. Fuck you.

One of the Dreaded Thirteen always stayed with me:

"If you can remember your first drink, you're an alcoholic."

New Year's Eve 1960—seventh grade—I stole a bottle of Scotch from my house.

My father was deputy superintendent of highways, a politically connected job. (His boss, superintendent of highways and later town supervisor, Thomas Pynchon Sr., was the father of world-class author and sometime recluse Thomas Pynchon.) On Long Island, in those days, the Republicans more than ruled the roost, and my father's uncle, Leonard W. Hall, had been Eisenhower's campaign manager in 1952 and 1956 and was national chairman of the Republican Party, thus the great gig for Pop.

So every Christmas, we'd get deliveries of case after case of booze— and the occasional fruit basket—that were sent by various contractors and builders, all vying for the ridiculously lucrative contracts to build and repair the roads in the Town of Oyster Bay, until the attic was so stacked with hooch there was hardly room for Pop's Christmas gifts. So the pilfered bottle of Scotch wasn't missed. Hell, a *case* wouldn't have been missed.

Me and the guys bought a bunch of quart bottles of Coca-Cola to mix with the booze and went to a new development where there were frames of partially built houses, a perfect spot for dopey kids like us to experiment with the demon sauce.

We poured some of the Coke out of one of the quarts and filled it back up with Scotch. As we drank it, we'd put in more Scotch, so each bottle got progressively stronger, and after repeating the pattern a few times we were pretty well embalmed.

I vividly remember staggering into the house and making it to the bottom of the stairs just as my parents were coming in from wherever they'd been . . .

My mother took a look at unsteady me and said, "John! He's been *drinking!*"

I could swear my father looked at me and yelled at me to get to bed as he was thinking, "That's my boy."

Case in point:

The smell of Scotch still takes me to that night.

Although I did do a pretty good job of trying to forget I ever read that article.

I was born in 1948, my brother Bobby came along in 1950, and my sister Kathy popped onto the scene in 1954. Until the late fifties, even the early sixties, we had a typical and truthfully pretty wonderful family, living in the quaint little suburb of East Norwich, just south of Oyster Bay on the glorious Gold Coast, the North Shore of Long Island, New York.

On a typical Sunday night, we'd be eating roast beef sandwiches made with the leftovers from that day's roast beef dinner. (Countless people shared those Sunday afternoon meals with my family and fondly recall them.) Us kids would be watching cowboy Roy Rogers' TV show, and before Ed Sullivan, Pop and my sister would hop in the car and fetch us all ice cream cones from Freddie's Luncheonette. We were a living, breathing Norman Rockwell painting.

My father's father had been a blacksmith, apprenticed by the generation of his family that preceded him, and though in very bad repair, his blacksmith barn still majestically stood on the corner of our property until the late sixties. So we were hardly what people conjured up when they were talking about our hunk of Long Island, then and now scattered with huge turn-of-the century mansions financed and owned by the moneyed class, the power brokers who basically controlled the country.

When my father moved to a better job that involved long, wet lunches with various businessmen, he started drinking more and coming home later and later. He'd miss more and more suppers and it got progressively more tense and continued to for years.

I imagine I started to drink because I'd watched my parents do it for as long as I'd been around.

But more importantly, I got used to being alone and finding ways to occupy my time. It was actually in many ways the perfect breeding ground for creativity.

My brother Bobby and I were pretty close in the early years, but when we got to our teens, I was a few years ahead, and we split off. He was smarter and more adventuresome, being one of the first in the neighborhood to smoke pot. He actually did the whole hippie thing before there was such thing as hippies.

I wasn't an anti-pot guy, I just couldn't imagine being able to have a better time than I was having—loving high school and the soccer team and the gymnastics team and the track team and chorus and school plays, playing in a rock and roll band, really enjoying my job as head busboy at Piping Rock Country Club (which was as much fun as going out), experimenting with girls as much as was humanly possible, and drinking. Lots of drinking. Who needed weed?

Even after I started smoking pot in the summer of 1967, which he was thrilled to hear, Bobby and I really never got close again. We had lots of fun together, with our many mutual friends, but over the years we drifted further and further apart. And though I'm aware and thrilled many people like and even love me, one of the ones who didn't was my own brother. And it festered to where he despised me. He died a few months ago, in late 2016, hating me. People have a hard time believing me when I tell them this, but I have no idea what fueled his hatred for me. And now I'll never know.

People suggest, "Maybe he was jealous of your success," but he hated me long before success looked like even a remote possibility for me. And as far as any other comparisons, he was very handsome and athletic and off-the-charts smart and funny—he was dealt an incredible hand in life—so that kind of jealousy is off the table. I truly have no idea. And it hurt, really hurt, for a long time. And of course, it still does. Truth be told, I was drinking too much long before he hated me (or was aware he hated me), so I have no idea if or to what extent that may have played into my habit(s).

In addition to whatever else he was dabbling in at any given time, Bobby drank way too much, for way too long, just as I had. That was the main cause of his passing. It of course haunts me that perhaps he was following in my misguided footsteps, but I'm fairly sure he never looked up to me. It's much more probable he took his lead from our very thirsty family.

My sister was much younger than me when we were in school, and moving at my whirlwind pace, I wasn't very close to her back then. But now she and her two great kids, Jessica and Brendan, make my life worthwhile. She's Katie Dunn to most people, having acquired that name from her late husband Jimmy Dunn, a guy who was as sweet as her. To me, she's caught right in the middle between Kathy Martling and Katie Dunn and I never know what I'm going to call her until I speak. She's always been a rock, has always done the right thing and came through the fire that was our family life remarkably unscathed—though I'm sure she's often put on a brave face while she was dealing with plenty. She's had a very rough road and has handled it unbelievably, is incredibly well loved and respected by all, has always been above-and-beyond-the-call-of-duty supportive of me and my follies, and I'm so proud of her I could burst. I spend a lot of time hoping there's some of her in me.

My mother had a scary quick, biting wit, and could be funny about anything and everything. Kathy's mind moves like lightning, too.

One day, a bunch of us were sitting at the kitchen table about to have tea and Kathy was standing behind me.

I said, "Kathy, give me a cup."

Throwing her arms out as she jumped up, mimicking a cheerleader, she yelled "Cup."

My little brother Jimmy, born in 1959, was eleven years younger and came in at the tail end of the good years, getting only a tiny taste of what our family had been. By the time he was coming up, things were pretty out of control, and he was raised in a war zone. If you look at the footprint of the first floor of our house, you'll see that my father sitting at the kitchen table in the northeast corner of the house and my mother sitting in her easy chair in the southwest corner of the house were for decades physically as far apart as they could be and still be in the house. They only barked at each other when it was absolutely necessary and gave Jimmy whatever he wanted because that was the path of least resistance.

He was so great, really smart and fun and funny, like all of us.

One day, when he was still a really little kid, my mother said to me, "Tell Jimmy you heard he buried his wife."

I said, "Hey, Jimmy, I hear you buried your wife."

Channeling W. C. Fields perfectly, he growled back, "Had to. She was dead."

But he had come along as the smoke was clearing from years of insanity and it's hard to guess what it looked like to a grade school kid, how he interpreted what had to be quite afar from anything he witnessed at his friends' homes.

Jimmy had a fascination with suicide from very early on—he had written a suicide note at age ten—and it got him in 1993. He was super brilliant, and at that time, he had been working at Cold Spring Harbor Labs mapping DNA with Dr. James Watson's team as he struggled with his many addictions.

I'm not sure how well I dealt with Jimmy shooting himself or if I ever even have. That's by far the worst by-product of our incredibly dysfunctional family, and Bobby's recent passing compounded everything. From a purely selfish (!) standpoint, I now have no brothers and two unnecessary deaths to somehow come to terms with.

The scene at my house back in those years, the sixties and seventies, is hard to describe. It was action central. We all gathered there, the usual suspects changing gradually over the years as each of we siblings got older. Me and my gang, then Bobby and his gang, then my sister and her gang, then Jimmy and his gang—often overlapping. And it continues to this day, with my sister's friends and her kids' friends.

As described by Frank ("Frankie No Clothes") Baer, a very dear friend since 1959:

"Your parents weren't necessarily bad parents. They were generous and open and caring about all of us; but there were lots of parenting tools they didn't have. A lot of people of that generation grew up in families that relied on structure to raise children. They, like my parents, didn't have a real emotional connection with their children (although they were good friends). In my family, raising children was an intellectual process; in yours, it was almost camaraderie."

We'd all go out and get so damn loaded and do all kinds of crazy stuff and somehow my mother, who seemed to always know everything that was going on, would know whatever had taken place. My pal Peter

DeGuzman swears mornings he'd come up to my house from Oyster Bay to find out from my mother what he'd done the night before.

As nuts as the place was, it was a safe haven, a harbor for some who needed it. Everybody knew they could trust and talk to my mother.

Our friends would sit with my father and/or my mother—rarely, if ever, at the same time, of course—and talk for countless hours, about anything and everything under the sun and over it, often when none of us kids were home and perhaps not even living in the state. Many were envious of our family—though it was the family that wasn't.

Many continued to visit Dot and Doctor John—my mother and father—long into adulthood, which was very special. My late pal J. R. had affectionately given my father the nickname "Doctor John" in the early seventies and Pop seemed to get a kick out of it, though he never mentioned it.

Whatever it was, for better or worse, that house and that family made me whatever it is I am. And, not counting our many tragedies, I wouldn't change a thing...

...Or would I?

For many long years it had been brewing in the recesses of my mind that I had to one day (always in the future) stop drinking. Throughout college and then through the seventies, I rarely went three days without drinking. Whenever I tried to stop I simply could never follow through. Seemed there was always a good reason to drink. I have no idea if I couldn't stop or merely didn't want to—but they're about the same, no?

In 1972, during one of my attempts to abandon the sauce, I wrote a song about it, "Three Day's Rest," thinking if I wrote a song, I'd be proud of myself for having accomplished something, forget about the folly of quitting drinking, and go get nice and loaded ... which of course I did and I did.

As time flew by, and the seemingly endless party continued, I wound up writing lots of songs about getting high one way or the other. "The Beer Song," "Another Glass of Fool's Gold," "(Someone Else Can) Paint the Town," "The Pot Song," "And I'm Thinkin' About You." As they always say, write what you know.

One day, way back in the summer of 1974, I was once more trying to quit.

It had only been a few days when somebody said, "Come on, man. You gotta come out, it's [my dear double cousin] Lenny's last night in town."

And when I heard that it was the first time it had really occurred to me, the first time it made it to the forefront of my mind . . .

I said, "It's *always* Lenny's last night in town."

In the early nineties, I had been sober for about ten or twelve weeks in the throes of the nightmare that is the Nutrisystem weight loss plan. Nutrisystem was a main *Stern Show* sponsor and, being a good soldier over the years, I did it three times.

Nancy and I were out to dinner in Port Washington on Long Island. I remember it well, as I had hit my goal weight and was wrestling with whether to stay with not drinking. When the waiter served my appetizer he put a frosty cold ten-ounce glass of beer in front of me. I hadn't noticed when I ordered that it would accompany my particular appetizer.

I said to Nancy, "Enough," and took a big swig.

It was *electric*. It was a magical honey, cold and smooth and exquisite, like nothing I had ever experienced.

I called the waiter over and said, "My *God!* This is *unreal!* What *is* that? What kind of beer is that?"

He said, "Draft Budweiser."

After my time on the *Stern Show* ended—I never know how to express that, as I didn't quit and I wasn't fired, we just didn't come to terms—my life changed dramatically. And being as confused as I was, my drinking wasn't helping matters.

As I've already mentioned, Nancy and I had been basically living together as pals for a few years. I need to tell you a little more about our split, because the excruciating pain of our long relationship ending was one of the huge reasons why I needed to get my head at least a little clearer.

Many things had driven us apart. Six unsuccessful IVFs (in vitro fertilization, trying to get pregnant) and what she perceived as my lack of support throughout those very difficult procedures, which I'll always contest. My lack of support for her and her career, which surprises people as I seemed to the outside world to be doing a lot, which I certainly was financially (it was *our* money, but I had no problem with us spending it), but I really didn't give her what she *so* needed: my whole-hearted endorsement and respect for her many talents, and I admit it and have taken full responsibility for it. And my drinking, which actually was nowhere near as big a factor as the others.

We still lived together as I was doing the radio show five days a week and doing stand-up many weekends, so when I had a weekend off, as I said previously, I wasn't going to spend it looking for a bachelor pad where I envisioned I'd be, after finally getting a bit of financial success, a millionaire cooking on a hot plate.

We always had great sex and continued to. Thank Heaven for small favors.

Even those years when we weren't getting along, merely cohabiting, she'd say, "Want to get me from the back?" and I'd of course say hell yes. Not anal sex—doggie-style, so we wouldn't have to look at each other and acknowledge how much we were enjoying it.

In 1999, an incredible home on Long Island Sound became available. It's at the end of the street where we already owned two houses.

We looked at each other and said, "We're getting this house, divorce or no."

We bought it, and pretty soon I asked Nancy if she wanted to start over in the new house. She said we were too far gone, and I guess I agreed, because I didn't go to the mattresses on it. Very gradually I started to move my stuff in and to stay there.

By the first week of March 2001, I was off the show. So I had lost my wife and my job, and was living in a house by myself for the first time in my life.

So I had nothing but time, the devil's workshop. I sat on my porch and drank coffee and read, walked on the beach endlessly, piddled at making my house a home, started the immense task of making the coal-heated car mechanic's garage into a media studio . . .

I tried to keep busy, but every night the end of the day rolled around. And there was no real reason not to drink.

At the end of April 2001, our mutual friend, the terrific drummer John Michel, was getting married in Memphis, so we treated ourselves to a four-day weekend.

I can vividly remember spending the days in Memphis waiting for five o'clock, which I must have randomly decided was when my imbibe gun would go off.

We spent Saturday night downtown. Rock and roll, blues, folk . . . every kind of music was blasting out of the open doors as we strolled along Beale Street. There were outdoor courts with incredible food of all kinds being barbecued, steamed, and fried, I was starving and I was loaded to the hilt.

We walked into a food court and they had smoked turkey legs, just like we'd run to Frontier Town to get the moment we'd enter Disney World. (At forty-four and thirty-five years old, Disney World had been a childhood fantasy come true for both of us—we wept the first time we were walking down Main Street USA toward Cinderella's Castle.)

I vaguely remember thinking, "I'm so hungry I can eat *two* of these."

But they were huge and I just got one. The place was jammed, and it was a while before Nancy and I finally found a seat at a big round table with about five or six very large black women. She patiently waited for me to eat my turkey leg, then we got up, I grabbed my second turkey leg, all wrapped up in aluminum foil—a turkey leg I hadn't bought—and we turned to walk away.

One of the women leapt up and screamed, *"Where you goin'?* That's MY turkey leg! That's MY turkey leg!" And she went on and on, ranting louder and louder.

I have no idea what I managed to say in my stupor, but I imagine I apologized as fast and as sincerely as I could as a crowd quickly surrounded us.

After calm was eventually restored, we walked away, me a bit sobered up by what had just happened—and what had almost just happened. I think something may have clicked. The waiting for five o'clock every day, the near brawl, and mainly having *wayyy* too much free time . . .

Whatever the multitude of reasons, by the time we got home on Monday night, I had decided to quit drinking. And I did.

But . . .

That Friday, Nancy and I were having dinner with Stuttering J. Johnny Johnson and his adorable wife Suzanna on Central Park South, and when I announced I wasn't drinking, John ranted, "Wh-wh-what do you m-m-mean, y-y-you're not drinking? Y-y-you're f-f-fucking drinking."

And so I did. And with our city apartment a few blocks away and not having to drive, I drank plenty. An hour later, John and I were with our two beautiful wives, in a romantic horse-drawn cab tooling through Central Park . . . with two six packs of Budweiser in a brown bag.

Thinking about it still makes me sick. But it was one more thing that underscored what I had to do.

That Sunday, Nancy and I went to a christening. And it had been my usual modus operandi.

I always made sure we were first to the wedding, birthday party, whatever event—to take full advantage of the cocktail hour.

After years of the same routine, I stopped tapping my foot impatiently while Nancy was getting ready. I'd open my first beer and drink it while I waited. *Voila!* No angst. If I was close to finishing it before she came down, I'd guzzle the rest, put the empty in the downstairs refrigerator, and grab a fresh one for the ride. It may even have gotten to where I'd sometimes polish two before she was ready. And I always left the house with a beer or two for the ride, even if we were just going down the street.

I'd drink throughout the event and when they came around with coffee I'd always order a few drinks or beers to make sure I was backed up before the bar closed. And we'd be the last ones to leave. When I could, I'd smuggle out a drink for the trip home or wherever we were headed next.

At the end of the christening dinner that Sunday afternoon, May 5, 2001, the waitress came around with a pot of coffee in one hand and a pitcher of beer in the other. As she made her way to us, I pushed my water goblet of beer away, pulled in my coffee cup and saucer, turned over the cup and gestured to it. Nancy must have thought she was hallucinating.

I looked over at her and said, "I'm done."

And I was.

Looking back, it sure seems quitting booze was easier than I ever imagined it would be. Of course, maybe I don't remember the agony if there was any. There were no shakes or physical withdrawals of any kind. My life was completely different, of course, but for many, many reasons.

Like I typed, it's been fifteen years, and back in February 2001, the thought of not having a drink for fifteen *days* would have been inconceivable.

After a few weeks off the hooch, I realized anybody could sit home and not drink if they were isolated like that. I knew I couldn't live like that. I had to go out and rejoin the living.

But I imagined that if I went into a bar all eyes would be upon me, as they were thinking, "What's *he* doing in here? He's not one of us. He doesn't drink anymore. He's an imposter."

I'd always been invited to lots of great show business gatherings and movie screenings I never was able to attend because I had to be up at the crack of ass, and now I could. And the invitations were still coming in.

Before I knew how I'd handle it, my pal Burf wisely said, "You should go to everything you're invited to. Just go deal with it."

I knew he was right. I remember so clearly making the decision that I was going to tough through it and learn how to be out on the town sober.

And?

And there was nothing to tough through. I'd get a seltzer or a Diet Coke, put in a piece of lemon and a stirrer, and not only did no one know I wasn't drinking, they couldn't have cared less. And I quickly noticed that most people don't drink like I had. They hold the same drink forever.

I'd be amazed, almost wanting to say, "Jesus *Christ*, are you going to drink that or what?"

So going out and mixing socially—bars, parties, media events—was instantly no problem. Now I could go and I did. And once I started talking to anybody, it was off to the races.

It really helped that a lot of the people who, much like me, had the gods on their side, making it this far, had also gotten sober. It's an instant bond when you encounter another war-torn veteran of the mahogany.

Very often, people ask me if it's okay if they drink when we're together—a girl I'm out to dinner with would ask if it'd bother me if she had a glass of wine, a couple my girl and I are out with might ask, and so on. And it's never, ever been even the slightest problem. There's no temptation. I have tons of beer and wine and liquor in my home for my many friends and family who drink, which is damn near all of them. I spend tons of time in situations where people are drinking.

Hey, if I wanted a drink, trust me, it wouldn't matter how close or far away it was, I'd get one. I made a decision and I've stuck to it. And as everybody who knows me will sadly vouch for, I vacillate on everything more than any ten people—but somehow I've adhered to this. I'm as proud of it as anything I've ever done, and many people are proud of me for it, too.

One thing that often strikes me is that it's weird taking congratulations for something I *don't* do. But I quickly stopped trying to rationalize it and think, "Hey, it's late in the game, I'm taking my bows wherever I can get them."

I went to a few AA meetings a couple months into my sobriety, but they were all pounding what seemed like too much coffee and the places reeked of cigarette smoke. Everyone was wonderful, but it wasn't for me. Nowadays, I'll occasionally go to a meeting with a fellow nondrinker and it's always a nice time, but AA ends there for me.

Once not long after I quit, I was at a New Year's party in Minnesota (sober or no, I have no idea whatsoever how I wound up in Minnesota on a New Year's Eve) and at midnight, somebody poured champagne down the very ample cleavage of a woman in a very low-cut dress who was standing next to me. Instinctively I bent down and slurped it right up.

Realizing what I'd done, I jumped back and said, "Wow, I wasn't thinking . . ."

I was talking to me.

I explained to her I had no problem with having licked between her breasts, but the champagne was a no-no for me. Needless to type, it was quite the icebreaker, and . . .

I imagine other people who have stopped drinking have similar experiences. Licked a cleavage, shared a shtup . . .

No, I mean took a sip of booze by accident.

Whenever alcohol accidentally enters my system, I could swear that every cell in my body jumps up and screams, "*Yahoo!* We're drinking again!"

You had to notice that the precise reason(s) I quit drinking are a bit (a lot?) fuzzy. That's because so much factored in.

Each time I start a sentence with "the main reason" I realize there wasn't one.

It wasn't hangovers. I rarely got them, unless I had gone totally balls-to-the-wall bonkers the night before and deserved it, which as the years flew by became pretty infrequent.

I never, ever woke up physically shaking, needing a drink to get right, but I was alone for the first time in twenty years, no wife or girlfriend, and was living by myself in a home that I had very recently moved into.

I had no job, but, more importantly, no longer had the relationships I had forged over nearly twenty years with my radio cast mates.

And as I said earlier, I had way too much free time.

If there really was one "main" reason why I quit, it was because I was waking to demons, wrestling with craziness like I'd never experienced. It constantly amazed me what would burst into my mind—negativity on top of negativity, inner conversations that were scary and depressing, so much so that often I'd find myself lying in a puddle of sweat as I awoke.

There was no rhyme or reason to the demons, to the ugly thoughts. They flew at me totally at random. Family problems, childhood memories, financial fears, loneliness pangs, much of it unfounded, but a decent amount of it right on the money. Right on the fucking money.

And each morning, I'd trek through that maze of these mostly bad thoughts, in a sometimes futile search for the positive, trying to convince myself all was not so bad.

It seems with jumping out of bed when the alarm sounded at 4:20 a.m. for fifteen years, all that crap never had a chance to rear its nastiness. I certainly concede a lot of it must have been residing within me for decades.

Were these daily trips through hell due to drinking and then waking up depressed and confused and so damn low?

It always made (makes?) me think of a classic Rodney bit that wasn't necessarily a joke:

Every morning I wake up to a heaviness . . .
Sometimes I talk to it . . .
I say, "Hi, heaviness . . ."

I was never a belligerent drunk and rarely was a flaming asshole (that is, more than whatever is my normal) due to alcohol. That said, many forces had met and it seemed the time was right.

I had wavered a lot about quitting alcohol as I tried to decipher my move to let the *Stern Show* slip away. Even through the constant vacillation, most often when I stood back, I realized it was a must-do.

I didn't specifically toss the greatest job on the planet (yes, of course I realized that) due to booze, but I certainly could never have quit drinking had I remained on the show—due to me, no one else.

One thing I credit myself for is finally knowing a bit about myself.

The processes of getting sober and going through a divorce while I was on the *Stern Show* looked to me to be, at the time, insurmountable tasks. Call me immature or weak, fine, but at least I knew myself well enough to recognize the cold facts. They both had to happen, and the sooner the better.

And now I had an open field, the space to make my break from the decades of drinking.

There were nights and mornings—more than a few—that I'd jump out of bed and drive over to Nancy's house and climb in with her and hold on for dear life. Close to no words would be spoken—we're that kind of friends. And always will be. That is, that close . . . no more bedmates.

So here it is, 2017.

Did I win? No.

To me, winning the battle with alcohol would be being able to have a few beers or a few glasses of wine and then let it go for however long.

My favorite analogy is tuna fish. I love tuna fish, love a tuna fish sandwich, probably as much as anything on this earth. But I might go a week or even a month without having one. But I'll love it when I do. And then who knows when I'll have another one? The point being is it isn't any kind of an issue.

I wish to me booze was like tuna fish.

I was talking about my drinking to a new and wonderful friend, Elizabeth Serkin, an octogenarian who'd been an alcohol counselor for over fifty years. As always, the question still nagged at me, did I really have a problem? Am I really an alcoholic?

I told her, "I never woke up and needed a drink. I never watched a ball game on television and drank beer. Nancy and I never drank while we were watching our prime time shows during the week."

She stopped me cold and said, "Jackie dear, if you use the word *never* in the description of your drinking, you're an alcoholic."

Interesting, eh?

Again, like way too many of us, I'm so very fortunate to still be here, let alone having never hurt anyone else, after decades of drinking and driving and whatever other roads all that booze led to. I've been to jail six times, four of them overnight, two of them for DWI, and in all but one case booze was directly responsible.

I'm long divorced but have a terrific relationship with my ex. I love my family more than life itself and I'm going to say it's reciprocal. I have the most wonderfully eclectic group of friends. I still thoroughly enjoy performing, no matter the venue (for the most part). When I'm not traveling, I split my time between two wonderful worlds, my home on Long Island Sound and my apartment in midtown Manhattan, most of it with Barbara Klein, a beautiful and very talented woman I adore more than I ever imagined I could. Meeting her gave me a whole new meaning to the term "getting lucky." Many breakfasts or lunchtimes find me and my pal Francis Galluccio at Brigitte's Bridge Café down the street, eating and complaining and arguing about whose turn it is to pay. And for the most part, I remember to feed my kitty, Jake. So I'm thinking I've escaped relatively intact.

Yeah, I'm a slow learner. But somehow I made it to now—and I don't drink anymore. Roll it up.

Two drunks are sitting at a bar when the first one pulls down his zipper and starts pissing into a beer bottle.

The second drunk says, "Wh-what're you doing?"

The first drunk says, "Th-this shit's so good I-I'm gonna drink it again."

A drunk's sitting at the bar, his pecker's out and he's yanking on it.

The bartender says, "Man, you gotta get outta here."

The drunk says, "A-are you kiddin'? I can't leave. I-I can't walk. I'm so drunk, I-I don't even know who I'm fuckin'."

2017

AND AFTER-ALL-IS-SAID-AND-DONE-WORD

So there it is. A pretty decent rundown of parts of my life.

Would I like to do it all again?

Absolutely, from square one. Pull me out, smack me on the ass, and let the games begin again.

What would I change if I had it to do over? Nothing. It was just ducky. I enjoyed every second . . . the good, the bad, and the ugly (after enough beer).

After almost seven decades, I've come to believe that all the religion anyone ever needs is the Golden Rule: do unto others as you would have them do unto you.

That's all I have to say about that.

I could start in about how I can't believe we have cretins in this country who don't believe in evolution, but that gets way too unfunny way too fast.

It hit me the other day that it may be a signal you've become a grown-up when you stop calling attention to and being proud of your farts. Can't wait.

I have tapered off, as I've reached the age where I really should cross my fingers before I fart.

One of my regrets is being so poorly read. If I had one wish, it'd be that I had read everything I was supposed to have read in the course of my education, all the way from grade school through graduating as a mechanical engineer from Michigan State.

Really.

I'm smart but I don't know anything. I know just enough about things to (hopefully) be funny.

Hey, maybe a preponderance of knowledge would've inhibited that. So let's say it was a fine strategy crafted by a boy with a plan.

As was probably evident as you glided through the events of my life—as I made my way like a pinball, bouncing this way and that—I love people. All people. Kids, elders (fuck, that's me now), and as I keep saying, I live to make them smile. For whatever reason.

Again, I gave up long ago trying to figure out why making someone smile or laugh makes me feel good. For many years I've just done it (or attempted to do it) with no introspection or hesitation, none whatsoever.

If you like chocolate, eat it. Do what you enjoy. It's a very short visit here.

If I order a sandwich and I make the deli guy laugh, it warms me.

Shallow? I don't give a fuck. I love it.

Years ago, I was one of the celebrities at a local guy's charity event in Bayville. Former New York Knick John Starks, Olympic figure skaters Sarah and Emily Hughes, and me were sitting at tables under a canopy. Everybody in town knows me and has had plenty of me, so I felt like an idiot sitting there with 8 x 10s and a Sharpie. Jackie being there was a big yawn.

The event had originated for the guy's very young son, who had beaten leukemia, so there were a lot of kids there. The kids hear there are famous people under the tent, so they start coming over—four- to eight-year-olds, that ballpark.

They have no idea who I am, but they want an autographed picture of me, because they were told I'm famous.

Of course, I'm thrilled. Business at my table!

I say to the first kid, "You want a signed picture?"

And she says, ever so shyly, "Yes."

I say, "What's your name?"

And she says, "Linda."

As I go to write her name on a photo, I say, "Okay, Linda . . . L-U-N . . ."

She says, "No, L-*I*-N-D-A . . ."

I said, "Okay, N-I-L . . ."

More animated, she says, "*NO!* L-I-N-D-A . . ."

So I continue to get it wrong until she's going totally nuts and then I sign it and she thanks me. I do the same routine for kid after kid. They work into a frenzy very fast, and it's a hoot.

The kids soon catch on, and after they get their signed picture they start standing around to watch me nail the next victim. Pretty soon we're all laughing and howling and it's a free-for-all. Just pure silly, crazy, innocent fun.

A few of the parents put their heads together and glancing over they start asking each other, "Is he telling them dirty jokes?"

Idiots.

The point of the story is I enjoyed that hour with those kids as much if not more as any dirty joke show I've ever done to a thousand people. It's the connection. It's what I do, what I really enjoy.

For a long time, it haunted me that I'm pretty intelligent, and maybe it's a shame I didn't use my intelligence to do something to better mankind, or at least attempt it.

And after sharing that thought with enough people, and having them reflect back to me, I realized I *have* made a contribution. A big one.

If making people laugh, whether on the radio, or on CD, or in a club or wherever and however, made them feel a bit better and gave them a nice jolt so they'd be just a bit more ready to go fix the world, then I damn well helped with the Shake 'n' Bake of life, no?

For over six decades . . . and I hope with my last breath.

It never fails to amaze me that very few of us ever really think about death. At least nobody I know has ever talked to me about it. I know I can't think about it. Whenever I try to address it in my mind, I quickly change the subject.

This is about as serious as I can get about death:

Two guys are drinking and the first guy says, "When I'm lying there in my casket, I'd like to hear them say, 'He was a nice guy, a true friend, and a good family man.'"

The second guy says, "I'd like to hear them say, 'I think I saw him move.'"

Since 2001, since I've been off *The Howard Stern Show*, most everybody I meet asks, "What're you doing now?"

And I'll start explaining, "I still do stand-up, I guest on lots of radio shows and podcasts, I tweet jokes, I send out joke emails, I update my dirty joke line . . ."

And it dawned on me the concise, simple answer is, "I try to make people laugh."

Because it makes me feel good.

I'm going to give my nephew Brendan a dick joke to read as they lower me into the ground.

And hopefully it'll get a laugh.